# a handb
# woodworking

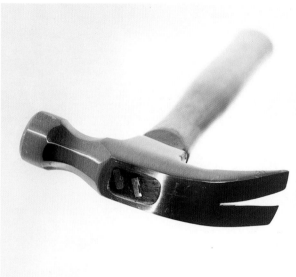

# a handbook of
# woodworking

the comprehensive guide for the home woodworker,
with techniques and over 20 projects

## stephen corbett

**southwater**

This edition is published by Southwater

Southwater is an imprint of Anness Publishing Ltd
Hermes House, 88–89 Blackfriars Road, London SE1 8HA
tel. 020 7401 2077; fax 020 7633 9499 www.southwaterbooks.com; info@anness.com

This edition distributed in the UK by The Manning Partnership Ltd,
6 The Old Dairy, Melcombe Road, Bath BA2 3LR
tel. 01225 478 444; fax 01225 478 440; sales@manning-partnership.co.uk

This edition distributed in the USA and Canada by National Book Network,
4501 Forbes Boulevard, Lanham, MD 20706
tel. 301 459 3366; fax 301 429 5746; www.nbnbooks.com

This edition distributed in Australia by Pan Macmillan Australia,
Level 18, St Martins Tower, 31 Market St, Sydney, NSW 2000
tel. 1300 135 113; fax 1300 135 103; customer.service@macmillan.com.au

This edition distributed in New Zealand by The Five Mile Press (NZ) Ltd, PO Box 33–1071 Takapuna,
Unit 11/101–111 Diana Drive, Glenfield, Auckland 10
tel. (09) 444 4144; fax (09) 444 4518; fivemilenz@xtra.co.nz

A CIP catalogue record for this book is available from the British Library

Publisher: Joanna Lorenz
Art manager: Clare Reynolds
Managing editor: Judith Simons
Senior editor: Doreen Palamartschuk
Text editor: Ian Penberthy
Designer: James Lawrence
Illustrator: Julian Baker
Photographer: John Freeman
Stylist: Annie le Painter
Contributors: Andrew Gillmore, Bob Cleveland
Editorial readers: Richard McGinlay, Jonathan Marshall
Production controller: Don Campaniello

Previously published as *The Complete Practical Woodworker*

1 3 5 7 9 10 8 6 4 2

Publisher's note
The author and the publisher have made every effort to ensure that
all instructions contained in this book are accurate and that the safest methods
are recommended. The publisher and author cannot accept liability for any
resulting injury, damage or loss to persons or property as a result of using any
tools in this book or carrying out any of the projects. Before you begin any
woodworking task, you should know how to use all your tools and equipment
safely and that you are sure and confident about what you are doing.

# Contents

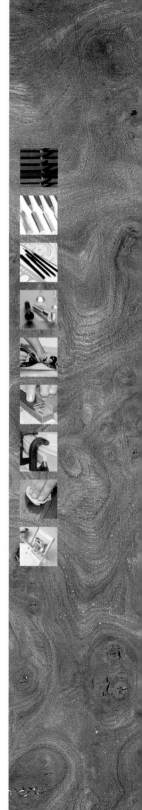

# INTRODUCTION

BY OPENING THIS BOOK, you have already displayed the first qualification to proceed further – a basic interest in wood and how it is used. Millions of people share this interest, and all of us benefit to some degree from its use. This book itself is made from paper, a universal product derived from the same raw material that goes into our houses, our furniture and many other items that we come into contact with daily. Despite the undoubted progress made by humankind in the development of metals, alloys, synthetic resins and plastics, wood, in its natural form, has been a part of our lives for thousands of years and will remain so.

## Why wood?

Wood has a universal and appealing presence to every culture and country. As a constructional material it is invaluable and very strong for its weight. It can be used to create complex structures at relatively low cost. Properly looked after timber (lumber) will last for years, as an examination of your surroundings will confirm.

Centuries of woodworking tradition have refined the techniques and tools we currently use, allowing a multitude of uses and styles. Best of all, wood is a sustainable resource – well managed woodlands can produce an inexhaustible supply of raw material, as well as playing a vital part in a balanced environment. Imagine

*Above* Houses being constructed from timber (lumber).
*Left* Wood has been used for sculpture for centuries. Here is a showering couple in the Grizedale Forest, Hawkshead, UK.
*Opposite* Wood is strong, attractive and in furniture joints can be used as a decorative feature in a design.

asking modern technologists to invent a synthetic material with so many qualities. Then ask them to add other properties – to make it feel warm and alive to the touch, and to look attractive at the same time.

The secret of being a successful woodworker or furniture maker lies in understanding that wood, as an organic material, was once alive, and that it can live again when shaped and formed by the human hand. No two pieces of wood are ever the same, and appreciating the variation will allow you to make the most of the material's natural qualities. All the tools and techniques in the world will be of no use without this feel for the material, which every woodworker shares.

When you have made your first piece of work, try this simple test – show it to someone else and wait for them to reach out and touch it. Then you will know that you have become part of a tradition of craftsmanship that will always be with us, and that you have taken the first step on a rewarding journey that has no end.

## How to use this book

The following pages provide an introduction to all the aspects of woodworking that will allow you to produce something that can be called your own work. From the recognition and selection of the right kind of timber (lumber) to the design and construction of the finished item, there is no area of understanding that a good craftsperson can ignore. The basics of every aspect of woodworking have been broken down into broad areas for easy reference.

The type and condition of the timber, the tools and techniques employed, the design principles and the basic safety rules that go with them all affect the finished

product. Taking short-cuts and making choices without exploring all the options can produce quicker results, but woodworking is not a race against time. Patience is one of the primary attributes of any good craftsperson. Take the trouble to consult each chapter in turn, using the information as the foundation of a thorough and sympathetic understanding of each task you approach. That way, you will always be learning something new and the benefits will be revealed in your work.

All the projects are suitable for the home woodworker, and range from simple, everyday household items to quite sophisticated pieces of furniture. They have been designed, made and photographed specifically and you will find all the information you need to recreate them. On the other hand, you can adapt the design and construction principles to suit your own ideas.

No two items made in wood are ever the same, and that is the way it should be. No woodworker is ever completely satisfied with the latest project, either – the next one will

always be better. There is no substitute for experience, and that is what you will find distilled in these pages. What you will not find is the reward that comes from your own efforts – the key to this lies in your own hands, and the understanding of the tools and materials you use.

## Note on measurements

Making accurate measurements is one of the most important skills to acquire if you want to achieve good results. The task can be made more confusing by the fact that different countries and timber suppliers work to different standards, using either the metric or imperial system (or sometimes a combination of the two), when sizing the raw material.

The same applies to tool manufacturers and suppliers of fixings and hardware. The way through this maze is to develop an understanding of both systems until mental conversion becomes second nature. A pocket calculator will help, but actually can slow the process.

In this book, dimensions are given in both metric and imperial form, but you should always check that the accuracy of any conversion is sufficient for the task in hand. Fractions of an inch, or 1 or 2 millimetres, either way are less critical in gauging large quantities of timber than when setting out detail, and converted values are often rounded up or down to make life easier. The table shown below provides some useful conversion factors and short-cut methods for estimating larger quantities of wood.

### Conversion table

| Multiply | by | to obtain | short-cuts |
|---|---|---|---|
| inches | 25.4 | millimetres | divide by four and add two zeros (4in = 100mm) |
| feet | 305 | millimetres | multiply by three and add two zeros (1ft = 300mm) |
| square feet | 0.093 | square metres | divide by ten |
| cubic feet | 0.028 | cubic metres | divide by 35 (35cu ft = 1cu metre) |
| lb/cu ft | 16.05 | kg/cu m | add two zeros, divide by six |
| pounds | 0.45 | kilograms | divide by two and subtract 10% (2.2lb = 1kg) |

# WOOD

**T**o most people, wood comes ready to use from a timber (lumber) yard or home improvement store, cut to standard lengths and planed to a smooth finish. Modern processing and marketing practices demand that the natural variation of the product is eliminated as far as possible. But wood is not a manufactured material, and its qualities are as varied as the trees from which it is derived.

As a discriminating woodworker, you will soon discover that the real pleasure of woodworking comes from exploring the potential of each species and using it to its best advantage. The knowledge and careful selection of the raw material is one of the most important steps to take in developing a feel for your craft. This chapter describes the immense variety and options available to you as the living tree is processed to arrive in usable form at your workbench.

# THE RAW MATERIAL

**Trees are arguably the most prominent members of the plant kingdom. They have been around for millions of years, forming a vital part of the natural biological cycle that keeps this planet alive. Like all plants, they depend on a process called photosynthesis to harness the sun's energy, combine it with carbon dioxide ($CO_2$) from the air and produce the nutrients they need to grow. In return, oxygen is emitted to the atmosphere and vast quantities of water evaporate from the leaves.**

### Tree trunks

The most useful and important part of the tree is the trunk, or bole. This performs three roles: it conducts water, or sap, from the roots; it supports the weight of the tree; and it stores the nutrients produced in the leaves to lay down new growth. Different parts of the trunk are adapted to each function, but all use the same basic building blocks: the cells, which have walls made of cellulose, the raw material of wood. When pulped and processed, cellulose can be made into paper; when it is left intact, it provides one of the most versatile constructional materials available.

### Living cycle within the tree

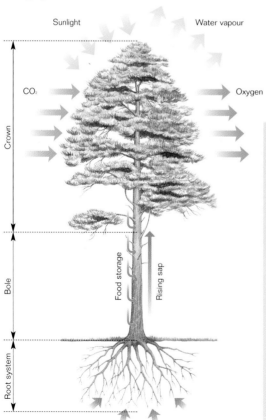

Sunlight

Water vapour

$CO_2$

Oxygen

Crown

Food storage

Rising sap

Bole

Root system

*Above* A western yellow pine (*Pinus ponderosa*), a softwood species, in spring.
*Opposite top* A Californian redwood, a softwood species, (*Sequoia sempervirens*).
*Opposite below* Mature oaks, a temperate hardwood species, (*Quercus robur*), from a post-Napoleonic-war plantation.

## Timber properties

| Softwoods | Hardwoods |
| --- | --- |
| low density: 400–600kg/cu m (25–37lb/cu ft) | high density: up to 1,000kg/cu m (65lb/cu ft) |
| great strength with lighter weight | heavier and sometimes more brittle |
| less durable in wet or damp conditions | more suitable for exterior use |
| less resistance to insect attack | more resistant to decay and rot |
| generally pale colouring | light to very dark colouring |
| generally more open grained | close-grained and harder to work |
| tendency to shrink or swell | more stable |
| low cost and more readily available | more expensive and harder to obtain |

flexibility, brittleness, and, of course, appearance. Understanding these qualities will help you select the best material for the job in hand. One of the first choices to make is not as straightforward as it may seem – softwood or hardwood?

Trees are divided into two botanical groups: *Gymnosperms* and *Angiosperms*, or conifers and broadleaves. These groups are popularly and respectively known as softwoods and hardwoods, but the terms can be misleading. Some so-called softwoods from coniferous trees, such as yew and pitch pine, are considerably harder than certain tropical hardwoods, not least balsa wood, which is the lightest of all.

The strength of timber (lumber) is determined by its density, which can vary within the same species according to its country of origin and rate of growth. Conifers are concentrated primarily in the cooler regions of the world, in both the northern and southern hemispheres, while tropical hardwoods, as the name implies, are found in the equatorial belt.

A third group, the temperate hardwoods, occupies the middle zone and is of special interest to woodworkers. Great variation can be found in the colour, distinctive grain figure and working properties of this group, and commercial supplies from sustainable sources are readily available at reasonable cost.

Whatever group timber belongs to, the woodworker will want to know its workability: how it behaves when worked by hand or machine tools, the quality of the grain, and how it takes to different adhesives and finishes. For most practical purposes, the more commonly available commercial softwoods all have certain similar features, with particular advantages and disadvantages as you can see in the table opposite.

**Softwoods and hardwoods**

Depending on the species and conditions of growth, wood possesses a wide range of characteristics in varying degrees: strength, durability,

# STRUCTURE OF WOOD

A good woodworker does not have to be an expert in botany, or even dendrology (the study of trees), but it does help to have a basic knowledge of a tree's internal structure. This allows the selection of the best material for the job at hand and assists in spotting potential defects, which can show up and spoil the finished product.

### Drying wood

An important part of the design process is knowing how wood behaves as it is worked and as it dries, which can vary depending on the part of the tree from which it originates. The cutaway section below of a tree trunk shows the principal elements that are common to most commercially available softwoods and temperate hardwoods.

### The layers of a tree trunk

The outer layer is the *bark* of the tree, which protects it as it grows. Just beneath the bark is the *bast*, a vital part of the tree's make-up. It conducts the sugars manufactured in the leaves down toward the base of the tree for storage, while the narrow *cambium* alongside it is responsible for creating new growth each year. The outer

layers are attractive to pests in search of the food products they contain, so most of the seasoned timber (lumber) supplied for woodworking will have had them removed at an early stage.

In the *sapwood* layer, each year's new growth is laid down and the cells conduct the sap upward from the root system. In some species, the sapwood is distinct, being pale in colour, while in others there is no visible barrier between sapwood and *heartwood*. Sapwood has the same strength as heartwood, but is more vulnerable to attack by furniture beetle, so as a rule it should be cut away. It can develop unsightly greyish-blue stains and is porous, making good glued joints and smooth finishes difficult to obtain.

The heartwood makes up the bulk of the tree and is the most usable part.

*Above* Growth rings are clearly visible in the end grain of these boards.

The cells of the heartwood are not alive, but they provide all the strength of the tree. As the tree grows, sapwood becomes heartwood, which is more durable and often of a darker colour. Each year's new growth forms another layer, and these rings enable the age of the tree to be determined.

In many species, especially from temperate climates where there is a distinct growing season every year, the rings are clearly visible, giving rise to an attractive striped grain figure. When a board is cut radially, through the growth rings to the centre, the *rays* will be revealed in cross-section. These run horizontally through the tree, storing food deposits as it increases in girth. They are very visible in oak, producing a characteristic silvery band; in other species, they are barely detectable by the naked eye.

The *pith*, at the very core of the trunk, is the oldest part of the tree; however, it is not the strongest. It is the growth laid down when the tree is immature, and it is softer and less durable than the true heartwood. It can flake out when being worked, and is prone to decay and uneven shrinkage as the wood dries. Defects can arise at the centre of the pith, and often it is removed when the log is processed.

### The structure of wood

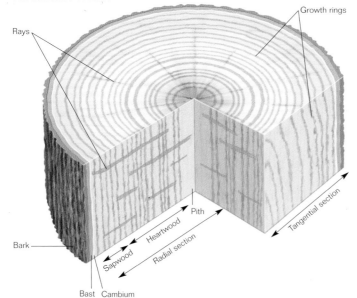

Growth rings

Rays

Bark

Bast  Cambium

Sapwood

Heartwood

Radial section

Pith

Tangential section

## Wood grain

Some species of timber (lumber) are termed straight-grained, where the growth rings are tight and concentric around the heart of the tree; they are a pleasure to work with.

*Above* These American white oak boards display the attractive striped grain figure common to woods with distinct growth rings. They have been cut tangentially – that is, cut across the face of the growth rings to reveal the cone-shaped formation.

## Knots

A knot is simply the remains of a branch where it grew from the main trunk of the tree, but it should not always be regarded as a defect. Small knots can create interesting effects in an otherwise bland piece of timber.

*Above* This panel of black walnut contains a good example of a dead knot. The small "pin" knot lower down creates an attractive pattern, but the large dead knot above it is a defect to be avoided.

However, they do cause problems when working the wood, and joints and fine detail should be positioned away from them if possible. A dead knot, encased in a ring of bark where a dead branch has been absorbed by the growing tree, should be avoided. It is likely to shrink and fall out, and, in softwoods particularly, can be very resinous, causing problems when applying a finish.

## Defects

Short- or cross-grain defects still occur, however, as a result of uneven growth or the grain being deformed around a knot. Very short or close grain is almost impossible to work successfully with hand tools without it tearing. It drastically weakens the material and should be avoided for constructional members and sections of wood close to joints. Certain species, particularly some tropical hardwoods, can always be expected to have difficult grain, growing naturally in spiral or interlocking patterns.

*Above* In this panel of European beech, the rays appear as small oval flecks distributed liberally across the face of the timber.

## Reaction wood

This occurs where uneven growth in the trunk of the tree puts the fibres under great pressure. It can be identified by tight bands of growth rings that are much darker than their surroundings. These areas are much weaker, more difficult to work and subject to abnormal movement or shrinkage. Large areas of reaction wood should be cut out when selecting stock.

*Above* Sapele is an example of a hardwood with a difficult grain, the alternate formation of each band of cells producing a striped effect. The right-hand panel in this photograph not only shows unacceptable short grain, but also another defect known as reaction wood.

## Shakes and checks

Small fissures, or *checks*, in the outer surface of a sample are not serious. Of greater concern are *shakes*, which arise within the tree due to decay or high stresses, or even old age. Star-shaped *heart shakes* can develop in the centre of a tree that has passed maturity. *Ring shakes* form between the growth rings and can be caused by the shock of being felled. A board with these defects should be rejected – it is unsound and will only deteriorate.

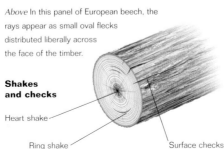

**Shakes and checks**

Heart shake

Ring shake

Surface checks

# PRODUCTION AND CONVERSION

Imagine a tree with a trunk that is 610mm (2ft) in diameter, with a useful length of 12m (40ft) stretching up toward the crown. This represents a volume of timber (lumber) of 3.5cu m (124cu ft). Imagine a billion such trees and you will have an idea of worldwide timber consumption in a year. Not all of this is converted into useful wood products, however – in fact, more than half is burned for fuel. Much of the remainder is converted into wood pulp for the paper and packaging industries.

### Tree felling

Timber production is a massive global industry, and the route taken by a piece of wood before it reaches your workbench is complex and varied. The home woodworker has a vast range of options available when specifying the correct quality and form of material to give the best results and reduce waste.

From the moment a tree is selected for felling, it is subjected to a continual process of evaluation to grade its quality and most useful content. When it reaches the sawmill, it will be allowed to "rest" for a period to allow the natural tensions within the trunk to equalize, before being converted into large slabs for seasoning. A skilled operator will know how to convert the log into the greatest quantity of usable timber with the minimum of waste.

As with most things, the higher the quality of product, the higher the cost, and the way in which the log is converted into convenient sizes can affect this dramatically.

Understanding the different methods and terminology will help you to specify the correct type of wood for your needs, and predict its behaviour under different conditions. The appearance of the cut surface,

*Above* Resawing an oak board to remove the heart shake.
*Below* A typical log storage yard.

the amount of waste and the way in which the wood shrinks as it loses moisture are all affected by the conversion method.

The quickest and least wasteful method of converting the log, or baulk, of timber is to make a series of parallel cuts along its length. This process is known as through and through cutting, sometimes abbreviated to T/T.

## Through and through cutting

This style of cutting is normal for most large-scale commercial sawmills. It produces large quantities of boards with a tangential figure, the cuts being made across the growth rings and producing the familiar cone-shaped pattern on the face of each board.

Such boards are described as plain sawn, flat sawn or slash sawn. Many species of wood with distinctive or contrasting growth rings are shown to their best advantage when converted in this way. To maximize the yield of highly figured boards, the entire baulk can be plain sawn.

*Above* Sawing a prime ash log on a bandmill.

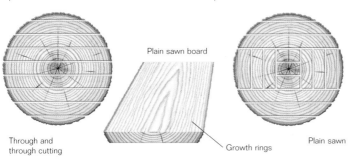

Plain sawn board

Through and through cutting

Growth rings

Plain sawn

*Above* Quarter sawing oak on a bandmill.

## Quarter sawing

In contrast, when a log is cut into quarters, and sawn radially, at right-angles to the growth rings, with the cut passing through the centre, the figure displayed is markedly different.

The photograph on the right shows a good example of quarter-sawn oak, the silky blaze of the rays being clearly visible in cross-section and the growth rings reduced to fine parallel lines. As the diagram below shows, however, this method is wasteful of timber and time-consuming, since the log needs regular repositioning on the saw table. True quarter-sawn timber, with the cut surface intersecting the growth rings at a right angle, is only

produced when the quality or the decorative value of the timber warrants it.

Boards described as quarter sawn from the supplier will have been cut by one of several methods, as shown. These are a compromise and accept the rings running at any angle of more than 45 degrees from the face.

Another possibility is rift-sawn boards, where the log is split horizontally, then sawn through and through vertically to produce boards with a higher proportion of quartered grain. Sometimes this is described as one square edge and it can yield good-quality material at a much lower cost.

*Above* A fine example of black walnut, with a plain-sawn panel on the left, quarter-sawn on the right and rift-sawn in the centre. The changing angle of growth rings across the panel can be seen clearly.

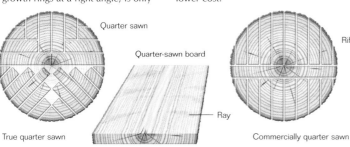

Quarter sawn

Quarter-sawn board

Rift sawn

Ray

True quarter sawn

Commercially quarter sawn

# SEASONING WOOD

**Newly felled timber (lumber) loses moisture rapidly at first as free water evaporates, then more slowly as water within the cell walls is given up. The woodworker should look for well-seasoned timber, which will have been dried at the sawmill under controlled conditions in two distinct stages.**

*Above* This shows how not to air dry timber. The boards have been piled in irregular fashion, unprotected from the heat of the sun. Rapid, uneven drying can split a board quite easily. Note the discolouration where the sticks were laid.

## Shrinkage

When newly felled, timber has a high water content and is termed "green". It is heavier and more vulnerable to decay than seasoned timber. However, it can be worked quite easily and is more flexible. As it dries, it will shrink slightly and can distort in shape.

The cherrywood bowl below shows how dramatic such changes can be. It is a section that was cut from the base of a cherry tree when it was felled. Note the deep colour of the heartwood in contrast to the sapwood. Without encouragement, within three months, the flat disc had formed a natural bowl shape. In this case, the result was turned to advantage, but such deformation would create havoc in a worked piece of furniture.

*Right* A cherrywood bowl. Note the contrast between heartwood and sapwood.

*Below* An air-dried timber (lumber) stack.

## Air drying

Outdoors, timber will dry naturally to a certain extent. It must be stacked carefully to allow good ventilation. When treating hardwood, a sawmill will air dry the converted timber for a period of up to two years before further processing. The stack should be protected from the elements, and the layers separated by small sticks to encourage an even rate of drying and to reduce distortion. Some pale species of timber, such as sycamore, are prone to staining when very green, particularly where the sticks are laid. Initially, these may be *end-reared*, or stacked on end, to avoid this.

## Stability and movement

Shrinkage describes the behaviour of timber as it dries, whereas *movement* is the tendency of wood to expand or shrink after it has been seasoned depending on its surroundings. Wood species with high stability are less likely to deform if the rates of tangential and radial movement are similar.

Certain species of wood, such as Douglas fir, teak, iroko and yellow pine behave much better than others and are preferable if this is an important consideration when choosing your wood.

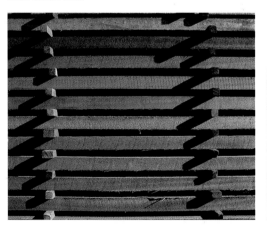

## Wood species
with low movement and good stability

| Softwoods | Hardwoods |
| --- | --- |
| Western red cedar | Muninga |
| Douglas fir | Teak |
| European spruce | Mahogany |
| Yellow pine | South American cedar |
| Western hemlock | Iroko |

## Kiln drying

Air drying is a lengthy process and can be unpredictable, as it is subject to varying weather conditions and seasonal changes. Kiln drying allows quicker production, while the quality and performance of the timber can be improved by careful control of the drying conditions. Today, nearly all commercially available timber is kiln dried, apart from beams of large section. Softwoods are normally kiln dried immediately after conversion, any preservative treatment also being applied at this stage. After drying, the timber may be cut into smaller sizes for distribution; it is in this condition that it usually reaches the home woodworker. Timber will produce disappointing results if it is worked before the seasoning process is over.

## Moisture content

The moisture content of wood is measured as the percentage of its dry weight. A sample of fresh-sawn softwood weighing 10kg (22lb) might contain as much as 5kg (11lb) of water

### Moisture content

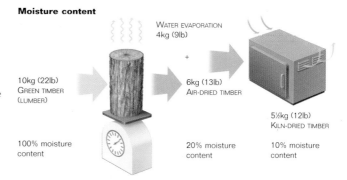

WATER EVAPORATION
4kg (9lb)

10kg (22lb)
GREEN TIMBER
(LUMBER)

100% moisture content

+

6kg (13lb)
AIR-DRIED TIMBER

20% moisture content

5½kg (12lb)
KILN-DRIED TIMBER

10% moisture content

and the same amount of dry wood. It would be described as having 100 per cent moisture content. In practice, wood is never dried completely to a zero per cent moisture content, but eventually it will reach a level consistent with its environment, which is called the *equilibrium moisture content* (emc). This can range from 18 to 20 per cent outdoors down to as low as 8 or 9 per cent in a warm, dry atmosphere. Kiln-dried timber is usually produced at a level of 10 to 12 per cent moisture content. It is essential to understand how changes in

the emc can affect the performance of a finished piece of woodwork, as the wood continues to absorb and lose moisture in response to changing levels of temperature and humidity. This is why doors and windows tend to stick during the cold months. A cabinet door that fits perfectly in the workshop can shrink or distort when installed in an air-conditioned, heated house. Consider storing the timber where it is to be used to allow it to acclimatize before being worked.

Moisture content can be estimated using a moisture meter. The meter must be suitably calibrated for the species concerned, and it will give only local values for moisture content, which will vary through the thickness of the wood. It provides a guide when monitoring timber as it dries.

---

### Drying defects

As wood dries, it shrinks, and distortion can occur in the finished boards, partly because the shrinkage will be uneven. This is predictable to an extent, depending on how it is converted. It moves more readily in the direction of the growth rings, and a plain-sawn board can lose as much as ten per cent of its original width in drying. Quarter-sawn boards are more stable, and are often used for wide areas of panelling for this reason. Uneven grain and tensions within the timber can result in defects in a board as it dries, or when it is worked. Here are some of the common problems:

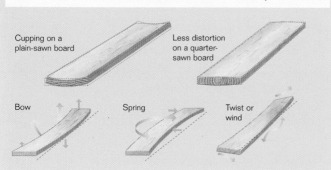

Cupping on a plain-sawn board

Less distortion on a quarter-sawn board

Bow

Spring

Twist or wind

*Above* Wood stacked high in a kiln.

# SELECTING AND STORING WOOD

**There are so many different species of timber (lumber) that it may seem difficult to decide where to start when making a selection. Your choice will depend on a number of factors, not least the cost and availability. It is well worth tracking down one or more suppliers who understand the needs of woodworkers, and striking up a good working relationship with them.**

### Choosing

Many stockists are set up to provide for the construction trade and do not take kindly to requests for small quantities of less common types. On the other hand, sometimes bargains are to be had from such companies, when they are left with short lengths of wood (sometimes sold as shorts or short ends) that are less useful to the trade. Also, bear in mind that boards with constructional defects, areas of sapwood or wild, knotty grain can be used to good decorative effect if selected carefully.

Although certain species of timber are specified for many of the projects in this book, the information should be used as a guide. Quite often, the first stage in the process of deciding what to make is to consider what timber is available and how its potential can be realized to the full, rather than sticking to fixed ideas. It is very rare that a substitute wood cannot be found that possesses the desired properties.

*Right* Stacking wood the correct way in a timber (lumber) yard.

### Workability

Some timbers are noted for being easily worked, with a low cutting resistance and blunting effect on tools. They tend to be quite bland in appearance, but are ideal for making solid frameworks where accurate jointing and stability are important. Straight, even grain gives good glued joints and resistance to splitting when nailed or screwed. These timbers can be obtained at relatively low cost.

### Finish

Not all species of timber will take a good finish – if the grain is very coarse, the surface can "pick up", requiring a lengthy process of filling the grain and rubbing down to produce a satisfactory result. Some species, such as teak, have a natural oily content that inhibits the bonding of the finish. Over the years, some woods have become highly prized for their lustrous qualities and their ability to take a high polish. Naturally they tend to be more expensive and hard to obtain.

## Wood species with good working properties

Agba
Alder
Basswood
Obeche
Pine (most species)
Western red cedar

*Left* American basswood, or American lime, is fine grained, and easily worked without blunting your tools.

## Wood species with good finishing qualities

Afrormosia
Ash
Cherry
Hemlock
Jarrah
Mahogany
Rosewood
Walnut

*Left* American black walnut, with its marked grain figure, is popular for high-quality cabinet-making and carving. It polishes to an excellent finish.

## Durability

Timber (lumber) should be selected for durability if it will be exposed to moisture, not only outdoors, but also in areas of high humidity or condensation, such as kitchens and bathrooms. Sapwood is perishable and prone to staining in most timbers, but even the heartwood of some species is vulnerable. Many tropical hardwoods, and softwoods such as yew and cedar, are highly resistant to rot because of their oily nature.

## Density

The density of wood (expressed as kilograms per cubic metre or pounds per cubic foot) is not only a measure of its relative weight, but is also linked to its strength and durability. Where these are important, your choice of species should reflect this. Bear in mind that most figures quoted are based on averages at a fixed moisture content, and the density of a single piece of wood can vary depending on its origin and growth conditions.

## Storing

Many woodworkers will hoard timber (lumber). A piece of prime quality will be set aside until the right job comes along, or because it is "too good to use". There is nothing wrong with this, provided you have the space: the timber will come to no harm if stored in the correct manner and conditions, and may even improve with age. Do not let this hoarding instinct get out of control and keep track of your stock and manage it sensibly. Record the origin and date of purchase of each batch, and do not mix them in the same piece of work.

If you do not have enough space to keep all your stock in the workshop, it will survive perfectly well outdoors until it is needed. Bring it indoors well before working it though, to allow it to acclimatize to interior conditions.

Store long lengths of timber under cover, and ensure good ventilation. Warm, damp conditions encourage decay, and an attack of fungus in a wood store must be avoided at all costs. The spores that spread fungi are everywhere, and all they need are the right conditions to take hold.

### Common durable wood species in order of durability

| Less durable | Very durable |
|---|---|
| Alder | Teak |
| Birch | Iroko |
| Lime | Afrormosia |
| Ash | Jarrah |
| Poplar | Chestnut |
| Spruce | Oak |
| | Cedar |

*Above right* Cedar of Lebanon (a true cedar), has a high resin content, and it is light and durable, one of the few softwoods suitable for exterior use without preservative treatment.

### Common wood species in order of density

| Softwood | Temperate hardwoods | Tropical hardwoods |
|---|---|---|
| Western red cedar *(least dense)* | Basswood *(least dense)* | Obeche *(least dense)* |
| Spruce | Poplar | Agba |
| Hemlock | Alder | Meranti, Idigbo |
| Scots pine | Sycamore, Ash | Mahogany, Abura |
| Douglas fir | Elm, Chestnut | Iroko, Muninga |
| Larch | Walnut, Cherry | Utile, Sapele |
| Parana pine | Beech, Birch | Teak |
| Pitch pine | Oak, Rock maple | Afrormosia |
| Yew *(most dense)* | Jarrah *(most dense)* | Ebony *(most dense)* |

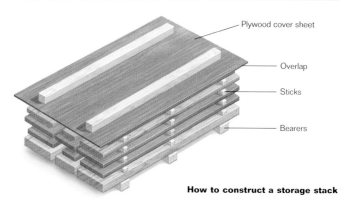

- Plywood cover sheet
- Overlap
- Sticks
- Bearers

**How to construct a storage stack**

# BUYING WOOD

Over a quarter of the land area of the globe is occupied by forested regions, and we reduce it at our peril. Unlike many other materials that we consume, trees are a renewable resource – it makes no sense to ignore the potential for endless supply by not replacing them as we use them. Gradually, the timber (lumber) trade is becoming aware of this, and the responsible woodworker should encourage the attitude by seeking out suppliers who operate environmentally sound purchasing policies.

**Timber awareness**

There are organizations such as the Forestry Stewardship Council (FSC) and the American Forest and Paper Association (AF&PA) that are working worldwide to encourage certification schemes that promote the sustainable management of our forests.

Seek out the sources of timber available to you and satisfy yourself that your local supplier is aware of the issues involved.

**The timber trade**

The trade market has a great responsibility, not only in forestry management and purchasing policy, but in promoting the efficient use of the raw material. Poor-quality timber can be directed toward the mass needs of industry while the best is reserved for the most demanding use. Everyone in the chain of supply, from foresters down to individual woodworkers, has a part to play in grading and selecting the correct timber for its purpose. When

specifying and buying timber, be prepared to consider alternatives to avoid wasting a valuable resource. Already some species are endangered and no longer available commercially, such as Brazilian rosewood; others are in short supply or are best converted into veneers. There is nothing wrong with using sheet materials, manufactured from timber trimmings (wood scraps) too small to use as solid wood, to provide a stable base for veneered panels or to make the components that will not be seen in a finished piece of work.

There are real cost savings to be made, too, if timber of the correct size and quality is purchased. Buying timber that has been dimensioned, or re-sawn to a predetermined size, saves handling large boards if you do not have the facilities. If timber has been *prepared*, or planed all round with square edges and smooth faces, it is ready to use without further machining. Bear in mind that each stage of the preparation process adds more cost. In the long term, it may pay you to invest in the space and equipment to machine your own stock from rough-sawn boards, allowing you to use the stock more selectively.

**Identifying timber**

The timber trade has its own terminology for describing the different grades and appearance of the product. Some of the more common terms are specified in the accompanying panel; look out for them when specifying timber. There is a comprehensive range of common

*Above* The country of origin of imported product is identified by distinctive shipping marks on the wood.

timbers suitable for practical woodworking. One of the first hazards to be aware of when selecting timber is that the common name for each species can be a pitfall. Many species are known by various names in different parts of the world, or even in the same country; just as often, the same name can be applied to more than one species.

The system of naming timbers is not deliberately intended to confuse, although it does seem that way sometimes. It came about because suppliers from different countries used their own systems of timber identification to suit their own market, sometimes for convenience, and even, it must be said, to give their product more value. "Mahogany", for

*Above* For a wood-product manufacturer, the use of wood from FSC sources shows a commitment to the conservation of the world's forests.

example, is used to describe completely different species of timber from South and Central America, Africa, and Australia. "Douglas fir" is not a true fir, and although it is also known as "Oregon pine", it is not a true pine either. You have every right to be confused!

The best way through the maze is to refer to the botanical name of a species, which is unique to each one, and should always be checked with the supplier when specifying the product you wish to buy. The first half of the name describes the genus or botanical group; the second part is the particular species within that group.

*Above* Douglas fir, or Oregon pine, is a softwood with a distinguishing grain.

## Timber trade terminology

|  |  |
|---|---|
| **Rough-sawn** | Sawn on a bandmill or circular saw to approximate dimensions. |
| **Prepared** | Planed in a sawmill. |
| **Surfaced** | Only small areas of a board are planed to give the buyer an idea of the colour or grain figure of the timber. |
| **PAR** | Prepared all round: square-section timber with machined faces. Beware: exact finished sizes will vary (see below). |
| **Nominal size** | The original size of the stock before machining: "ex 50 x 100mm" ("ex 2 x 4in") describes the nominal size. |
| **Finished size** | The true size of prepared stock after machining. Approximately 3mm (⅛in) will be removed from each face during this process. |
| **A/D** | Air-dried timber. Expect it to be no less than 18% moisture content. |
| **K/D** | Kiln dried. Usually timber is dried in the kiln to around 12% moisture content. |
| **T/T** | Through and through. Boards converted by through-and-through cutting will be plain sawn. |
| **1/SE** | One square edge. Boards with one square edge and one waney (crooked) edge, likely to be rift sawn. |
| **Waney edge** | Board with the sapwood and uneven edge still present, although the bark will have been removed. |
| **Unsorted** | Surprisingly, this describes the best grade for joinery-quality softwoods. Also termed clears, or clear and better. |
| **4ths & 5ths** | Lower-grade softwood stock. |
| **FAS** | Firsts and seconds. The best grade to look for in hardwoods graded for good-quality work. At least 83% of each board will yield clear, defect-free usable timber in large sizes. |
| **Commons** | Second-grade hardwood, yielding between 67 and 83% clear timber in smaller lengths. Acceptable for cabinet-making and small projects. |

## Timber and the environment

Forests Forever is encouraging companies to adopt an Environmental Timber Purchasing Policy. Companies are encouraged to set environmental objectives and targets, and to internally audit their progress towards these targets. In particular, they are encouraged to implement a programme to assess and monitor the environmental and legal credentials of all their timber products suppliers, and to trace timber as far as possible to the forest of origin.

While you shouldn't boycott individual species, it is possible to play a positive environmental role by seeking to specify a wider range of timber species. The use of "lesser-known species" can assist certain countries, usually in the tropics, with the implementation of their national sustainability programmes by taking pressure off those species which have, in the past, formed the mainstream of business. With a larger number of commercially valuable tree species, forestry departments have greater flexibility in planning harvesting regimes to ensure a better species balance in the future.

Bear in mind that in seeking to increase the range of species used, you shouldn't compromise on quality or performance. Your choice of species should always be governed by the need to ensure that it is technically suited to the application. However, keep an open mind to alternatives and don't be put off simply because a species name is unfamiliar.

# SOFTWOODS

This type of wood is not necessarily soft, but all softwoods have in common the property of being conifers, or cone-bearing trees, and mostly evergreen, although the larch is a notable exception. Usually low in cost and readily available, most common softwoods are suitable for all forms of general carcassing and construction work.

   If better appearance and good finishing qualities are required, more careful selection is necessary. Softwoods are generally light in weight, less durable, and more susceptible to insect attack and fungal decay than most hardwoods. Pitch pine, cedar and yew are three notable exceptions.

*Opposite left, centre and right*
*The storage chest is made from reclaimed pine floorboards; the magazine rack is pine; and the bar stool is constructed from Southern yellow pine.*

| | Common name | Other names | Botanical name | Origin |
|---|---|---|---|---|
| | Cedar of Lebanon | True cedar | *Cedrus libani* | Middle East, Europe |
| | Douglas fir | Oregon pine | *Pseudotsuga taxifolia* | USA, Canada |
| | Hoop pine | Queensland pine | *Araucaria cunninghamii* | Australia |
| | Kauri pine | Queensland kauri | *Agathis* spp. | Australia, NZ |
| | Larch | European larch | *Larix decidua* | Europe, Asia |
| | Parana pine | | *Araucaria angustifolia* | S America |
| | Pitch pine | Longleaf pitch pine | *Pinus palustris* | USA, Central America |
| | Ponderosa pine | Bull pine | *Pinus ponderosa* | USA, Canada |
| | Rimu | Red pine | *Dacrydium cupressinum* | New Zealand |
| | Scots pine | European redwood | *Pinus sylvestris* | Europe, UK |
| | Sequoia | Californian redwood | *Sequoia sempervirens* | USA |
| | Silver fir | European whitewood | *Abies alba* | Europe |
| | Southern yellow pine | Carolina pine | *Pinus echinata, Pinus eliottii* | USA |
| | Spruce | European whitewood | *Picea excelsa, Picea abies* | Europe |
| | Western hemlock | Alaska pine | *Tsuga heterophylla* | USA, Canada |
| | Western red cedar | Shinglewood | *Thuja plicata* | USA, Canada |
| | Yellow pine | Quebec yellow pine | *Pinus strobus* | USA, Canada |
| | Yew | | *Taxus baccata* | UK, Europe |

Cedar of Lebanon

Larch

Southern yellow pine

Yellow pine

| Description | Other properties | |
|---|---|---|
| Light brown heartwood, with distinctive growth rings | Very resinous, durable, easy to work, but low in strength | |
| Yellow to pinkish brown with marked growth rings | Slightly coarse, quite dense, durable with good workability | |
| Yellow brown heartwood, pale sapwood, as Parana pine | Not a true pine. Works and finishes well, very stable | |
| Fine, straight grained, creamy brown colour | Again not a true pine, but works well and is durable | |
| Resinous with pale sapwood and reddish heart | Heavier and more durable, but harder to work | |
| Attractive reddish brown heartwood with dark streaks | Straight grained and good workability, but poor stability |  Douglas fir |
| Marked figure with yellowish to reddish heartwood | Coarse grained and resinous, but very durable | |
| Yellowish white, straight grained with delicate figure | Very stable, works well, excellent finishing | |
| Reddish brown heartwood with fine texture | Not a true pine, but equivalent working properties | |
| Pink to reddish heartwood with distinct growth rings | Resinous, good all-round working and performance | |
| Prominent growth rings, reddish brown heartwood | Similar to Western red cedar, but non-resinous | |
| Very similar to Spruce, sold generally as Whitewood | Soft and lightweight especially when fast grown | Scots pine |
| Yellow to reddish brown heart with marked growth rings | More durable and stable than Yellow pine | |
| Pale white with sapwood and heartwood very similar | Can be knotty and contain pockets of resin | |
| Fine, straight grain with dark red growth rings | Good workability and finish, but prone to movement | |
| Attractive heartwood varies from light pink to dark brown | Very stable and durable, but soft and low in strength | |
| Light tan to pinkish heartwood, good even texture | Good quality, stable, and slightly resinous | |
| Pale sapwood and reddish heart with colourful figure | Dense, oily wood works to a fine finish | Western hemlock |

Yew

# TEMPERATE HARDWOODS

There are thousands of species of hardwood to choose from, but those listed here have been selected because of their ready availability, cost and performance. Temperate hardwoods are grown away from the tropical belt, in Europe, Asia, North America and the Southern Hemisphere. They offer a vast range of different properties, making it possible to find a particular species to suit virtually any purpose.

*Opposite left, centre and right*
*The occasional table is constructed from white ash; the picture frame from white oak; and the settle from sweet chestnut.*

| | Common name | Other names | Botanical name | Origin |
|---|---|---|---|---|
| Alder (American) | Alder (American) | Red alder | *Alnus rubra* | USA |
| | Ash | European ash | *Fraxinus excelsior* | USA, Europe |
| | Australian blackwood | | *Acacia melanoxylon* | Australia |
| Basswood | Basswood | American lime | *Tilia americana* | USA, Canada |
| | Beech | | *Fagus sylvatica* | Europe, Asia |
| | Birch (European) | White birch | *Betula alba* | Europe, Asia |
| | Boxwood | | *Buxus sempervirens* | Europe |
| Birch (European) | Butternut | White walnut | *Juglans cinerea* | USA |
| | Cherry | American cherry | *Prunus serotina* | USA |
| | Chestnut | Sweet chestnut | *Castanea sativa* | UK, Europe |
| | Elm (European) | English elm | *Ulmus procera* | Europe |
| | Hornbeam | | *Carpinus betulus* | UK, Europe |
| Chestnut | Jarrah | Australian mahogany | *Eucalyptus marginata* | Australia |
| | Maple (Hard) | Sugar maple | *Acer saccharum* | USA, Canada |
| | Maple (Soft) | Red maple | *Acer rubrum* | USA, Canada |
| | Oak (American Red) | | *Quercus rubra* | USA |
| | Oak (American White) | | *Quercus alba* | USA |
| Jarrah | Oak (European) | | *Quercus robur* | Europe |
| | Sycamore (American) | Buttonwood, Lacewood | *Platanus occidentalis* | USA |
| | Sycamore (European) | | *Acer pseuodplatanus* | Europe |
| | Walnut (Australian) | Queensland walnut | *Endiandra palmerstonii* | Australia |
| Oak (European) | Walnut (Black) | Virginia walnut | *Juglans nigra* | USA |
| | Walnut (European) | | *Juglans regia* | Europe |
| | Yellow poplar | American whitewood | *Liriodendron tulipifera* | USA |
| Sycamore (American) | | | | |

| Description | Other properties |
|---|---|
| Light brown, fine straight grain | Works well, but non-durable |
| Pale honey colour with marked growth ring figure | Good working and bending properties, excellent finish |
| Gold or red to dark brown with sometimes curly figure | Strong, works well and polishes to a high finish |
| Creamy white with close even grain | Low in strength and durability, works and carves very well |
| Pale brown with distinctive flecks | Hard, but good to work and finish |
| White or pale brown with little figure | Soft and easy to work |
| Pale yellow brown, fine even grain | Very dense and hard, good carving and turning wood |
| Light brown, straight coarse grain | Easily worked and very stable |
| Reddish brown with pale sapwood | Hard-wearing, but tough to work |
| Light brown, similar to oak, but without silvery ray figure | Bends well, easy to work and reasonably durable |
| Brown heartwood with twisted grain | Attractive, but hard to work |
| Uniform close grain, yellowish white | Very hard-wearing, but hard to work |
| Rich red heartwood, wavy figure | Strong, durable, but low in stability |
| Very close grain, creamy brown | Dense and hard wood, polishes well |
| Pinkish tinge to heartwood | Softer and lighter than above |
| Pinkish brown compared to *Q. robur* | Less obvious ray figure |
| Lighter, but similar to *Q. robur* | Less durable than European oak |
| Pale to dark brown; distinct growth rings and silvery rays | Strong and durable, bends well, harder to work |
| Light brown, straight even grain with wide rays | Ray figure produces attractive "lacewood" when rift sawn |
| Very pale, sometimes wavy grain | Stains and finishes well |
| Similar to European walnut | Interlocking grain, harder to work |
| Dark brown with purple tints | Coarse grain, but good to work |
| Greyish brown with rich dark streaks and wavy grain | Excellent finish, hard and durable |
| Pale sapwood, dark streaks in heartwood, straight grain | Good working properties and good finishing, stable |

Ash

Beech

Cherry

Elm (European)

Maple (hard)

Oak (American red)

Walnut (black)

# TROPICAL HARDWOODS

Tropical hardwoods have become a sensitive issue in recent times, as large areas of tropical rainforest around the world have been cleared by indiscriminate logging. This is not to say that some sources of tropical timber (lumber) are not managed responsibly. Indeed, where they are, they should be encouraged as a means of supporting local industries in the sustainable management of the resource. Identifying the species at risk (see chart) and using alternatives with similar properties is a responsible approach to the problem.

*Opposite left and right* The legs of the dining table are constructed from teak and the top is from elm. The conservatory bench is made from iroko.

| | Common name | Other names | Botanical name | Origin |
|---|---|---|---|---|
| | Afrormosia | | *Pericopsis elata* | W Africa |
| | Balsawood | | *Ochroma lagopus* | S America |
| | Brazilian cedar | | *Cedrela fissilis* | S America |
| Afrormosia | ● Bubinga | African rosewood | *Guibourtia demeusei* | W Africa |
| | ● Cocobolo | Nicaragua rosewood | *Dalbergia retusa* | Central America |
| | ● Ebony | Macassar ebony | *Diospyros macassar* | Indonesia |
| | Greenheart | | *Ocotea rodiaei* | S America |
| Bubinga | Idigbo | | *Terminalia ivorensis* | W Africa |
| | Iroko | African teak | *Chlorophora excelsa* | Central Africa |
| | Jelutong | | *Dyera costulata* | Indonesia |
| | ● Kingwood | Violetwood | *Dalbergia cearensis* | S America |
| Idigbo | ● Lignum vitae | Ironwood | *Guaiacum officinale* | C & S America |
| | Mahogany (African) | | *Khaya ivorensis* | W Africa |
| | ● Mahogany (Brazilian) | | *Swietenia macrophylla* | C & S America |
| Iroko | Makore | African cherry | *Tieghemella heckelii* | W Africa |
| | Meranti | Lauan, Seraya | *Shorea* spp. | Indonesia, Philippines |
| | Obeche | African whitewood | *Triplochiton scleroxylon* | W Africa |
| | Padauk | African or Indian padauk | *Pterocarpus* spp. | SE Asia, W Africa |
| Makore | Ramin | Melawis | *Gonystylus macrophyllum* | Indonesia |
| | ● Rosewood (Brazilian) | Rio rosewood, Jacaranda | *Dalbergia negra* | S America |
| | ● Rosewood (Indian) | | *Dalbergia latifolia* | India |
| | Sapele | | *Entandophragma cylindricum* | W Africa |
| Meranti | ● Satinwood | | *Chloroxylon swietenia* | India, Sri Lanka |
| | ● Teak | | *Tectona grandis* | SE Asia |
| | Utile | | *Entandrophragma utile* | W Africa |
| Teak | Wenge | | *Milletia laurentii* | W Africa |

■ *Endangered species*

| Description | Other properties | |
|---|---|---|
| Orange-brown, straight and fine-textured heartwood | Stable and durable, good alternative to teak and less oily | |
| Pale beige, porous and open-grained | Lightest and softest of all hardwoods | |
| Pink to mahogany coloured heartwood | Durable and good to work, resinous |  |
| Reddish brown with dark figure | Hard and dense, coarse grained | Brazilian cedar |
| Dark brown with colourful streaks | Tough and dense with lustrous finish | |
| Dark brown with black stripes | Dense, used for turning and veneers in small quantities |  |
| Yellowish to dark olive brown | Extremely durable, hard to work | |
| Pale yellowish with some figure | Stable and durable, poor finishing | Ebony |
| Yellowish to golden brown, with coarse striped grain | Durable with lustrous finish; hard to work and blunts tools | |
| Straight grained, pale creamy colour | Lightweight and stable, works well |  |
| Even-textured with variegated figure from brown to violet | Lustrous and excellent finish, used for turning or veneers | |
| Olive to deep brown, interlocked grain and fine texture | Oily, hard and extremely dense, used mainly for turning | Mahogany (Brazilian) |
| Pale pinkish brown, with coarse or interlocking grain | Easy to work, reasonable substitute for true mahogany | |
| Light to dark reddish brown, straight and even grain | Stable with excellent working properties, good finishing | |
| Reddish brown, fine straight grain | Hard, dense and difficult to work | Obeche |
| Pink (White lauan) or reddish (Red lauan), coarse grain | Easy to work, often seen as Far Eastern plywood | |
| Creamy white to yellow, open grained | Light, but stable, easily worked | |
| Red to purplish brown; resinous and interlocking grain | Hard-wearing, very stable, hard to work and poor finish | |
| Straw to creamy brown with dark flecks, straight grained | Easy working, but poor stability, often used for mouldings | Ramin |
| Dark brown with variegated violet to dark bronze streaks | Attractive, but in short supply, used mainly for veneering |  |
| More dull brown to purplish black | As for Brazilian rosewood | |
| Reddish brown; markedly striped quartered figure | Alternative to mahogany, easy to work, but less stable | |
| Golden brown with lustrous figure | Good to work, hard fine texture | Rosewood (Brazilian) |
| Honey coloured to dark brown with strong figure | Dense, oily, durable, attractive but hard to work |  |
| Reddish brown, interlocking grain | Similar to sapele, but more stable | |
| Dark brown with black stripes | Hard and dense, attractive finish | Sapele |

# MANUFACTURED BOARDS

Manufactured boards in various forms are familiar and have revolutionized the principles of wooden construction. By processing solid timber (lumber) into sheets of stable material, glued together by various means, the suppliers have considerably increased their usable output and have improved the material's performance for many uses. Parts of the tree that otherwise would be pulped can be reformed to produce an economic building material. For the woodworker, the main advantage is the availability of large panels that are stable, easy to work and low in cost.

*Above* MDF is stable and easy to work, and ideal for making templates in the workshop.

### Plywood

This consists of several thin layers of wood, usually with the grain at right angles in alternate layers (cross-ply). It is dimensionally stable and very strong. Useful thicknesses range from 3mm (⅛in) up to 25mm (1in).

*Softwood ply* is usually made from Douglas fir, and is coarse grained, but durable.

*Birch ply* has more laminations and is pre-sanded to give a smooth finish that is ideal for painting or varnishing.

*Far Eastern ply* is cheaper, but more open grained and more useful for structural work.

*Exterior-grade ply* uses a WBP (water- and boil-proof) adhesive and hardwood laminations.

*Marine ply* is the most durable of all and correspondingly expensive.

*Flexiply* has the grain running in the same direction on every layer and can be formed into tight curves. It also has no "voids" in its structure.

*Decorative ply* has a veneer of decorative hardwood bonded to one or both sides and is perfect for enclosed panels and carcass construction.

### Blockboard

The core of blockboard is made from solid strips of softwood glued along their edges. It is faced with a layer of veneer on each side. Blockboard is lighter than plywood, resistant to bending, and is useful for large structures and shelving. Normally, it is available only in 19mm (¾in) and 25mm (1in) thicknesses.

### Laminboard

Similar to blockboard, laminboard has an internal core made of much smaller strips of softwood. As a result, the board is more stable. It is ideal for a smooth, ripple-free finish.

### Particle boards

In particle boards, no thin layers of solid wood are used at all. Instead, the board is made from small particles of processed timber bonded together with resin.

*Chipboard* is the most common type, being used as a base for laminated work or for utility shelving and carcassing. It has a smooth, hard surface and a softer core. Unlike plywood, it is prone to splitting when screws are driven into the edges.

*OSB* (oriented strand board) is similar to chipboard, but is made from larger, wafer-like particles and has uneven faces. Both types can be used to provide hard-wearing surfaces for bench tops and flooring, but they have poor moisture resistance and low integral strength. Chipboard shelving is prone to sagging unless well supported at close intervals.

*Pineboard* is like the core of blockboard, but without the outer layers. Small strips of pine are glued together on edge and sanded smooth,

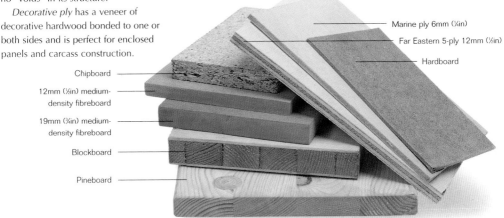

Marine ply 6mm (¼in)

Far Eastern 5-ply 12mm (½in)

Hardboard

Chipboard

12mm (½in) medium-density fibreboard

19mm (¾in) medium-density fibreboard

Blockboard

Pineboard

making it ideal for instant shelving, carcassing and many home improvement projects.

## Fibreboards

Wood is shredded into a fibrous form and bonded with resin under high pressure to manufacture various forms of fibreboard.

*Softboard* or *Insulating board* is extremely light and soft. It can be used as an insulating layer or as a pinboard.

*Hardboard* has one hard surface only, but is very stable and bends easily. It is useful for making templates.

*Tempered hardboard* is impregnated with resins to make it more water-resistant, but by no means is it completely waterproof.

*MDF* (medium-density fibreboard) is by far the most useful fibreboard product. It is dense, flat, stiff, has no knots and is easy to cut. It is very stable, and the fibres are compressed so finely that it can be cut and shaped without crumbling. It is best cut with carbide tools as steel cutting tools may dull easily. MDF makes an ideal substrate for veneer, and is available in decorative form with real hardwood veneers already bonded to both faces. Always wear a mask when working with MDF, as it creates fine dust particles which can be carcinogenic. Glues for MDF are also made with formaldehyde and are toxic.

## Standard sizes

Nearly all manufactured boards have a standard size of 1220 x 2440mm (4 x 8ft). Some suppliers offer a metric size, which is smaller (1200 x 2400mm), so always check, as this can make a critical difference to your cutting list. Special sizes of plywood and MDF, up

*Right* An indication of the wide range of finishes that manufactured boards can offer.

to 3m (10ft) in length, are available from some suppliers. Many stores will cut large sheets into smaller sizes if requested at the time of purchase.

## Grain direction

The direction in which the grain runs on the outer layers is always given first when describing plywood. This can be important when planning your cutting list. With birch plywood, for example, 1220 x 2440mm (4 x 8ft) in a supplier's catalogue will indicate that the grain runs across the width of the board, not down its length.

Most veneered decorative boards are manufactured with the grain running across the length. In this case, the catalogue entry would read 2440 x 1220mm (8 x 4ft).

### Common thicknesses of manufactured board

| Type | 3mm ⅛in | 6mm ¼in | 9mm ⅜in | 12mm ½in | 16mm ⅝in | 19mm ¾in | 22mm ⅞in | 25mm 1in | 32mm 1¼in |
|---|---|---|---|---|---|---|---|---|---|
| Plywood | X | X | X | X | X | X | X | X | |
| Plywood (D. fir) | | | | X | | X | | | |
| Blockboard | | | | | | X | | X | |
| Laminboard | | | | | | X | | X | |
| Chipboard | | | | X | X | X | X | X | |
| OSB | | | | X | | X | | | |
| Hardboard | X | X | | | | | | | |
| MDF | | X | X | X | | X | | X | X |

# MOULDINGS

This is the term used to describe any section of timber (lumber) that has been shaped, either by hand or by machinery, to alter the square profile of the original piece. This may range from rounding over the sharp edges of the finished work to adding more decorative detail. Ready-made mouldings, in a variety of different species, are sold by most timber suppliers and can be used to enhance your work. Alternatively, profiled cutters can be fitted in a router to make your own mouldings and create a range of decorative effects.

**Parts of a moulding**

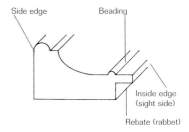

### General-purpose mouldings

A range of commonly used profiles is available in standard lengths, usually 2.4m (8ft) and 1.8m (6ft), and to different sized sections. They are ideal for fitting in corners and along edges to break up sharp angles or for trimming the edges of manufactured boards to conceal their exposed cores.

A close-grained timber is normally used to form ready-made mouldings, reducing the risk of splitting when nails are driven through them, but even so small pilot holes may be needed, especially when fixing close to the ends.

Common species include pine and spruce, pale coloured hardwoods such as beech, ramin and poplar (ideal for staining or painting), and darker hardwoods such as mahogany, utile and meranti.

In former times, the woodworker would have had to hand a variety of moulding planes to produce a detail on a piece of work. Nowadays a power router can be used to achieve the same effect. If you cannot find a suitable ready-made profile, or would prefer to use the same material to match your project, you will find it just as easy to make your own with a profile cutter of the right shape.

*Below* A range of ready-made carved and embossed mouldings.

## Common mouldings

**Quadrant moulding** A simple quarter-round moulding for breaking up the sharp edges of a corner.

**Ovolo** A stepped, convex profile that adds a visual break to a moulded edge.

**Scotia** (or cavetto) is a concave curve that works well on internal corners.

Angled

Hockey stick

**Ogee moulding** An S-shaped profile with reverse curve; often used as a panel moulding.

**Astragal moulding** Usually for small-section beading; suitable for dividing large panels into smaller areas, or as a cover strip.

**Angled and hockey-stick mouldings** These are commonly used for trimming edges.

TGV Cladding

TGB Cladding

**Skirting torus moulding** A half-round profile, one of several types often used for skirting boards (baseboards).

**Chamfer skirting** These may or may not have a rounded edge. Use them to remove the sharp edge, or arris, on the corner of a section.

**Tongued-and-grooved mouldings** can be used to make wide panels and wall cladding. Tongued, grooved and V-jointed (TGV) is the most common profile; tongued, grooved and beaded (TGB) incorporates a half-round bead along one edge. Also known as "bead board" in the United States.

# DECORATIVE MOULDINGS

These can be fixed to walls or flush doors or cabinets to create a panelled or decorative effect and are available in a wide range of styles.

### Panel mouldings

Ready-made sets of mouldings can be fixed to flat panels to create decorative effects. They may include curved sections for the top edges.

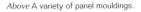

*Above* A variety of panel mouldings.

### Carved mouldings

For intricate designs, small sections of decorative carved moulding with repeated patterns can be used to good effect. These are carved by machine, or sometimes "embossed" by stamping a relief into the surface of the wood.

*Above* A variety of carved mouldings.

### Architectural mouldings

Certain mouldings are grouped together under the name "architectural" and are commonly used for interior joinery. However, they have many other uses, including adding decorative detail to cabinets and fitted furniture.

The wide range of sizes and profiles adds enormous potential to the woodworker's options when designing decorative pieces.

*Architrave* A moulded strip of wood that surrounds a door frame.

*Pediments* Pre-formed in fixed widths to suit standard door sizes, these can be used to good effect along the tops of bookcases and closets, matching the interior style of a room.

*Plinth blocks and corner blocks* A good method of producing a classical style, avoiding the need for mitred corners.

*Skirting boards (base boards).* Well-known features in any room and available in a useful range of profiles.

*Above* A variety of twist mouldings.

*Above* A variety of "egg and dart" style mouldings.

Architrave

Pediment

32

## Joining mouldings

This is a typical layout showing how architectural mouldings are put to use. They are so called because they would be used to produce a certain effect in the interior of a room rather than for individual items of furniture.

Notice how they combine a decorative effect with good practical points: the plinth blocks and corner blocks around a door frame convey a classic formality, but they also avoid the need to form complex joints where two wooden components meet.

Cornice

Corner block

Architrave

Dado (chair) rail

Plinth block

Skirting board
(baseboard)

# Veneers

Certain species of timber (lumber), which are expensive or have decorative properties (usually both), are frequently available as veneer forms. These are simply very thin sections of wood that have been peeled or sliced from the main trunk of the tree, allowing maximum use to be made of a valuable resource. When glued to a solid panel, they make all kinds of effects possible. As exotic timber from rare species becomes more difficult to obtain, the use of veneers is becoming more widespread. Decorative manufactured boards, already veneered with a range of hardwoods, are also commonly available.

Bird's eye maple

Fiddleback sycamore

Figured birch

Figured finegre

## Cutting veneers

To slice veneers from a log, it is mounted in a frame that rotates or slides up and down against a razor-sharp blade. Depending on the way the log, or *flitch*, is mounted, different sections of the figure in the grain can be displayed to their best effect.

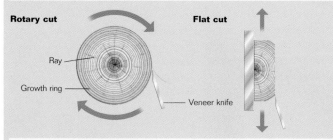

**Rotary cut**

**Flat cut**

Ray

Growth ring

Veneer knife

Figured sycamore

Pommelle

Figured makore

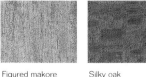
Silky oak

*Rotary-cut* veneers follow the growth rings in the log as it is "unpeeled" like a giant roll of paper. They are produced in large sizes. Commercially produced plywood is usually made from rotary-cut veneers.

*Flat-cut*, or *Crown-cut*, veneers are cut parallel to the centre line of the flitch, as in through and through conversion. Species with distinct growth rings are best sliced in this way.

### Distinctive grains

Veneers are made from a wide range of wood species to produce various effects. Certain trees develop distinctive grain patterns and can be sliced into veneers to display these to maximum effect.

Bird's eye maple is a highly prized effect that arises in certain maple trees, and is selected for veneers wherever possible. The veneer is rotary cut to display the dimpled grain that resembles birds' eyes, hence the name. Sometimes a distinctive ripple arises in sycamore, known as fiddleback, so-called because sycamore was often used for making violins. Other species produce curious mottled and lustrous patterns. When a log is quartered to cut through the horizontal rays, the silvery pattern in some species is unmistakable, as in oak or silky oak (see above), which is not a true oak, but a similar-looking wood from Australia.

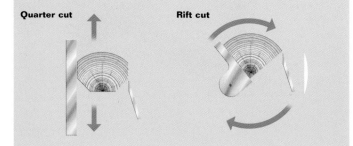

**Quarter cut**

**Rift cut**

*Quarter cutting* through the rings at right angles displays the rays in wide bands, as in quartered oak, where the silvery "flash" (rays) is distinctive. With the knife offset at a slight angle from the quarter position, a *rift* or *comb* cut is achieved. This produces a fine parallel grain figure and prevents the rays from flaking out of the thin slices of veneer.

## Burr veneers

Burr, or Burl, figure arises from an abnormal growth on the tree trunk, the grain becoming tortuous and disfigured. It can occur in many species and is sought after for veneering or turning.

Vavona (sometimes written vervona), is the name given to burr wood from the sequoia tree. Burr veneers need very careful handling as they are extremely fragile when sliced into thin sheets. They should also be well sealed and coated to prevent small fragments becoming separated.

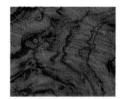

Walnut burr

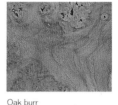

Oak burr

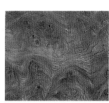

Elm burr

Ash burr

Vavona burr

Myrtle burr

## Colour

Veneers are selected to display the striking colours of some species, from the bright orange of yew wood to the dark olive green sometimes found in the heartwood of ash.

Some wood tends to darken naturally when it is exposed to sunlight, as in the example of weathered sycamore. It should be well sealed to prevent further bleaching or discolouration. Other veneers are actually stained or tinted to produce a variety of coloured effects which can be quite striking.

Yew

Olive ash

Red elm

Walnut

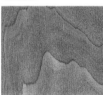

Bolivor

Weathered sycamore

## Exotic veneers

Rare species of wood are much more likely to be encountered in veneer form than any other.

Brazilian rosewood in its solid form has now been banned from international trade because of its scarcity. However, small quantities of veneer can still be obtained from specialist veneer suppliers. Even rare varieties of wood become available from time to time, and this is the most sensible and economical way of using a valuable resource.

Brazilian rosewood

Red gum

Santos rosewood

Madagascar rosewood

# TOOLS

**W**oodworking requires a range of specific tools, which have been developed and become increasingly specialized to suit every conceivable task. Despite the introduction of power tools in recent years, few jobs can be done without using hand tools at some stage of the process, and every woodworker will gradually collect more of them as the need arises. The following pages include most of the tools in common use, but there is no end to the variety and different levels of quality and refinement available, as browsing through any tool catalogue will reveal.

Tools can be grouped into families according to each stage of the woodworking process – measuring and marking, cutting and shaping and finishing, for example. Only a few basic essentials from each group are needed to begin, but the serious craftsperson will soon find that learning new skills and acquiring the tools that go with them is a never-ending process, and part of the rewarding experience of fine woodworking.

# THE BASIC TOOLKIT

"A bad craftsman always blames his tools." We have all heard this saying and understand what it means – you cannot expect a tool to do its job well if it is not handled correctly. This does not simply mean that you need to develop your woodworking skills; you also have to select the appropriate tool for the task at hand, understand how it functions and know how to keep it sharp and in good condition.

It will take some time and a little patience to gain confidence using hand tools, especially saws, chisels and planes but you will gain much satisfaction and increase your skills as a craftsperson.

### Buying the best

A common mistake made by novices is to start out with a cheap "beginner's" toolkit. This can be a false economy – not only will the tools be made of poor-quality steel that will not hold a sharp edge, but also their overall quality and balance will make hard work of simple operations. As a result, you may become frustrated at your inability to achieve good results, no matter how much care you take, and lose interest in persevering.

There must be many people who think that they do not have what it takes for woodworking, when in fact all they need is the correct guidance and a little tuition in selecting the tools for the job.

*Below* Build your tool collection gradually by buying the best tools you can afford.

## Starting a collection

|  | Basic toolkit | Next on the list |
|---|---|---|
| Measuring and marking: | Retractable tape<br>Try square<br>Marking knife<br>Bradawl or awl | Steel rule<br>Combination square<br>Marking gauge<br>Adjustable bevel gauge |
| Cutting: | Hardpoint saw<br>Tenon saw | Professional hand saw<br>Mitre saw |
| Shaping: | Bench plane<br>Bevelled chisels | Block plane<br>Firmer chisels |
| Assembling: | Screwdrivers<br>Claw hammer<br>Mallet<br>G-cramps (C-clamps) | Cordless drill/driver<br>Drill bits<br>Pin hammer<br>Sash cramps (Bar clamp) |
| Finishing: | Sandpaper/abrasive papers | Scraper |

### Getting the essentials

It is not easy to specify the tools that are essential for starting out, simply because the range of woodworking activities is so wide. A model maker needs different tools to a cabinet-maker; working with manufactured boards requires sharp, tungsten-carbide-tipped tools for best results, while softwoods can be worked easily with good-quality hand tools.

Nevertheless, most woodworking operations tend to have a definite sequence of work, and the basics will allow you to get started and explore further options as you progress. Included in the table are the tools that should form your "wish list" – the most useful items to save for.

## Buying tools

Most large hardware and do-it-yourself stores stock a full range of tools and offer good value where the more basic items are concerned. For the best quality and a wider range of specialist (specialty) tools, however, a professional tool shop is worth a visit. An expensive hand saw or plane must be handled and tested for balance before you buy.

A good tool supplier will understand this and should be able to offer a variety of different models so that you can choose the one that suits you best.

Spare parts and servicing are important, so try to develop a good working relationship with your supplier and discuss your needs. Remember that many expensive tools can be hired (rented) rather than purchased outright, if you need them only for the occasional project. This is also a good way of trying out different makes and models before buying a tool for yourself.

Browsing through tool catalogues is another habit that most woodworkers share. You cannot handle the tools or try them out, but a good mail-order supplier will offer a very wide range and can be a good source for really specialized items. Even second-hand tool shops are worth visiting if you get the chance. Examine the tools carefully to check that they are not damaged or incomplete; you may find a real bargain. Old tool steel was forged to a high quality and is definitely superior to some of today's cheap varieties.

## Storing tools

Well-made tools are works of great craftsmanship in themselves. They should be chosen with care and looked after well. Most accomplished craftsmen still possess some of the first tools they ever acquired, even though they may be many years old. Always protect the cutting edges of tools. A good-quality hand saw needs a cover that clips over the blade – you can make one from thin strips of plywood or plastic tube if one was not supplied with the saw. Keep chisels in a leather tool roll, with divisions to separate the blades. Planes should always have their blades retracted when not in use and be stored on their sides to preserve the surface of the sole plate.

When buying power tools, the more professional models will usually be supplied in a carrying case, which should be considered a necessity rather than a luxury. As well as protecting the tool from dust, it will prevent damage to the power lead (cord), and keep the accessories safe so that they are to hand when needed.

## Power tools

Portable power tools represent a greater investment than hand tools and must be chosen carefully. They are listed in order of versatility and usefulness.

- Jigsaw
- Cordless drill
- Router
- Orbital sander
- Circular saw
- Power drill
- Power plane (planer)
- Belt sander
- Biscuit jointer
- Mitre saw

*Below* A good set of chisels, with high-quality steel blades that are kept sharp, will last for many years.

# TOOLS FOR MEASURING AND MARKING

Accurate marking out is always the first step to a successful job. Poor-quality measuring and marking devices can lose their accuracy very quickly and spoil your work without you realizing until it is too late. Check them regularly for wear and damage, and if you think an item is suspect, put it to one side or dispose of it. A common mistake is to keep such a tool as a spare, but this is a false economy. A try square, for example, should form a perfect 90 degree angle – any variation makes it useless.

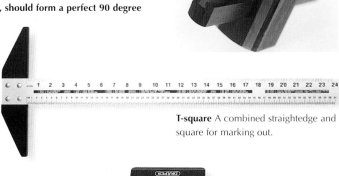

### Units of measurement

When buying measuring and marking instruments, always check which units are used on the scale. Even though metrication of the woodworking trade has been in progress for many years, there are no signs of the imperial system dying out and certainly not in the United States. Suppliers, toolmakers and timber (lumber) yards seem to manage to work to both systems in parallel, and woodworkers need to be able to do the same. It is not as confusing as it seems, but there is always room for misunderstanding. Double check the specifications of the tools when you buy them.

### Metric and imperial

A metric rule will be marked in millimetres or centimetres, or both; an imperial scale will be marked in feet and inches. Most useful of all might be a rule with both scales, on either side, but do remember to check that they are accurate. Some of the cheaper tools are poorly engraved or printed, and an inaccurate scale is not worth buying at any price.

**T-square** A combined straightedge and square for marking out.

**Straightedge** This is used as a measure and a guide for scoring and cutting. A large handle allows a firm grip and keeps fingers well away from the blade of a marking knife. A good straightedge will have thin friction pads on the underside to prevent it from slipping.

**Steel rule** For accurate setting out of joints and small dimensions, a steel rule with etched divisions is the best. It can be up to 1m or 36in long, but a 300mm (12in) rule will be more convenient for most marking-out tasks.

**Combination square** With a sliding scale and well-designed stock, this can be used as a try square, a mitre square and an adjustable depth gauge. This example even has a small spirit level mounted in the stock and a small pin for accurate marking.

**Bench rule** (*below*) A long wooden rule, less accurate for fine detail, but suitable for bench joinery and general cabinet-making. Brass-tipped versions prevent damage to the ends.

**Mitre square** (*above*) This is not a "square" at all, but an accurately machined blade and stock set at 45 degrees for gauging perfectly mitred corners.

**Bradawl** This is similar to an awl, but with a small flat end to the blade. It is used for marking hole positions and can be twisted into the wood without splitting the grain.

**Adjustable bevel gauge or sliding bevel** The hardened steel blade with locking lever can be adjusted quickly for measuring and transferring angles. A rosewood stock with brass strips ensures lasting accuracy.

**Try square** The classic carpenter's square, with a rosewood stock and brass facings for consistent accuracy. One of the first items for your toolbox.

**Craft knife** This has a multitude of uses, particularly for scribing and scoring the workpiece, as well as cutting. Choose a model with a retractable blade for safety.

**Retractable tape** An all-purpose measuring tape in a rigid case. Look for a good locking action, clear markings on the blade and a well-formed hooked end that allows both internal and external measurements.

**Spirit level** This is not vital for bench carpentry, but comes into its own when carrying out installation work. A small "torpedo" level can be kept in the toolbox.

**Chalk line** A quick method of marking out straight lines. Fill the reservoir with coloured chalk powder, clip the hook over one end of the work, pull the string tight and snap it lightly to leave a perfectly straight, temporary cutting line.

**Vernier gauge** Used for measuring both the inner and outer diameters of circular objects, or the widths of a mortise and tenon joint.

**Profile gauge** Small needles slide in the central stock, allowing the outline of any profile to be copied and transferred with ease.

**Engineer's square** An all-metal square, precision made with a hardened blade. Ideal for checking detail and can be obtained with a blade as short as 75mm (3in).

**Awl** A small pointed blade for starting holes or pricking out a mark accurately.

**Mortise gauge** This is used to mark out consistently accurate, parallel lines for cutting a mortise. The two brass pins are independently adjustable on accurate brass slides, while the sliding stock runs against the face of the work. There is a single pin on the opposite side of the shaft for marking a single scribed line.

# HAND SAWS

A well-balanced hand saw is an essential tool for any woodworker. Properly set and sharpened, it can produce a smooth, straight cut as quickly and even more accurately than a power saw. The performance of a saw depends on the size, shape and number of the teeth, which act as a series of miniature knives to slice through the wood. Each tooth is ground and sharpened individually, the quality of the steel determining how well it will perform.

**Crosscut saw** These are traditional saws. If they are well maintained, they will last a lifetime. Ideal specifications include a taper-ground blade, to prevent it from binding in the saw cut, with cross-ground teeth for splinter-free cutting across the grain. A 560mm (22in), 10- or 12-point saw is suitable for most tasks. A 10-point saw has ten tooth points for every 25mm (1in) of the blade.

**Hardpoint saw** Modern technology has produced saws with hardened teeth that remain sharp for longer, and have a specially ground profile for cutting along and across the grain with equal efficiency. However, hardpoint teeth cannot be resharpened.

**Utility saw** Consider using this "universal" saw for general-purpose use. It cannot be resharpened either, but can be considered as disposable when it has done its job. It is ideal for cutting manufactured materials, such as chipboard, which are less kind to traditional saws.

## Tenon saws

This family of saws (*below*) was designed for small-scale, accurate work, such as making joints and so on. The blade is stiffened with a strip of steel or brass along the back, and consequently these saws may be described as "backsaws". They have smaller teeth, typically 15-point, for a finer cut.

**Hardpoint tenon saw** Like the larger hand saw, this cannot be resharpened, but is ideal for general-purpose use.

**Classic tenon saw** A good-quality tenon saw for the cabinet-maker.

**Dovetail saw** A smaller version for very fine joinery work, with 20-point teeth.

## Special-purpose saws

Frame saws are designed for intricate work. The disposable blades are heat treated for hard wear and will cut wood, fibres or plastic. The frame allows the blade to be swivelled to any angle for cutting curves.

**Piercing saw** This has fine teeth (up to 80-point) for the finest modelling and engineering work. The quick-release facility allows the blade to be fed through the work and re-attached.

**Coping saw** Designed for quick adjustment, it allows curves to be cut by swivelling the blade within the frame.

**Hardpoint padsaw** This has a short, stiff blade that allows small cut-outs to be made in panels where access is restricted. Hardpoint teeth will cut fibre- or plasterboard with ease.

**Pistol-grip padsaw** This allows greater control of the blade with a pistol grip. Interchangeable blades, including hacksaw blades, can be used for cutting thin sheet metal.

**Fret saw** This can cut into the work as deep as 250mm (10in) from the edge before the frame impedes the cutting action. It works on the pull stroke for accurate control.

**Mitre box and mitre block** Useful sawing accessories without the expense of a mitre saw. To use them, insert a tenon saw blade into the pre-cut guide slots to make accurate square and mitre cuts. A mitre block has one slot, while a mitre box has two, to direct the saw blade.

**Mitre saw** This makes short work of cutting accurate angles and offers fine adjustment. It is well worth the investment if working with delicate mouldings or making picture frames. The hardpoint blade slides in nylon bearings, which, in turn, guide the cutting action.

Mitre box

Mitre block

# POWER SAWS

Power saws can save a lot of time and hard work, but they can also do a lot of damage if used incorrectly. Never force a saw through the work. If the blade is not sharp, or the motor is underpowered, not only will the cut be inaccurate, but also you'll be putting your safety at risk. Let the saw do the work, guiding it slowly, but surely, along the line. Use an adjustable fence if possible when making straight parallel cuts.

**Jigsaw** The all-purpose power saw with a multitude of uses. As well as making curved cuts, a jigsaw is ideal for quickly roughing-out work before finishing by hand.

Jigsaw

### Jigsaw key features:

- Pendulum action to reduce binding and increase the life of the blade.
- Variable speed for greater control to suit the thickness of material.
- A sawdust blower that directs the exhaust from the motor fan toward the cutting line to remove sawdust as you follow the line of the cut.
- An adjustable base plate to permit a variety of cutting angles.
- Scrolling action, allowing the blade itself to be swivelled for cutting curves of very small radius.

**Reciprocating or sabre saw** This is not really a common workshop tool, but it is useful for the rapid cutting of boards to length. Unless you do this frequently, a good, sharp hand saw will be just as effective.

Reciprocating saw

### Saw blades

Jigsaw blades come in a variety for many purposes, but check that the model of jigsaw you buy will accept standard-fitting blades. There are many specialized blades available for cutting all kinds of material, such as wood, manufactured boards, metal, ceramics, plastics and laminates. A knife blade has no teeth, and is designed for cutting leather or rubber sheeting.

Bi-metal blades, though more expensive, will last longer and are less inclined to bend. Most blades are 100mm (4in) long, allowing a depth of cut of 50–65mm (2–2½in), but heavy-duty blades are available up to 150mm (6in) long. These should only be fitted to a machine with a powerful motor designed to accept the extra load.

### Circular saw blades

Check that the bore of the blade (the diameter of the central hole that fits over the spindle) is compatible with the machine, as different makes vary. As with hand saws, the type of blade should suit the material and the cutting action, whether ripsawing along the grain, crosscutting, or making fine cuts in veneered or laminated panels.

Carbide teeth are cheaper for most general-purpose work; tungsten-carbide-tipped blades are sharper and much more hardwearing. They should be used when cutting composite materials and manufactured boards.

Powered mitre saws use special blades with teeth at a "negative rake" to suit the plunging action of the saw. They are not interchangeable with other machines.

Circular saw

**Circular saw** This is the best saw for cutting out large panels of plywood or similar manufactured materials. If it is used with a fence or purpose-made (custom-made) guide, it will make straight, smooth cuts with ease. The size of the machine and the diameter of blade determine the maximum depth of cut.

### Circular saw key features:

- Tungsten-carbide-tipped (TCT) blade.
- Adjustable base plate or "shoe" for depth and angle of cut.
- Sliding fence for cutting parallel to the edge of the work.
- Good visibility in front of the blade to aid control when cutting freehand.
- Spindle and also electric brakes to stop the blade spinning as soon as the trigger is released.
- Spindle lock for fitting blades quickly and safely.

Powered crosscut saw

**Powered crosscut saw** Sometimes called a mitre saw, this is a more costly item, but a useful workshop tool. It makes quick work of cross cutting timber (lumber) accurately to length with perfectly square ends, or can be adjusted to make angled cuts up to 45 degrees. The best models allow the saw body to slide out on parallel bars for cutting extra-wide stock up to 250mm (10in) and have a swivel mount for cutting compound angles.

**Cordless circular saw** This version of the circular saw comes into its own when working outdoors away from a power source. It does have the added safety advantage of not having a vulnerable power cord, and can be used one-handed for light work. Note how on the model shown, the blade is mounted on the left-hand side of the body for better visibility.

Cordless circular saw

# PLANES

Hand planes are among the most satisfying tools you can use. A finely set plane with a sharp blade will slice through the wood with an unmistakable sweet sound, leaving a smooth surface that scarcely needs any further treatment. As with other tools, different sizes and types of plane have been developed over the years to suit each particular task perfectly.

### Bench planes

This is the standard family of planes for two-handed use on the workbench. Each type is designed for a specific function, depending on the length of the body and the angle, or set, of the blade. Try planes or jointer planes have bodies of up to 600mm (24in) in length and are used for "trying", or truing-up (squaring), perfectly straight edges. Fore planes are slightly shorter, at 460mm (18in), and are used for much the same purpose as the try plane.

### Anatomy of a bench plane

The base of the plane is called the sole, or sole plate, and should be protected from damage to keep it perfectly straight and flat. The mouth in the sole allows the shavings to be cleared away as the plane is used. The frog is the machined block that receives the blade assembly; it can be adjusted to alter the width of the mouth. It is set to the ideal position during manufacture. Adjustment levers are mounted in the frog to control the depth of cut and to keep the blade perfectly straight. The blade assembly is removable for sharpening and maintenance, and consists of three parts: the blade itself, or plane iron, made of high-quality carbon steel for long life; the cap iron, which clamps over the iron to tension it and clear the shavings as they are produced; and the lever cap, which locates over a screw on the frog and clamps the whole assembly to the plane body.

A good-quality plane should be maintained whenever the blade is removed for sharpening. Clear all fragments of wood from the body, remove all dust and apply light machine oil to the moving parts.

### Jack plane

At 300–380mm (12–15in), this is a convenient size for most workshops. It is ideal for flattening the faces and edges of boards, and for preparing sawn timber (lumber).

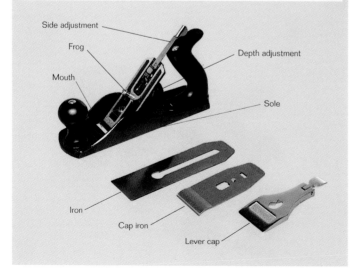

Side adjustment

Frog

Mouth

Depth adjustment

Sole

Iron

Cap iron

Lever cap

### Smoothing plane

The most useful plane for fine finishing in all kinds of woodworking. It is usually 225–250mm (9–10in) long.

### Block plane

This is not classed as a true bench plane, although the body has a similar design. The blade has a much shallower angle and can be set for the removal of the finest shavings when working across end grain. A versatile tool, shaped to fit the palm of the hand and often used one-handed.

### Shoulder planes

(*above and right*) Each of these narrow planes has its blade set at an acute angle for the removal of fine shavings when trimming joints. They are essential tools when forming tenons or cleaning-up small rebates (rabbets).

### Rebate, or filister, plane (*right*)

The best plane for forming a rebate (rabbet) along the edge of a length of wood. Like the shoulder plane, its blade spans the full width of the body. Fitted with a sliding fence to control the width of the cut, and a depth stop.

### Compass plane

A very specialized plane with a flexible sole that can be formed into a shallow arc for working on curved surfaces.

### Plough plane (*below right*)

A more sophisticated version of the rebate (rabbet) plane, having interchangeable blades of different sizes. Can be used to form grooves or rebates (rabbets) with great accuracy. A combination plane will accept other blades, or cutters, of different profiles to form beaded and tongued mouldings.

### Spokeshave

This is a two-handed tool for working on rounded stock. Available with a flat base or a rounded base for dealing with convex or concave surfaces. The name comes from the days when wheelwrights made spokes for wooden wheels.

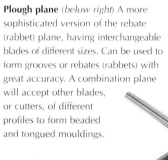

# POWER PLANERS AND ROUTERS

These are quite different tools to power saws, but they have in common the use
of rapidly rotating cutter blades, which remove the stock very quickly and
easily. When used safely they can be a powerful aid to most shaping operations.
Tungsten-carbide-tipped blades make it possible to work with manufactured
materials that can be very hardwearing on the sharpest of hand tools.

### Power planer key features:

- Reversible tungsten-carbide-tipped
  blades for longer life.
- Parallel fence for accurate rebating.
- Body design that allows a rebate
  (rabbet) depth up to 20mm (¾in).
- Dust extraction facility or collection
  bag for shavings.
- Automatic pivoting safety guard for
  cutter block.
- Safety switch and electronic
  speed control.
- V-groove in the sole plate to allow
  easy chamfering operations.

Power planer

**Power planer** This power tool is ideal
for the rapid removal of large amounts
of waste, but it should be handled
with great care, as it is extremely easy
to remove too much wood and ruin
the work. The depth of cut in one pass
ranges from 1.5 to 5mm (¹⁄₁₆ to ³⁄₁₆in) on
more powerful models; 3mm
(⅛in) is quite adequate for most
general purposes.

The cutter block, in which the
blades are mounted, rotates at very
high speed and should be treated with
great respect. Always make sure that
the power cord is well out of the way
when using a power planer, so that it
does not impede the work. Keep your
hands well away from the blades and
wait for the cutter block to stop
spinning before putting the tool down
on the workbench.

**Biscuit jointer** A biscuit jointer is a
handy tool for making quick work of
all kinds of jointing operation. The
"biscuits" are flat wooden dowels that
fit into semicircular slots formed by
the blade of the jointer. Its great
advantage is the ease with which
quick adjustments can be made to
suit any thickness of wood. The best
models have an adjustable carriage
that can be tilted up to 45 degrees for
dealing with mitred corners.

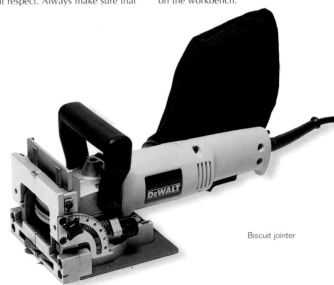

Biscuit jointer

**Router** A router is one of the most versatile and powerful tools a woodworker can have. It incorporates a rotary cutter mounted in an adjustable body, which removes small slices of wood with each rotation, allowing all kinds of profiling and shaping work.

The range of router cutters is huge, and a good way to begin is with a "starter" selection of ten or twelve cutters, which will cover a wide range of applications.

### Router key features:

- Safety switch and "soft start" feature to prevent kick-back when starting.
- Variable speed control for different materials and delicate work.
- Stepped-adjustment depth gauge, allowing a series of passes at different depths.
- Dust extraction facility.
- Spindle lock for easy cutter changing.
- Range of collets to receive cutters of different shank sizes: 6–12mm (¼–½in).
- Parallel fence with fine tuning adjustment.
- Template follower for copying patterns and routing curves.

**Router table** More powerful routers can be mounted upside-down in a work table, allowing very efficient machining operations. With a sliding fence and protective cutter guard, continuous profiling work will be accurate and safe. Large-diameter professional cutters make short work of mouldings and tongued-and-grooved panels.

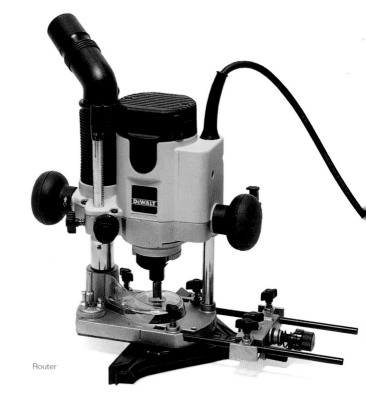

Router

Router table

# CHISELS

A high-quality forged steel blade set in a tough handle are the qualities to look for in a good woodworking chisel. Traditional chisels with hardwood handles should only be struck with a wooden mallet; more modern versions with shatter-resistant polypropylene handles can withstand hammer blows equally well. Most chisels are available in matched sets, ranging in size from 6 to 38mm (¼ to 1½in) or more, but for a more modest outlay, a set of three, comprising the most useful sizes of 12, 19 and 25mm (½, ¾ and 1in), will suffice.

### Bevelled chisels

Bevel-edge, or bevelled, chisels are the most versatile type you can buy for most woodworking tasks. They can be used for chopping out material when struck with a mallet, or for more gentle paring and shaping tasks when used freehand. A newly purchased chisel will have the main bevel ground on the end of its blade, but a secondary bevel will need adding to hone it ready for use.

| 32mm | 25mm | 19mm | 12mm | 10mm | 6mm |
|------|------|------|------|------|-----|
| (1¼in) | (1in) | (¾in) | (½in) | (⅜in) | (¼in) |

### Firmer chisels

A firmer chisel is just that: a stronger blade designed to accept heavier blows when chopping out a mortise or socket. The end bevel is designed for slicing across the end grain of wood, while the long edges are not bevelled, allowing the cutting of square, parallel-sided mortises. Usually, firmer chisels are sold only in four common sizes to suit the standard widths of mortise used in general joinery. Good quality steel is essential for these chisels, to give a good sharp edge, which can withstand heavy use.

| 25mm | 19mm | 12mm | 6mm |
|------|------|------|-----|
| (1in) | (¾in) | (½in) | (¼in) |

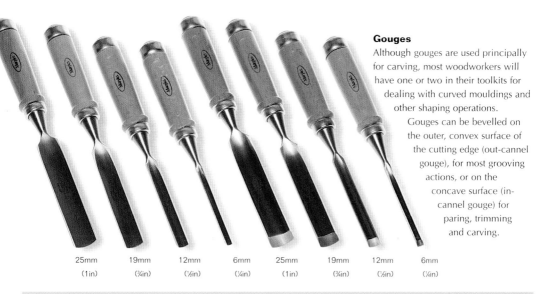

## Gouges

Although gouges are used principally for carving, most woodworkers will have one or two in their toolkits for dealing with curved mouldings and other shaping operations.

Gouges can be bevelled on the outer, convex surface of the cutting edge (out-cannel gouge), for most grooving actions, or on the concave surface (in-cannel gouge) for paring, trimming and carving.

| 25mm | 19mm | 12mm | 6mm | 25mm | 19mm | 12mm | 6mm |
|------|------|------|-----|------|------|------|-----|
| (1in) | (¾in) | (½in) | (¼in) | (1in) | (¾in) | (½in) | (¼in) |

## Sharpening equipment

A good sharpening stone is a vital part of the toolkit. Without a sharp edge, a chisel will be not only difficult to work with, but also dangerous. The chisel will follow where the wood directs it, rather than where you want it to go, and can easily slip.

Chisels should be sharpened at the beginning and end of every session. If they are attended to regularly, just a few minutes' work will keep the honed edges in prime condition. Once in a while, a longer honing session might be necessary – if the bevel loses its original angle or if the edge is chipped.

Natural sharpening stones are quite expensive, and synthetic versions are commonly used. Japanese water stones are of natural stone and need water as a lubricant. They can produce a finely ground edge on the best-quality steel. For more general use, oilstones are sufficient.

A combination stone is the best buy, two stones of different grades being bonded together back to back.

The coarse stone is for regrinding to the correct bevel; the fine stone for delivering a keen honed edge. A honing guide is a useful accessory and will assist in maintaining the correct angle of a chisel or plane iron when being sharpened. By clamping the blade in the guide and moving it gently to and fro on the stone, you will be able to grind a constant angle without difficulty.

Conical and cylindrical slipstones and wedges are sometimes used to achieve the correct profile on the blades of curved and angled chisels.

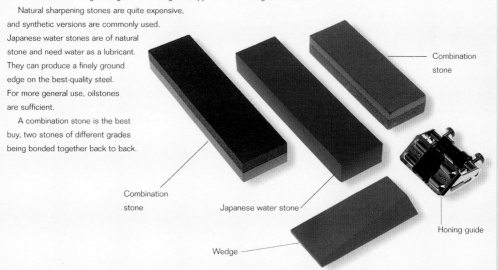

Combination stone

Combination stone

Japanese water stone

Honing guide

Wedge

# HAND DRILLS

There are few woodworking projects that do not require drilling holes of some kind, if only for fixing screws. To insert a screw correctly, a clearance hole should be drilled in the piece to be fixed to match the size of the screw's shank and prevent the wood from splitting as the screw is tightened. A countersink or counterbore may also be needed to sink the head of the screw below the surface. Finally, a pilot hole is usually advisable, of the correct diameter to suit the tapered, threaded end of the screw. All these operations can be carried out easily with a hand drill.

### Accurate drilling

This is an important woodworking technique, and it has been much simplified in recent years with powered hand drills and even more so with bench-mounted pillar drills. Hand drilling with a brace still has a place, however, especially in sites far removed from electric power. Even in the workshop, it is often quicker to reach for a small hand drill than to set up a power drill just for the few holes required before proceeding to the next stage of the job.

**Hand drill** A useful tool for quickly producing small holes when needed. Ideal for drilling pilot holes and countersinking. Its small size comes in handy in tight corners.

### Practical tip

Never interfere with the centre point of a drill if it has one – this will almost certainly affect its concentricity.

**Gimlet** The screw thread is for starting a screw hole without fear of splitting the wood when the screw is inserted.

**Carpenter's brace** This is a powerful drilling tool, which provides ample leverage from the wide sweep of its handle. Look for a "universal" jaw – a chuck that accepts both tapered and parallel drill bits – and a reversible ratchet action.

**Bradawl** Sharp pointed shaft for scribing and piercing holes for pins and nails.

## Drill bits

Great advances have also been made in the pattern of bits and there are now bits especially designed for setting dowels. This technique is often used in projects involving manufactured boards such as chipboard or ply and these produce flat-bottomed holes. There are also flat bits, which work with a scraping action and cut large holes very rapidly, although these are not as accurate as twist bits. For the home worker on a limited budget, an adjustable bit is a good investment but these can only be used in a hand brace and not in any powered tool. The ordinary twist bit is used for making small holes and for starting screws. Beware of buying cheap sets of drill bits. They can be made of poor-quality steel and can be easily blunted.

**Standard twist drills** (*left*) Sometimes described as HSS (high-speed steel), these bore holes easily in steel, but are equally suitable for woodworking. They are made in a wide range of sizes at small increments – 1mm (½₂in) – so there should be no difficulty in finding the correct size.

**Spade, or flat, bits** (*right*) These are the traditional woodworker's drill bit for larger holes up to 32mm (1¼in) in diameter. Drill vertically, using a brace, for best results.

**Centre-point (brad point), or "lip and spur", bits** (*right*) These should only be used for wood. The point centres the bit exactly, preventing slipping and helping to keep the hole straight as you work. Made in a smaller range of sizes than standard twist drills, but still adequate for most needs. They are also known as dowel drill bits, as certain diameters match the small wooden dowels used for aligning joints – 6, 8 and 10mm (¼, ⁵⁄₁₆ and ⅜in).

# POWER DRILLS

For any repetitive work, or removing large amounts of waste, a power drill is essential. Certain types of drill bit are designed specifically for use at high speeds and will not produce satisfactory results in a hand drill. Sometimes, a low speed with high torque, or turning force, is the best combination, and a power drill of the correct rating is ideal for this. The power source of the drill is all important – motors range in capacity from 300 watts (3 amp) for light duty to 1000 watts (10 amp) and above for really heavy work; a 600 watt (6 amp) motor is fine for general duties. A motor will soon burn out if the drill is overloaded.

Cordless drill

**Cordless drill** One of the first items in your toolkit should be a cordless drill. These are relatively recent products, but in the space of ten years or so they have been found to be so useful that there is now a vast range on the market. One of the advantages for the woodworker is that many cordless drills can be used as slow speed, powered screwdrivers.

The voltage of the battery determines the power of the drill and the length of time it can be used before recharging. Top-of-the-range models have 18 volt batteries – 9.6 or 12 volt is adequate for general use. Always check the manufacturer's instruction manual.

## Cordless drill key features:

- Spare battery, allowing uninterrupted use without having to wait for recharging.
- Carrying case and rapid charger.
- 10mm (⅜in) keyless chuck, allowing quick changing of drill bits.
- Screwdriver bits, clipped to the body of the drill when not in use.
- Two-speed or variable-speed facility.
- Reversible action (essential for screwdriving).
- Adjustable torque control to prevent breaking screws.
- Electric brake that stops rotation instantly when the trigger is released.

**Electric drill** For more regular use, there is no substitute for a power drill operating on mains voltage. This will run continuously at higher speeds and is ideal for mounting in a drill stand. Many power drills have a percussion facility useful for drilling into masonry, stone or brick, but this can be switched off for normal use when working with wood. A depth gauge is useful, as is a variable-speed/reversible action. A side handle provides extra grip and makes it easier to hold the drill vertical when used freehand. Some drills even have a side handle containing a small spirit level for greater accuracy. The extra power means that a 13mm (½in) chuck can be fitted to accommodate the largest drill bits.

Electric drill

**Percussion drill** A hammer, or percussion, drill is only required for drilling into masonry, using specially hardened masonry bits. It will be useful for installing items that need fixing to plaster or brickwork, but unless you intend doing a lot of work of this kind it could be an expensive luxury. Consider renting one when necessary – do not be tempted to overload a smaller drill that is not designed for heavy duty use.

Percussion drill

### Specialized drill bits

Plug cutters are a useful addition to any workshop, especially where quality work is undertaken. Another common accessory to drilling is the countersink. This allows the head of a screw to be sunk cleanly flush with the surface of the wood.

Forstner bits are designed to drill large flat-bottomed holes that do not go through the wood, such as might be needed to fit kitchen cabinet hinges. They are also accurate for drilling deep holes even in the end grain of timber.

**Boring bit** Used for boring holes for concealed hinges or other fittings of a standard size. Available in 25 and 35mm (1 and 1⅜in) diameters. Drills a shallow, flat-bottomed hole, with a centre point to keep it centred accurately.

**Counterbore, or 3-in-1, bit** This device will drill a pilot hole, clearance hole and counterbore for a screw in one operation. Obtainable in different sizes to suit a range of screws and usually sold with a plug cutter of the same gauge.

**Plug cutter** This makes small wooden plugs for concealing fixings. Ideally, it should be used in a drill stand, as it is not self-centring.

**Countersink bit** A "rosehead" countersink creates a recess for the screw head so that it is flush with the surface. Use with care, as it is very easy to spoil the work by drilling too deep.

**Masonry bits** Available in many different sizes. You will need to use this bit when attaching fittings for wooden cupboards, shelves and other types of furniture to masonry walls.

### Circular hole cutter

This must be used in a fixed drill stand or a drill with an additional side-mounted handle for safety. Select a low drill speed with a high torque setting, as the teeth remove a large amount of waste. Various sizes are available and fit a common arbor, which contains a 6mm (¼in) pilot drill to centre the hole. Holes up to 100mm (4in) in diameter are possible.

**Auger bit** This will drill deep holes quickly, removing waste. If used with a power drill, the motor must have a reverse facility, otherwise you will not be able to remove it.

# TOOLS FOR FIXING

No tool box is complete without a hammer and a screwdriver for straightforward assembly work. There are different types to suit every need. Even though they are familiar items, they should be selected and used carefully.

## Hammers

The head, or poll, of a hammer should be of good quality steel, heat treated and hardened for a long life. Hammer sizes are ranged by weight measured in ounces, even in these days of metrication: from 4oz for a small pin hammer up to 20oz.

**Cross pein, or pin, hammer** The small cross pein opposite the striking face comes into its own when fixing small panel pins (brads). Hold each pin between finger and thumb, and the narrow blade will be small enough to slide between them to deliver a few gentle taps to start it.

**Ball pein hammer**
More of an engineer's tool; the most heavy-duty hammer in common use and not often called for in woodworking.

**Rubber mallet** A useful tool for assembly work, when a reasonably firm blow may be required to knock a component into position. The rubber head will not bruise the surface of the wood. You can also buy a dead-blow mallet, which is a synthetic hammer with a hollow head, which is filled with lead shot. It delivers a sharp blow with little effort and no bounce. It is useful for assembly work.

**Carpenter's mallet** A solid beech mallet is of the correct strength and density to deliver a sound blow to a chisel without jarring. An essential tool for any carpenter.

**Claw hammer** A good-quality traditional claw hammer has a handle made of hickory, selected for its great shock-resistant properties. The precision-ground head should be fixed firmly to the shaft with hardwood and iron wedges, and feel well balanced for driving nails straight.

Slotted screwdrivers (*left*) and cross-head (Phillips) screwdrivers (*right*)

## Screwdrivers

Screws come in all shapes and sizes, with different types of head, and there are just as many types of screwdriver to suit them. The quickest way to strip the head of a screw is to use a screwdriver that does not match. Worse still, it can slip out of position and damage the work. Screwdrivers with interchangeable bits, which can be quickly inserted into a socket on the screwdriver shaft, make life easier, but there is still no substitute for the traditional cabinet-maker's tool.

Screw heads vary in size according to their gauge, common sizes ranging from a No.4 (the smallest) up to a No.12 or greater, and you will find a screwdriver to fit each perfectly. A longer shaft will provide more torque; a short screwdriver makes up for this with a larger handle for extra grip. Slotted screws are steadily being replaced by screws with cross-heads, which prevent the driver from slipping out of position, provided it is of the correct size. Make sure you have a set of screwdrivers handy to cover most needs. Never use a screwdriver blade as a lever to open a can of paint – the tip of the blade is tempered steel and can easily shatter if misused.

## Screwdriver bits

Small bits with hexagonal shafts are designed for use in special socketed handles, but some can also be clamped into the chuck of a cordless power drill.

A selection of driver bits will take up far less space than a set of separate screwdrivers. They range from long bits for heavy-duty work to short, 25mm (1in) bits, which must be fitted in a holder. All have a standard 6mm (¼in) hexagonal shank. A magnetic bit holder makes quick work of changing bits and will hold a steel screw on the tip for one-handed operation. Cross-head screws are available in two

*Above* Screwdrivers range considerably in size, from large heavy-duty drivers with a flared tip to the smallest stubby screwdrivers. The tips are described according to the size of screw they are designed for: gauge sizes for slotted screws, and point sizes for cross-heads.

types, which require different screwdrivers. A Phillips head has a simple four-way cross design, while the Pozidriv version gives a more positive grip with four additional flutes between the main slots.

It is important to be able to recognize the difference and select the right bit to suit the screw, otherwise the head will strip as you tighten up the screw.

Double-ended bits

Long heavy-duty bits    Phillips-head bits    Pozidriv-head bits    Flat bits

# ABRASIVE PAPERS AND SCRAPERS

"Sandpaper" has always been used to give a final finish for wood, although it is not made with sand. Small abrasive particles, glued to a backing paper, are graded according to their size: the finer the grit, the smoother the finish. Grades range from 40 grit up to 1200 grit, so fine that sometimes it is called flour paper in some countries.

### Varieties of paper

Many different types of material are used to make abrasive papers. For the woodworker, the most useful include garnet paper, silicon carbide and aluminium oxide paper. Garnet paper is dark red in colour and fairly coarse. It is used for flattening rough-sawn surfaces. Glass paper is paler in colour and available in the full range of grit sizes. It tends to wear quite quickly, but is economical to use.

Silicon carbide paper is more hardwearing and quite efficient. Light grey silicon paper is self-lubricating, providing a smoother finish. Dark grey paper is sometimes called "wet and dry" paper and needs lubricating with water. It is available right up to 1200 grit and is used for fine finishing.

Aluminium oxide paper is sometimes called production paper. It is the hardest wearing material and is the best option for heavy-duty use. However, it is not generally available in much finer grades than 180 grit. For woodworkers, the grades of silicon carbide and aluminium oxide papers most used are 80, 100, 120, 150, 180, 240 and 320 grit.

Use a square of sandpaper wrapped around a cork or rubber sanding block for best results. A small wooden block can be used with some success, but using a more flexible material allows better control and reduces wear on the paper, making it last longer. Make sure the face of the block is free of defects to avoid scoring the surface of the work.

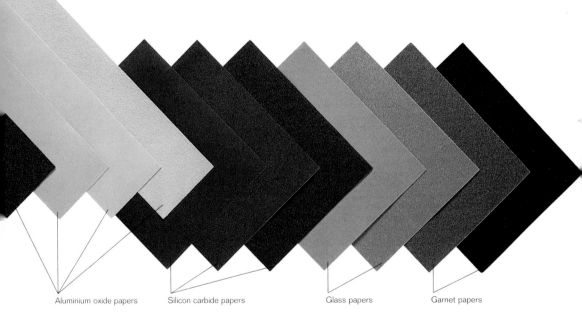

Aluminium oxide papers     Silicon carbide papers     Glass papers     Garnet papers

## Scrapers

A cabinet scraper works by cutting the wood fibres rather than wearing them down through abrasion, but is capable of delivering a very smooth finish. It is well worth acquiring the knack of sharpening and using one. A set of scrapers of different profiles will allow the finishing of curved and moulded surfaces. Whereas sandpaper tends to round off sharp edges, the profile of a gooseneck scraper can be matched to almost any curved moulding, thus preserving fine details.

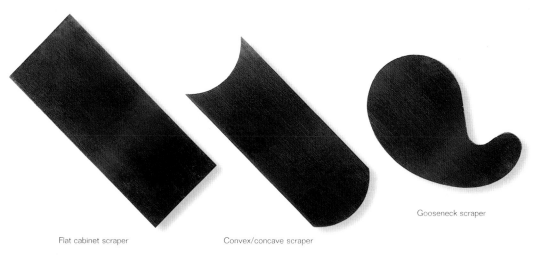

Gooseneck scraper

Flat cabinet scraper

Convex/concave scraper

## Rasps

Rasps are useful for roughing out or smoothing the edges of wood when working freehand. A wood file can then be used to achieve a finer finish. Both tools come into their own if you are dealing with variable or uneven grain where using a plane produces poor results. They can be flat or round, and a half-round profile is the most versatile. The pointed end of the file is the tang, and is generally fitted into a separate wooden handle. A surform rasp has holes in its teeth and does not clog up as much as normal rasps.

## Wire (steel) wool

This is useful for final finishing. It is available in nine grades and from 5 at the coarse end for stripping and 0000 at the fine end. It is clog resistant.

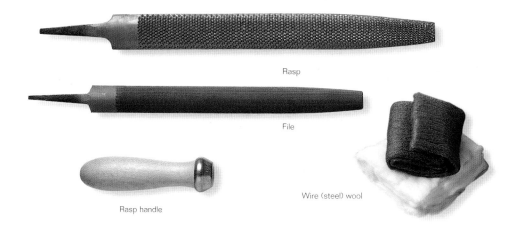

Rasp

File

Wire (steel) wool

Rasp handle

# POWER SANDERS

**These come in two main types. Belt sanders employ a cloth-backed sanding belt, usually of fairly coarse grade, for the rapid removal of stock. Orbital sanders have a backing pad that makes rapid circular movements and is capable of fine finishing work.**

**Belt sander** This should be used with great care, as it can easily dig in to the surface, leaving deep scour marks. The most important feature to look for is efficient dust extraction, as large amounts of waste are produced. A dust collection bag is essential, but the facility for connecting to an extractor unit is even better.

Different models of belt sander use belts of varying sizes, and for some reason no common standard size has been adopted by manufacturers, so check that the belt size you need is widely available.

## Belt sander key features:

- Two-speed or variable-speed motor to suit different surfaces.
- Automatic tracking control to keep the belt running smoothly.

Belt sander

**Orbital sander** More useful than a belt sander for general use. The sanding action is less severe, and by using progressively finer grades of paper, a fine finish can be achieved. Three common sizes of sander are available: half-sheet, one-third sheet and quarter-sheet. These denote the size of sandpaper that needs cutting from a standard sheet thus avoiding waste.

## Orbital sander key features:

- Effective dust collection pouch.
- Perforated base and sanding sheets that prevent dust from collecting under the sander.
- Quick-release clips for changing sanding sheets.
- Variable speed for delicate work.

Orbital sander

## Multi-function sanders

For intricate modelling and restoration work, a family of sanders with specially shaped sanding pads are worth considering. Delta sanders have a triangular base ideal for reaching into the corners of panels. Self-adhesive sanding sheets can be changed quickly without clips, but are more expensive.

Multi-function sanders

**Palm sander** This allows one-handed operation and is not suitable for heavy work, but it is ideal for a light touch to produce a fine finish. The sanding base vibrates at a higher speed than a large orbital sander. It takes quarter-sheet of standard sized sandpaper, and as with larger models, a dust-collection pouch is advisable.

Palm sander

**Random orbit sander** This is a versatile tool, combining two functions in one. Hold the sander lightly and the circular sanding disc spins in a circular motion for the rapid removal of rough surfaces. Apply more pressure and the action changes to a reciprocating orbital motion for finer finishing.

Random orbit sander

# CRAMPS, TOOLBOXES AND WORKBENCHES

There are many varieties to meet the needs of different workshop tasks. Most woodworking adhesives depend on high pressure to form a solid bond and need to be clamped for long periods. Cramps, often called clamps, have other uses, too, such as locating components temporarily when setting out and holding wood steady while working. Clamping the work firmly before any operation is a vital part of safe woodworking practice. The well-equipped workshop will have a collection of several types and sizes of cramp.

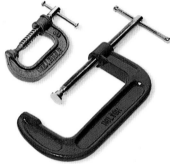

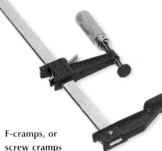

**Sash (bar) cramp** (*above*) Two cramp heads on a steel bar deliver firm parallel pressure, on which accurate joinery depends. Available in lengths up to 1.2m (4ft) and more, and most useful when employed in pairs.

**G-(C-)cramp** (*above*) The traditional woodworker's tool – you can never have too many G-cramps. Good-quality forged steel is essential; cheaper cast versions can shatter if overtightened.

**Mitre (frame) cramp** (*above*) A specialized tool that is ideal for frame making. Slide two components together to meet at the centre of the cramp, which guarantees a true right angle.

**Web cramp** (*below*) Useful for furniture making and assembling objects of irregular shape. The strong nylon webbing extends around the work and is tightened with a small spanner (wrench), applying tension equally around the assembly.

**F-cramps, or screw cramps**
(*above*) These versatile cramps are quickly adjustable. Slide the movable arm along the bar until it locks against the work, then tighten the screw.

**Quick (spring) cramp** (*above*) This only applies light pressure, but is useful for a temporary fixing, as it can be used one-handed, leaving the other hand free to locate the components.

## Toolboxes

Good tools need to be well organized and protected from damage. In earlier times, the first task of the woodwork apprentice was to make his own toolchest or toolbox, designed for his own personal toolkit. A simple box made from a few pieces of plywood, with internal compartments to keep tools separated, is well worth making when time allows. Alternatively, there is a good range of ready-made items to choose from.

A robust steel engineer's toolbox is good for smaller hand tools, with easily accessible compartments in a compact form.

Cheaper versions in rigid plastic are useful for keeping screws and nails tidy and ready for use.

Larger tools, such as hand saws and planes, can be protected in a heavy-duty canvas toolbag, while a leather tool roll is ideal for chisels. When buying a power tool, a purpose-made carrying case is a good option to look for. It will keep the tool free of dust and protect the power cord.

Engineer's toolbox

Plastic toolbox with separate compartments

## Workbenches

A good workbench will have a solid flat top with a vice fixed at one end. Even in the workshop a folding portable workbench comes into its own as a temporary support. The adjustable jaws are ideal for clamping lengths of timber (lumber).

A foldaway portable workbench

A permanent wooden workbench

# MACHINE TOOLS

Equipping a professional workshop with heavy-duty machine tools is a costly process, but the serious woodworker can benefit from smaller versions, designed for semi-professional and home workshop use. For your own safety, these machines should not be used without proper training. Many local technical schools and colleges offer evening courses in woodworking, and this is a good way to learn the principles of operating powerful machinery and to expand your abilities. If your workshop space and budget allows, this overview of woodworking machinery will give you an idea of the most popular machines and their function.

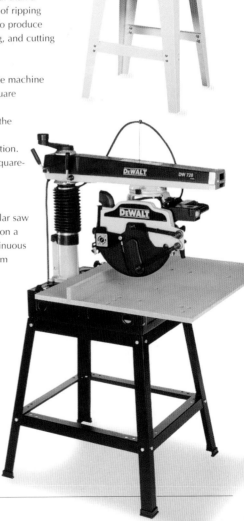

**Saw bench (Table saw)** The heart of a workshop, allowing solid timber (lumber) and sheet materials to be cut to precise dimensions with ease. The saw motor is mounted beneath the table, having a rise-and-fall action to control the height of the blade and a tilting carriage for cutting angles up to 45 degrees. A parallel fence, which slides on a calibrated scale, allows quick adjustment.

**Bandsaw** (*right*) A continuous blade of flexible steel, running through an adjustable table, makes all kinds of woodworking operations possible. A bandsaw is less powerful than a circular saw, but capable of ripping wide boards lengthways to produce thinner stock, crosscutting, and cutting curves and angles.

**Jointer surfacer** A separate machine that produces straight, square stock, as with a planer thicknesser, but removes the necessity to reset the machinery for dual operation. It is ideal for producing square-edged boards for joining together in wide panels.

**Radial saw** (*right*) A circular saw body mounted overhead on a radial arm; ideal for continuous crosscutting work. The arm can also be swivelled through 90 degrees, permitting ripsawing and angled cuts.

**Morticer** (*above*) A real time-saver when making mortises. An auger revolves in a square chisel, removing waste and forming a perfectly square mortise. The key to accurate work is a solid table that keeps the work square to the direction of cut at all times.

**Planer thicknesser (Combination jointer)** (*right*) One of the most useful machines for the home workshop. Two sets of operations are possible. On the overhead table (jointer), a length of timber (lumber) is fed over the cutter block, which is exactly square to the side fence. This produces a perfectly square edge on rough stock as a first stage. Below the table, a length of timber is fed between an adjustable bed and the rotating cutter block to produce parallel, smooth faces to accurate dimensions.

**Lathe** (*left*) Unlike any other machine tool, the lathe makes possible a whole new dimension of woodworking, by turning the stock lengthways against the tool. Any cylindrical form can be produced, from spindles to bowls and goblets.

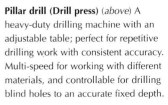

**Spindle moulder** (*left*) Similar to a powerful router. The spindle carries a set of steel cutters, revolving at high speed, for making mouldings and shaping wood. A high degree of precision is possible, allowing the production of large quantities of profiles with consistent accuracy.

**Pillar drill (Drill press)** (*above*) A heavy-duty drilling machine with an adjustable table; perfect for repetitive drilling work with consistent accuracy. Multi-speed for working with different materials, and controllable for drilling blind holes to an accurate fixed depth.

# GETTING
# STARTED

**N**o one simply decides one day to become a woodworker. The introduction to the craft of woodworking is a gradual process, as one increasingly finds that handling and working with wood produces a feeling of satisfaction and reward.

A useful way to begin is to use ready-made plans to make something you need or that you find attractive, where the design and method of construction are already worked out. It will become more important to understand how and why things are done in a certain way, and to broaden your experience with other projects, different types of wood or new tools and techniques. From there, it is a small step to want to make variations, try out new ideas and develop your own designs.

There is no need to feel restricted by a fixed set of rules – the attraction of working with wood stems from the infinite possibilities that the material offers. Nevertheless, certain principles should be followed to avoid early disappointment. This chapter provides an introduction to the planning and design process, and gives a few pointers to safe and successful woodworking practice.

# WORKSHOP PLANNING

The novice woodworker might start out by working on a portable workbench in the backyard, a garage or a spare room, only to discover the frustrations of limited space and lack of opportunity to tackle more elaborate projects. Defining a viable workspace, whatever its size, is the first step to working safely and efficiently. A workshop will often be expanded as one's skills and ambitions develop, but if this happens without forethought, confusion and inefficiency are inevitable.

### Workbenches

The centre of operations for any woodworker is the workbench. Above all, it must be stable and able to resist the forces applied to the work when clamped to it. Also, it must have a perfectly flat top for accurate assembly tasks. If the surface of the workbench is not true, it cannot be relied on for setting out accurate joinery: anything you make on it will reflect the deformity when assembled.

Hardwood workbenches can be purchased in a kit form at fairly low cost, or you can make one yourself along the same lines. A good workbench will have a solid flat top with a vice fixed at one end. For a right-handed woodworker, the left side of the bench is the best position for the vice. Holes at suitable intervals in the top of the bench act as locations for "dogs", or bench stops, against which a piece of wood can be wedged to hold it while planing or sawing. The traditional bench has a recessed well along the back edge to store tools while working.

A drawer for small items that otherwise may go astray is well worth having, while a stout lower shelf will help to stiffen the construction and keep it square. Strong legs provide support – when hammering or using a

**Benchhook**

mallet, the work should be positioned directly over one corner to avoid straining the top. Some woodworkers prefer to attach a "sacrificial" top of cheap plywood, which can be replaced from time to time as it wears.

### Bench accessories

A vital piece of equipment is a bench vice, which should be of good quality as it is a precision instrument for holding your work squarely and securely. A woodworking vice can be obtained as a separate item from any tool shop and fitted to your own bench if required.

You can add a variety of useful accessories to a workbench, such as a simple tool rack made from a strip of plywood and a series of hardwood blocks screwed to the end of the bench. A bench hook is a square of plywood with a lip that hooks over the front of the bench, and a backstop to support the work.

Screw a board to the wall directly above the workbench for storing other tools and workshop items. Fit it with spring clips for holding chisels and screwdrivers, and wooden pegs for suspending hand saws.

**Workbench**

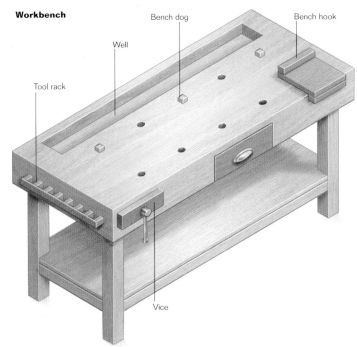

Bench dog

Well

Bench hook

Tool rack

Vice

### Practical tip

Spend time getting your bench at exactly the height that suits you. An incorrect height can prove to be tiring. Never shorten the legs of a bench if it is too high, work off a duckboard if necessary.

## Workshop layout

If you have plenty of space at your disposal, give some thought to the overall layout of the workshop. Think of the route taken by the wood as it is worked into the finished article, and treat the workshop as a small production line, with separate areas for each stage of the operation.

Setting out your work needs a large flat area along one side. The workbench, with tool or wood storage above, should be alongside this, with a clear space in the centre for any tasks involving power or machine tools. Keep the finishing area separate from the work area and, if possible, behind a partition to keep dust to a minimum. Use a dust extractor when creating large quantities of shavings or fine sawdust.

If you have room for a sawbench (table saw) or other machinery, a central position with plenty of clear space around it will be required to accommodate large sheets of plywood and long lengths of timber. Build a table at the right height to support the work as it passes beyond the saw, and economize on space by using the same area for feeding planed timber back toward the saw in a circular route. The table can also act as an assembly area for large projects, with good access from all sides and room for timber storage below.

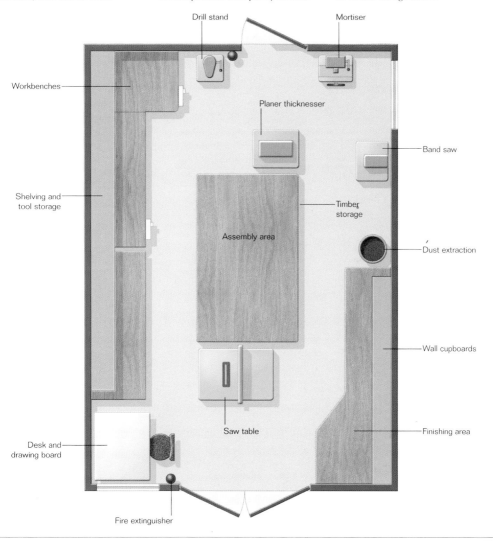

Drill stand

Mortiser

Workbenches

Planer thicknesser

Band saw

Shelving and
tool storage

Timber
storage

Assembly area

Dust extraction

Wall cupboards

Saw table

Finishing area

Desk and
drawing board

Fire extinguisher

# HEALTH AND SAFETY

Your personal safety should underlie every stage of woodworking practice, including the layout of a workshop. It is better to plan your work to eliminate hazards rather than accommodate them – for example, using a dust extractor on a machine that creates a lot of dust is a better solution than wearing a dust mask. Because woodworking depends on the use of cutting tools, this may seem a risk that cannot be avoided, but any experienced craftsman will confirm that a sharp tool is actually less dangerous than a blunt one or a tool that is used incorrectly.

Fire extinguisher

## Working practice

Working safely is largely a matter of common sense and awareness. More accidents occur as a result of losing concentration than for any other reason. Develop a sense of rhythm and routine when working, so that you are in tune with what you are doing. Never rush to finish a job, whatever the motivation. There is no advantage in quick results if you risk ruining the work, not to mention suffering injury.

If someone enters your workshop while you are working, finish the task and switch off any machinery before addressing them. They will soon learn to follow your work discipline. For obvious reasons, do not lock yourself in to avoid being disturbed when working alone. On the other hand, do keep the workshop locked in your absence for the safety of others.

### Personal safety

Avoid wearing loose clothing and jewellery when working, especially with machinery and power tools. A stout pair of boots should be worn in case of accidents – a sheet of plywood will be painful if it slips and lands on your toe. You can prevent this by wearing a pair of leather or canvas gloves when handling timber. Always inspect a piece of wood for splinters and protruding nails before picking it up. Always have a first aid kit in the workshop for minor injuries. When you work on large machines, do not work alone in case of injury.

## Workshop safety

Observe the following points to reduce the risk of accidents:

**Keep the workshop tidy** An obvious point, but at times it may be tempting to leave the chore of sweeping up until another day. Make a habit of tidying the workshop at the end of every session and dispose of dust and debris sensibly. Keep a check on small offcuts (scraps) that tend to collect wherever you are working and present a real hazard underfoot. Wood and sawdust are biodegradable, so they can be disposed of easily at a local recycling depot.

**Treat chemical waste with care** Many finishing products are inflammable or harmful to the environment and should be stored separately in a secure place, inaccessible to children and animals. Used chemicals should be collected in resealable containers and disposed of safely at an appropriate waste depot. This even applies to finishing cloths and wipes. Certain volatile products are highly inflammable in concentrated form; spread out contaminated rags so that solvents can evaporate before disposal.

**Consider the fire risk** Avoiding all naked flames can reduce the risk of fire and, it goes without saying, the workshop should be a non-smoking zone. Install a powder-filled fire extinguisher at every exit door, and fit a smoke alarm. A pile of sawdust can smoulder for hours before bursting into flame. A well-kept workshop has no piles of sawdust, of course, but a smoke alarm guarantees peace of mind.

**Observe electrical safety** Install a safe power circuit, protected by a circuit breaker to cut off the power in case of any wiring fault or accident. Make sure the circuit is adequate for the load of any machines likely to be used, and fit a master switch near the entrance to the workshop so that switching off all the power becomes routine at the end of every session.

Extension cords trailing across the floor are common causes of accidents, so keep them clipped out of harm's way if they have to be used. Examine all power cords regularly for wear, replacing any that have damaged outer sleeving. Make sure the workshop is well lit with bright fluorescent lighting.

## Safety equipment

Even though a private workshop is not required to comply with health and safety legislation, which applies to commercial premises, it makes sense to observe the same safety disciplines and use the personal protection equipment that is recommended and readily available.

**First aid kit** Obtain the correct size of kit recommended for small workshops, and keep it in a prominent position ready for use. If any of the contents are used, replace them immediately.

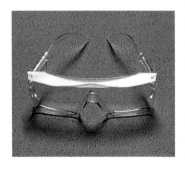

**Eye protection** Always protect your eyes with safety glasses or goggles when sanding, finishing or using power tools. When operating a machine that produces large quantities of chippings at high speed, wear a full-face visor.

**Ear protection** When using power tools or machinery, wear approved ear defenders (protectors) or earplugs to keep noise to an acceptable level. Some people think that it is safer to operate a machine by listening to its performance. They are wrong, and they risk permanent impairment of their hearing in the future.

**Dust masks** There are several types of mask to choose from, including the frame mask with replaceable pads and disposable masks that cover the whole of the mouth and nose. Choose the right product for the level of dust generated in the workshop. The dust produced by sanding machines is the most hazardous and needs a mask with a fine filter. Use sanders that are fitted with their own dust collection bag to cut down on the amount of dust produced. Clear, full-face safety masks are available now and are easy to put on and comfortable to wear, especially when using power tools.

When working with hazardous finishing materials, keep the workshop well ventilated and wear a respirator if necessary. Always be guided by the manufacturer's safety data, which by

law must be supplied with any hazardous product. In general, if a product is so dangerous as to cause serious problems, you should consider an alternative.

**Gloves and boots** It is advisable to wear heavy-duty rigger's gloves when handling sawn timber (lumber) or large, heavy sheets of material. When you are using adhesives or finishing materials that are harmful to the skin, wear rubber or latex gloves. It is best to wear sensible and sturdy boots to keep toes protected in case you drop any wood.

*Above* Wear gloves when handling large pieces of wood.

## Dust extraction

By far the best way of reducing the risk of inhaling sawdust is to install a dust extraction system. Compact units designed for the small workshop are available from all good tool suppliers. Many portable power tools are supplied with adaptors for direct connection to an extraction unit.

# PLANS AND DRAWINGS

Drawing plans before starting a job is an important part of the design process. They will help you to visualize how the different components of your woodworking project fit together and how the two dimensions on the paper are translated into the three dimensions of a solid object. They also take the guesswork out of calculating the quantity of materials required, keeping costs down. No special skills are required, merely the same methodical approach that is part of any woodworking operation. Even a quick sketch on the back of an envelope can be enough to clarify an idea or reveal any discrepancies of scale or measurement before proceeding.

### Views

These are usually the most helpful drawings when designing a project. The plan view shows the object viewed from above, and the elevation as viewed from one side. A section view shows a slice through the object. For a complex design with many components you may need more than one section to develop the idea.

There is no need to spend a long time on a complicated piece of artwork – a good drawing shows just the right amount of detail, clearly set out, and no more. Include the scale you have used to avoid errors and get a feel for the proportions of the design.

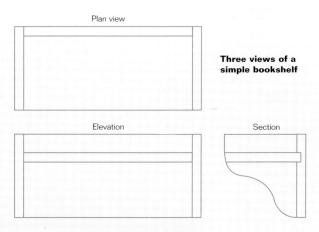

Plan view

**Three views of a simple bookshelf**

Elevation

Section

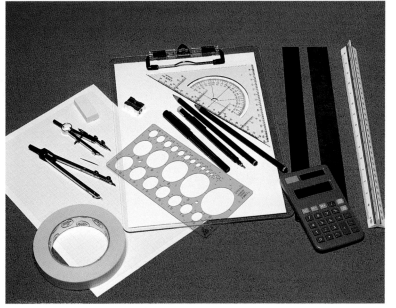

*Left* All of these items will prove invaluable for drawing plans for your projects: graph paper – useful for scale drawings and templates; plain paper or a sketch pad; a clipboard or drawing board; masking tape; a pair of compasses (compass); dividers or callipers – for the accurate transfer and duplication of measurements; drawing pens, pencils and a carpenter's pencil; eraser and pencil sharpener; a set square and protractor; templates for circular cutouts or other necessary shapes; rules (imperial or metric scales); scale rule and a pocket calculator for converting measurements and making calculations.

## Scale drawings

Scale drawings are the best way to design a job accurately. They will allow you to get a feel for the proportions of the finished article. A scale rule converts dimensions on to the paper automatically; otherwise an ordinary rule can be used for simple scales such as 1:10 (when working in metric units) or 1:12 (imperial units – 1in equals 12in). You can also use graph paper, in either metric or imperial scales, to establish a grid on to which quite complex shapes may be plotted. Choose any scale that allows the overall dimensions of the object to fit neatly on the page.

## Cutting lists and plans

From an accurate scale drawing, it is easy to work out a detailed cutting (cut) list for all the materials needed for a project. This helps when selecting the wood, making sure that you do not run short. When making an item where the grain of the timber is to be displayed at its best, it is important to purchase one batch of material so that all the components are of a matching colour and figure.

Label each part to identify it on the cutting list, and mark each piece of wood as it is finished to avoid confusion. Record any alterations you make on the cutting list and file it

away safely as you might want to repeat the project in the future or use it as the basis for a similar job.

Cutting plans are slightly different: if you need to cut large sheets of plywood or MDF (medium-density fibreboard) into a set of different sized pieces, it is worth taking a few minutes to sketch out the most efficient layout to avoid waste.

All components of a similar width, for example, can be cut from one strip, then cross cut to length one at a time. Try combining different sizes to make up the full width or length of a sheet so offcuts (scraps) are kept to bare minimum.

## Scaling-up

When dealing with complex curved profiles, it is useful to be able to scale-up a detail to produce a working template. Make a tracing of the small-scale drawing and lay it over a sheet of graph paper. Then transfer each section to a similar grid on a larger scale to reproduce the full-size pattern. The more intricate the design, the finer the grid should be to capture every detail.

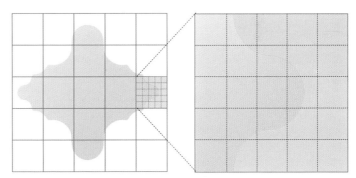

## Isometrics

This simply means "of equal measurement". An isometric drawing does not give a true idea of shape or perspective, but to the draughtsman or designer it is invaluable, allowing true measurements to be scaled from a drawing in all three dimensions. Simply divide a circle into three equal segments of 120 degrees to establish an axis for each side of a three dimensional object. When drawn to this format, the exact measurements in any direction can be reproduced faithfully on the page to establish how a construction will fit together.

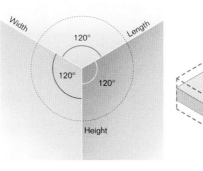

**Isometric axes**

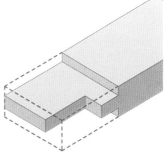

**Isometric sketch**

# DESIGN

Wood has so many variable qualities and such wide potential as a construction material that it is difficult to make any hard and fast design rules. Every piece of work is unique, and a common creed among woodworkers is to allow the wood to "speak for itself" and the natural qualities of each piece to suggest the best way of using it.

## Grain direction

The pleasure of woodworking lies in working with it and not against it to express organic forms. Designing around the material in this way is an intriguing process of developing ideas in new and unexpected directions. As you will generally not be making free-form sculpture, to produce a well-constructed design requires the careful selection of material, tools and techniques to achieve the best results. Over the years, certain species of wood have become associated with specific types of furniture for the qualities they possess.

When working a piece of wood with hand tools, you will discover that it will behave better when cut or shaped in a particular direction, and can be most "unfriendly" if you try to force it in another. Thus, you should have no qualms about altering a design to reflect this changing quality as you work; this is one reason why no two pieces of work will be the same.

*Right* Directional table by Christopher Rose, made from maple with a veneered top and detachable solid leg frames.
*Below* Boxwood stringing provides a hardwearing edge to this steamed pear desk by Nicholas Pryke.

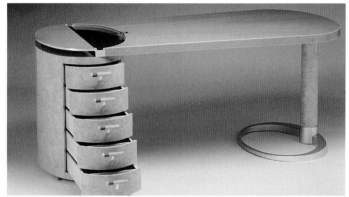

## Design properties of wood

*Beech* was used for making chairs because of its good bending properties. The resistance to splitting of *elm*, with its knotty grain, makes it ideal for chair seats and table tops. *Ash* possesses a natural flexibility and springiness, and traditionally was used for carriage making. The high density of *maple* makes it ideal for hardwearing applications, notably chopping boards and butcher's blocks. *Oak* is uniquely impervious to water, but can be softened with steam and bent into shape. It was widely used for boatbuilding.

*Above* An elegant bureau designed by Tony McMullen, using a mixture of solid wood and veneers in contrasting colours.

*Above* Mapa stacking dining chair by the vk&c partnership. The design benefits from the contrast between native cherry and sycamore.

## Ergonomics

Whatever the appearance of a piece of furniture, certain principles should be carefully observed to ensure that it performs its function correctly. A chair that is impossible to sit on comfortably could be said to have failed as a chair, no matter how striking, inventive or original the design.

A desk or workstation at the wrong height may encourage an unhealthy posture and you could easily do yourself harm without realizing it. By maintaining certain basic dimensional relationships when making furniture, you can still develop original designs while making sure that form and function work together to make a well-balanced product.

Therefore, good woodworking design is achieved by combining well-established principles with a feel for the potential of the material. The colour and figure of different types of wood are so variable that there is no limit to the effects that can be achieved. Even so-called defects in the grain can be displayed to advantage by emphasizing the natural qualities of the wood.

Choosing the finish can make a difference to the design – a high gloss will scatter light and add depth and colour, but also it can seem cold or formal in the wrong context. A simple wax finish generally adds warmth and lustre, which grows deeper with every new coat. Although the natural colour of wood is highly regarded, the creative use of stains or coloured polish can produce unusual and quite striking results.

Good contrasts can be obtained by working with light and dark woods. For example, a light wood interior will "expand" the space inside a cabinet and dark wooden legs on a light coloured table top will give it a more solid appearance.

## Chair to table height

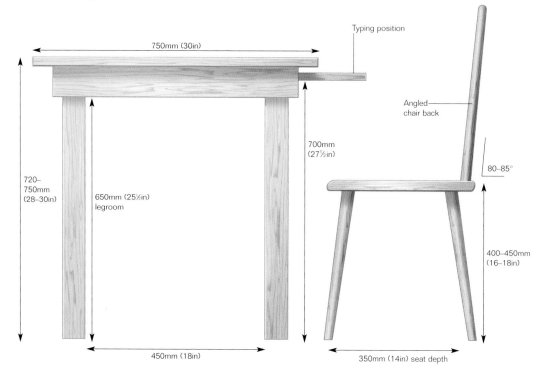

Typing position

750mm (30in)

Angled chair back

700mm (27½in)

80–85°

720–750mm (28–30in)

650mm (25½in) legroom

400–450mm (16–18in)

450mm (18in)

350mm (14in) seat depth

# CONSTRUCTION TIPS

No matter how creative your design, it is sensible to observe sound
construction principles to make your work safe to use and give it a long life.
Some of these are common sense; others have been developed from years of
experience. Depart from traditional techniques by all means, but not without
considering their purpose.

### Strengthening a shelf

The shape and size of a storage cupboard or bookshelf
should not encourage overloading. Strengthen shelves by
adding a length of rebated (rabbeted) moulding along the
front edge.

### Fittings for safety

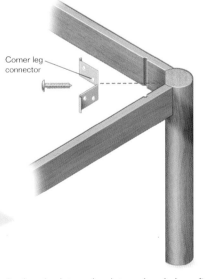

Fall flap stay

Fall flap

Choose the correct fittings so that moving parts do not
open too far and strain the hinges or cause injury. A fall
flap stay allows the flap of a bureau, or the lid of a box, to
fold out and come to rest in the right position.

### Stiffening corners

Stiffening members can be added, concealed if necessary,
to hold a wooden frame square and prevent the joints from
working loose. In a wall cupboard, even two relatively thin
strips across the back will stiffen the structure without the
need for a solid back panel.

### Using knock-down fittings

Corner leg
connector

Steel angle plates or brackets, or knock-down fittings, can
be used to strengthen joints, as well as allowing a piece
to be taken apart if required. These ingenious corner
brackets are used to fix the detachable legs and connect
the side rails at the same time.

## Movement

Even well-seasoned wood is prone to movement under different conditions of humidity and temperature. Understanding the behaviour of wood helps in developing construction methods to allow for its natural tendency to move. Even though modern adhesives are much more permanent than those used previously, they will not prevent wood from swelling or splitting.

A moisture-resistant finish coat may help to stabilize a piece, but as soon as the film is penetrated, it can lift or craze. In earlier times, woodworkers understood this and designed furniture to allow for natural movement.

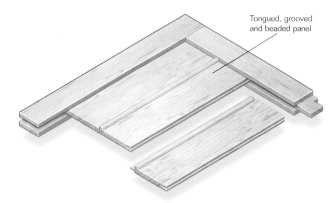

Tongued, grooved and beaded panel

It is better not to fix panelling into its surrounding frame, but allow it to move naturally within a groove. The beaded edge on a tongued-and-grooved moulding is not merely decorative – it creates a shadow line to distract the eye from the gap caused by natural shrinkage.

## Gluing boards

When several boards are glued together on edge, the direction of the growth rings should be alternated to counteract the "cupping" tendency of the wood. Quarter-sawn boards, with the rings running at right angles to the surface, are much more stable in this respect.

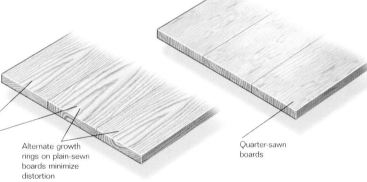

Growth rings in same direction – will lead to cupping.

Alternate growth rings on plain-sewn boards minimize distortion

Quarter-sawn boards

## Table top fixing

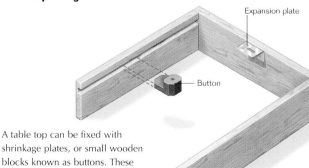

Expansion plate

Button

A table top can be fixed with shrinkage plates, or small wooden blocks known as buttons. These are slotted into a groove to accommodate the greater movement of the wide boards relative to the narrow members of the supporting frame.

## Finishing

Safety principles should also be observed when selecting the finish for your work. Never use oil-based paints or varnishes on toys or children's furniture – acrylic-based stains and coatings are non-toxic and safe. Oiled wood is heat-resistant, but modern finishing oils contain mineral extracts and should not be used on items that come into contact with food, such as bowls and countertops.

French polish provides a high-quality finish, but is not heat-resistant and will soften on contact with alcohol, so it is not always the ideal choice for a table top.

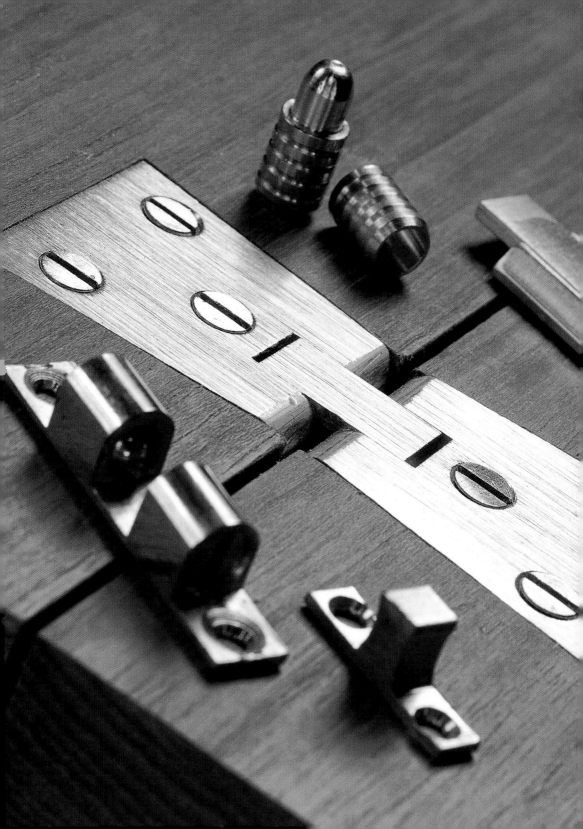

# FIXINGS AND FITTINGS

**F**ixings and fastenings, or hardware, play an important part in almost every wood project, and it is worth getting to grips with the different types to be able to choose the most suitable. There is a wide range of sizes and patterns, but each has been devised and developed over the years to meet a specific need. Nails and screws, whether designed for mechanical strength or more decorative qualities, can make all the difference to a job when used correctly.

In the same way, the choice of hardware fittings is so vast that you are certain to find the right item to complete a project. Some have a purely functional purpose, while others are more decorative. A pair of well-designed brass hinges, for example, has both qualities and can really add the finishing touch to a well-made piece of work.

# SCREWS AND NAILS

Given the many types of nail, pin and screw that are manufactured, you can be sure that there will be one to suit any application. Inevitably, over time, you will build up a huge collection of fixings (hardware), and it is always worth the effort to keep them sorted into different sizes and types ready for use. Nothing is more frustrating than to reach the assembly stage of a piece of work and find you cannot complete it for the lack of the right size of screw and nail. It is very easy to ruin the work by making do with something fairly close, but if it is a little too long or too wide, it can easily split the wood. Use small jars or tins to store different types, sorting them by size and length, and labelling them so that they are easily identified.

### Screws

These provide a more positive fixing than nails and generally are more useful for strong construction work. The size of the screw is determined by the size of the shank or the diameter of the gauge, and is denoted numerically. A No. 4 gauge is slightly smaller than 3mm (⅛in) in diameter and about the smallest size in common use; a No. 12 is 6mm (¼in) in diameter and used for heavy-duty constructional work. The gauge of the screw does not change with the length of the screw.

In general, the smaller the gauge, the shorter the range of lengths that will be available. For general cabinet work, a No. 8 screw is a convenient size, and is available in lengths from 19–75mm (¾–3in).

Regardless of size, all screws should be long enough to pass through the piece to be secured and penetrate approximately three-quarters of the depth of the second component. If there are lots of screwholes in a piece, wrap a piece of tape around the bit to mark the depth on the bit.

**Wood screw** The standard traditional wood screw, with a single slotted head and tapered shank. It requires a clearance hole of the correct size, counter-sunk to accommodate the head. It is the cheapest type of general-purpose screw and it is made in mild steel with a "self colour" finish. This means that the steel is untreated and will corrode easily in damp conditions.

**Roundhead screws** These are intended to be seen; the flat underside of the head provides extra grip.

**Raised and countersunk wood screw** This has a shallow domed head, which projects slightly above the surface and looks quite decorative.

**Pozidriv head** This is a more modern and very popular form of wood screw with a cross-head for extra grip. It is countersunk with a cross-head slot and zinc plated for rust-resistance. The shank is parallel, rather than tapered, making it suitable for driving into manufactured boards, using a suitably sized pilot hole, without splitting. Made of hardened steel, it is suitable for use with a powered screwdriver.

**Black japanned roundhead screws** are commonly used with black iron fittings for decorative purposes.

**Brass screws** These are less strong than steel screws of the same gauge, but have the great advantage that they will not rust or bind in the wood. Brass countersunk wood screws are perfectly acceptable in cabinet-making. They look neat when they are sunk flush with the surface. In hardwood, first drive in a steel screw of the same size as the brass screw, and then drive in the brass one.

**Surface screws** Modern furniture is frequently assembled using these, with the heads being concealed by plastic caps. These allow the unit to be taken apart if required. Each small plastic cap clips on to a washer under the screwhead. Different colours are available to suit the material's finish.

**Brass cup and washer** This is a more decorative version of the screw cap. It is designed for use with a brass countersunk screw and is ideal for fixing removable panels, such as bath panels. Screw cups and washers spread the pressure of the screw.

**Security screws** have shaped heads, allowing them to be inserted with a flat-bladed screwdriver, but making removal impossible. The slot in the screw head is shaped so that the screwdriver will only grip when turned clockwise.

**Mirror screw and cups** This has a chrome-plated cap that screws over the head after fixing it. Domed (top) and flat versions are available as above.

**Recessed cup washer** Available for recessing into the wood. Drill a counterbore of the correct size to sink the cup flush with the surface.

Nail set
(punch)

## Nails and pins

By far the most common type is the standard wire nail, which is available from 19–150mm (¾–6in) in length. These are fine for structural work, but are best used where they will be concealed, as the heads are difficult to sink down below the surface of the wood without causing it to split.

Lost head nails solve this problem. As their name implies, they can be set just flush with the surface and filled in if necessary. They are ideal for nailing battens (cleats) down and some larger components.

Oval nails have an oval section throughout their length, making them less likely to split the wood.

Annular, or ring, nails have small rings or grooves formed in the shank in order to to grip the wood. They are ideal for permanent attachments, as they are difficult to remove.

Panel pins (brads) come into their own for fixing small sizes of wood and delicate mouldings.

Brass panel pins will not rust or cause stains and can be left with their heads showing if desired.

Carpet tacks have wide, flat heads and are made of hardened steel.

Upholstery pins provide a decorative means of securing upholstery work and have wide, flat-bottomed heads so that they grip the fabric.

When working with small sections of timber, or particularly brittle components, it is worth drilling small pilot holes for fixings to prevent the wood from splitting. Use a cross pein or pin hammer for delicate work, and leave the head of each nail protruding just above the surface.

To punch, or "set", the nail head below the surface of the wood, use a nail set, which has a small-cupped end to fit over the head and punch a neat hole in the wood. Nail sets are available in a range of sizes to suit different nails. The resulting hole can be filled with a coloured stopping for an undetectable fixing.

**Varieties of nails and pins**

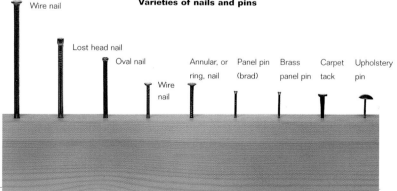

Wire nail

Lost head nail

Oval nail

Wire nail

Annular, or ring, nail

Panel pin (brad)

Brass panel pin

Carpet tack

Upholstery pin

# ASSEMBLY FITTINGS AND HINGES

The introduction of modern flat-pack furniture has generated a large range of custom-made assembly fittings, sometimes called knock-down or K-D fittings, which enable the home user to assemble and dismantle them without special tools. They are equally useful for making your own furniture, as they provide very rigid joints. All that is required is some care in drilling the correct locating holes. K-D fittings are obtainable from many good hardware stores, do-it-yourself stores and mail-order suppliers.

**Brass guide dowel** Used in conjunction with a cross-dowel to ensure perfect alignment as the joint is pulled up tight, preventing it from twisting. Guide dowels are equally useful for lining up the leaves of a table or an inserted panel.

**Panel connector** A device for connecting two panels side by side, as in a row of fitted base units. Also known as a *barrel nut* or *sleeve nut*. The bolt screws into the sleeved connector, clamping the units together and providing lateral location.

**Expansion, or shrinkage, plate** This angled bracket is ideal for attaching a table top or countertop made of solid boards. The slotted screw holes in the upper flange allow the top to expand or shrink slightly without becoming loose. It is also useful for attaching any kind of panel or fascia, and allows for accurate alignment.

**Corner bracket** Ideal for attaching a work surface or table top, it holds the corners of the framework square at the same time.

**Cam fitting** This ingenious cam fitting allows two panels to be joined at a right angle. A quarter turn of the integral screw tightens it against a cam, drawing the two components together. They can be disconnected easily when required.

**Worktop connector** Sometimes called a handrail connector. It uses a positive bolt action to draw two components tightly together.

**Corner bracket** This is designed for attaching table legs and strengthening the corner joints at the same time. The two lugs on the bracket locate into slots in the rails of the table and lock them together as the central bolt is tightened into the leg.

**Countertop connector** When attaching countertops made of chipboard and other man-made boards, expansion plates are not required as the materials are stable. These connector blocks are fitted into holes drilled inside the top edge of a cabinet and have holes for the screws. The holes are angled to allow easy access for a screwdriver.

**Confirmat screw** Designed for fixing into the edge of chipboard without splitting the material. A pilot hole of the exact size removes the chipboard core, and the parallel thread grips the chipboard fibres without expanding the board.

**Cross-dowel connectors** The small steel dowel, threaded to receive the bolt, is inserted into a hole drilled in the face of a panel. The bolt that connects the second component, passes through a hole drilled in the edge of the first panel that intercepts the dowel hole. The recessed bolt provides a strong, square connection.

**T-nut** This is tapped into the reverse side of a panel. A T-nut acts as a captive nut when access is restricted.

## Hinges

Any device that includes a pivot action can be called a hinge, and there are many different variations. Some are designed to be concealed within the framework of a cabinet, or the carcass, while others are intended as decorative features in their own right.

It is important to choose hinges of the correct size and robustness when hanging a door so that it is well supported when it swings open. If a hinge or hinge pin is strained in any way, the door will not fit in the frame and may become detached, causing injury.

## Fitting hinges

Attaching small hinges to cabinet doors requires patience. The style of door will determine the type of hinge required.

Doors which overlap the front of the cabinet can be fitted with butt hinges screwed to the front of the frame, or concealed hinges which are invisible when the door is closed.

Flush doors, which fit inside the cabinet frame, are normally fitted with butt hinges. They need to be recessed into the wood. Mark around the leaf of the hinge with a craft knife or sharp pencil, and form a recess with a chisel.

Flush hinges have very thin leaves, which avoid the need to cut a recess. They are small enough to fit into the small clearance gap surrounding the door.

**Concealed hinge** Originally designed for use in self-assembly base units, this hinge is concealed from view when the door is closed. It clips on to the base plate, allowing the door to be removed easily, and is adjustable in all three directions. A mounting hole is required, using a boring bit to suit the hinge boss.

**Cylinder hinge** Even more discreet, the barrel of the cylinder hinge is concealed in the edges of the door and frame, and is almost invisible when the door is opened. This is only suitable for light-duty use.

**Counter hinges** These are decorative brass hinges, suitable for bar flaps, counter tops and table leaves. Double hinge pins allow the hinge to fold back on itself without binding.

**Lay-on hinge** This is also a concealed hinge, but it requires no mounting holes. It is laid on the surface of the door and frame, and simply screwed in place. The linked pivot arms allow 180 degree opening and are spring-loaded for a positive closing action.

**Pivot hinge** A very discreet and neat hinge, suitable for small cabinet doors. One half screws directly into the frame; the matching half (not shown) screws into the edge of the door and slips over the brass pin of the former, allowing the door to be lifted on and off.

**Lift-off hinge** A decorative hinge in polished brass with finials at the ends, which can be separated, allowing the door to be lifted on and off at will.

**Flush hinges** The slimline design of these hinges allows them to be fitted without the need for chiselled recesses. One leaf folds inside the other to provide a very neat connection.

**Butt hinges** The classic hinge style that is machined from solid brass for a smooth action. It requires a recess chiselled in both door and frame. Butt hinges are available in sizes from as small as 12mm (½in), for use in a jewellery box for example, up to 100mm (4in) for hanging full-size doors.

**Piano hinge** A continuous brass-strip hinge, sold in lengths up to 1.8m (6ft) and having all kinds of use. It is ideal for fitting a lid to a box or, indeed, a lid to a piano.

# STAYS, CATCHES AND DOOR FITTINGS

You should consider buying these fittings in advance. They are an important part of making and designing furniture and especially in the case of door and drawer handles, they will add the finishing touches to your design. There are many specialist outlets that sell all manner of stays, catches and door fittings and most can be ordered by mail order. The style and size of fittings should be chosen with some care to suit the overall design.

**Shelf support**
A small torpedo-shaped shelf support that fits into a 5mm (³⁄₁₆in) hole in the side of a cabinet, making a very unobtrusive fitting.

**Stays and catches**
Features such as nylon bearings and spring-loaded magnets make all kinds of ingenious fitting possible, expanding the range of hardware available to the cabinet-maker. For example, they can be used to design a cabinet door that springs open with a slight touch, requiring no handles at all. If you intend using any of these devices, it is advisable to obtain a sample first and study its operation before building the project. Although any hardware may be the last item to be installed, it must be included in your plans at the design stage.

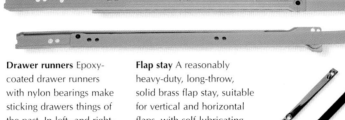

**Drawer runners** Epoxy-coated drawer runners with nylon bearings make sticking drawers things of the past. In left- and right-handed pairs, these runners are available in various lengths to suit different sizes of drawer, but are a consistent 12.5mm (½in) wide when assembled. Therefore, a drawer box should be made exactly 25mm (1in) smaller than the internal size of the cabinet or cupboard.

**Flap stay** A reasonably heavy-duty, long-throw, solid brass flap stay, suitable for vertical and horizontal flaps, with self-lubricating nylon glide bearing. Reversible for fitting to the left- or right-hand end of a unit.

**Glass shelf support** A small shelf support made of transparent plastic so that it is hardly visible. Incorporates a safety catch to prevent the shelf from being knocked accidentally out of place.

**Lid stay** A light-duty stay for less demanding operations, and only in plated brass. There are many varieties of lid and flap stay available to suit a wide range of applications.

**Brass shelf support**
Small brass clips that fit into a slotted bookcase strip, allowing shelves to be positioned at will.

**Keeper plate**
Used with a furniture bolt.

**Keeper plate**
Used with an auto latch.

**Magnetic touch latch**
This latch is spring-loaded so that a light touch on the closed door will release it and throw it open. To close the door, gently push it until the keeper plate and latch connect, and it clicks shut.

**Bed fitting** Used for connecting two panels at a right angle, such as the end and side panels of a small bed or cot. Screw one half to each panel, slot together and they interlock with a tapering fit. However, they can be detached easily when required.

**Miniature magnetic catch**
A very discreet catch, suitable for small cabinet doors. The barrel containing the magnet is recessed into the door frame, while the tiny striking plate is simply tapped into the door like a drawing pin (thumb tack).

**Furniture bolt** Unlike a barrel bolt, a furniture bolt has a flat profile and is much less obtrusive. It is spring-loaded to prevent it from rattling.

## Door fittings

Whether the style of your project is traditional or ultra-modern, there is sure to be a range of door hardware to suit. Cabinet doors can be fitted with a variety of handles and knobs. Often, changing the handles can improve the appearance of a cabinet considerably.

For a set of doors or drawers, you can fit knobs or drop handles ranging from a reproduction style in Florentine bronze to slimline chrome or satin aluminium. Natural wood, ready for staining and polishing, or ceramic knobs to match a painted finish are other options. The size of fittings should be chosen with care to suit the overall proportions of the design.

**Door handles** D-shaped handles in oak and pine, can be unfinished for staining or polishing to match the finish of the unit. A recessed oak handle, for flat mounting to a door or drawer front, provides a finger pull with no holes required.

**Escutcheon** A key hole can be covered with an escutcheon plate, or a discreet insert can be pushed into the hole, protecting it from wear.

**Fall-flap lock** This type of lock is designed for the fall flap of a bureau or cocktail cabinet and has a special security feature: the key can only be removed when the flap is locked shut.

**Wooden door knobs** Turned knobs in oak, beech and pine, a few examples of the different sizes and styles available. Although these are sanded ready for finishing, they can also be obtained ready-lacquered.

**Cabinet locks** A rim lock fits on the inside of a cabinet door or flap, mounted on the surface. A mortise lock is neater and more secure, and is inserted into a mortise cut in the edge of the door.

**Reproduction handles** A wide range of pull handles is made for reproduction furniture, offering different decorative styles with interchangeable base plates. These items are made with a copper, brass, bronze or pewter finish.

**Auto door latch** A spring-loaded door latch that allows a cabinet door to be closed or sprung open by gentle pressure, so you do not need a handle.

**Magnetic door catch** A simple device, with a small keeper plate that is screwed to the inside of a door. The magnet in the body of the catch keeps the door closed.

**Ceramic knobs** White, cream and decorated ceramic knobs are made in a range of sizes and look good on painted furniture.

**Satin aluminium knob** Metallic knobs give a contemporary look. They may be made in aluminium, steel or brass, with a highly polished, brushed, chromed, satin or even gold-plated finish.

**Shell handle** Typical of Shaker-style furniture, this nickel-plated handle is suitable as a drawer pull.

# 5

# BASIC TECHNIQUES

**S**tudy the finest example of cabinet-making, and no matter how complex it may seem, you can be sure of one thing: when it was made, the same skills were used as in the simplest of projects. Selecting wood and cutting it to size, shaping the individual components, assembling and gluing them together, then sanding and preparing for a final finish – all woodworking, at all levels, depends on these elementary principles. To develop your ability from novice to expert requires time, patience and application: persevere until experience begins to make the difference.

There are no easy short-cuts, but in the following pages you will find plenty of advice that will help you achieve your goals. An understanding of how hand and power tools work, and how wood behaves, will provide a good grounding for improving your skills and expertise.

# MEASURING AND MARKING

There is a saying often repeated in woodworking: "Measure twice and cut once." It may seem obvious advice, but when woodworkers repeat it, you can be sure that they speak from experience – there is not a woodworker in the world who does not occasionally forget this basic rule. By adopting a simple discipline for measuring and marking out, you can reduce the risk of making mistakes in your work. Before even laying hands on your tools, check and double check. The simplest of errors can produce the most costly results.

### Measuring tapes

A retractable measuring tape is a basic essential. Choose one with a lockable blade and clear markings – the quality can vary considerably. A double scale showing both imperial and metric measurements can be useful, allowing quick conversion across the scales.

Inspect the hooked end of the tape measure regularly for wear – this is a common cause of inaccuracy, so try not to let the tape spring back into its casing out of control, which could damage the end. The retracting spring in the centre of the tape will lose its effectiveness if fully extended, so if you find this occurring regularly, you should consider buying a longer rule. A 3m (10ft) or 5m (16ft) rule should be adequate for most workshop tasks.

It is a good idea to lubricate and clean the blade from time to time by applying a drop of oil with a soft cloth as the blade is retracted.

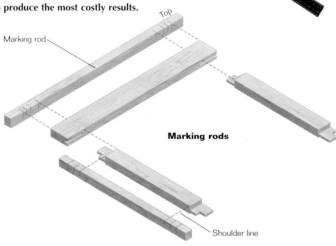

Marking rod

Top

**Marking rods**

Shoulder line

*Above* Use a combination square as a try square or as a normal rule.

### Steel rules

A fixed steel rule with a permanently engraved scale will be better than a retractable tape where accuracy is required, such as when setting out joints and fine detail. A combination square is even more useful – it combines a steel rule with a sliding stock that acts as a try square and adjustable gauge all in one. If there are curves, you will achieve greater accuracy with a flexible steel rule.

### Marking rods

When marking out a number of identical components, use a marking rod to reduce measuring errors. This is a straight length of square batten with suitable reference points marked on it. It is a simple matter to set out all the details of complex joinery on this master pattern without discrepancy. Keep it safe as a permanent record of each job you do – you never know when it might be useful again.

### Marking divisions

To divide the width of a board in half, or into any number of equal strips, you can save calculation and the risk of error with this quick method. Lay a steel rule at a 45 degree angle across the work with an even number of divisions from edge to edge. Simply use the scale to mark off the intervals you need; repeat at the other end of the board, and join the marks with a straightedge or chalk line.

## Face and edge marks

Wood is an organic material and by its nature will be subject to variations in size, even after it has been cut from the tree. Woodworkers deal with this by always using one edge as a basis for all their measurements and setting out. Establish a procedure for marking up your work and follow it every time until it becomes second nature.

Select every component individually, bearing in mind its position in the construction. Grain pattern and direction, possible shrinkage, how much it will be seen, how it will be finished, and the strength and design of any joints required are all factors that should influence your decision in selecting the "face side" of any piece of wood. This attention to detail is the secret of quality woodwork. True-up (square) the face of the wood with a try plane or jack plane. The surface must not only be straight, but free of any "wind" or twist between opposite corners.

1 On a wide piece of wood, use a pair of winding rods – place a straightedge at one end of the board and sight across it to another at the far end.

2 Use a try square or a combination square to check that one long edge is square to the face. Place the stock of the square against the face edge, with the blade on the face side.

When using a try square to check if the edge is square, sight along the surface toward a light source and slide the square from one end of the wood to the other – any small gaps will be visible. Adjust with the plane if necessary and mark the wood as shown where the two faces meet. Take all your measurements from the face edge/face side and you will eliminate any discrepancies in width or depth that might affect the overall dimensions of the finished piece.

### Face and edge marks

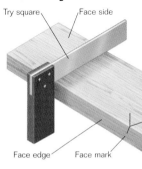

Try square    Face side

Face edge    Face mark

## Marking and mortise gauges

A marking gauge has a single point and adjustable stock, and is used for scribing a line at a fixed distance from an edge; a mortise gauge (left) has two adjustable points, allowing parallel lines to be scribed.

To set up the mortise gauge, adjust the points and slide the stock to approximately the correct position, then turn the locking screw of the stock until it just "nips" on to the beam. Gently tap one end of the beam against the bench to make fine adjustments before finally tightening the screw. When gauging lines on timber (lumber), always run the stock of the gauge along the face side and edge. Set the points to the width of the chisel you intend to use to cut the mortise, not from a rule.

## Scribing

When setting out lines for cutting or making joints, score across the grain of the timber with a bradawl (awl) or sharp knife. This prevents the wood fibres from tearing out along the grain, and provides an accurate guide when paring down to the line with a chisel or plane for a final fit.

# USING HAND SAWS

Cutting the material to size is the first stage of any project, and without doubt the art of sawing straight and true is the first vital skill to acquire. You should persevere with the correct technique until it becomes instinctive. Understanding how a saw works, and how the wood behaves as it is cut, is the key. If the teeth lose their cutting edge, or the set of the teeth becomes uneven through constant use, you will find it impossible to saw straight.

### Sawing technique

Hand saws come in many types and sizes. An all-purpose panel saw and a good-quality tenon saw are the two basics to get you started. As your technique improves, and you explore the different demands of woodworking and the different properties of hardwoods, softwoods and sheet materials, you will soon find your collection of saws expanding. Nevertheless, the essential technique remains the same.

First of all, clamp the wood firmly to the bench. Forgetting this simple step is the most common cause of accidents – sawing accurately requires both hands for good balance, even though a hand saw looks like a one-handed tool.

Position yourself squarely over the piece, with your line of sight directly above the cutting line. Always make sure the saw cuts just to the waste side of the line to allow for the width of the cut, or kerf.

Start the cut slowly and form a groove. Some saws have a group of finer teeth at the tip of the blade for this very purpose. Hold the blade at a steep angle, sighting down and over the edge of the work to keep the cut absolutely square and vertical. This first step guides the saw for the rest of the cutting action.

Gradually decrease the angle of the cut and lengthen the strokes of the saw blade. Allow the blade to do the work – do not force it through the wood. You will learn what it means to hear a good sharp hand saw "singing" as it cuts rhythmically. Use all your arm to generate the sawing action, keeping the upper arm, elbow and wrist in line; use your forefinger to direct and steady the saw. When cutting large boards, arrange a support to take the weight of the scrap, but make sure it does not force the work upwards and cause the saw blade to bind in the cut.

1 Start the cut very slowly with the tip of the saw blade, drawing it back and forth to form a groove, and guiding it with your thumb.

2 As you near the end of the cut, support the waste with your other hand and use shorter, gentler strokes to sever the last few fibres.

| Ripsaw | Crosscut saw | Fleam cut saw |
|---|---|---|
| Use this for cutting along the grain of wood with a ripping action. The teeth are coarse set with a deep gullet to clear the waste quickly and prevent the saw from binding, particularly in resinous softwoods. The size and spacing of the teeth are specified as Teeth per Inch (TPI) – very coarse ripsaws can have as few as four or five TPI. | A crosscut saw is designed for cutting across the grain of timber. Each tooth is sharpened at an angle to the grain to prevent it from tearing. The teeth are smaller and finer than those of a ripsaw, up to 12–13 TPI. | Many modern saws are made with dual-purpose teeth for general use. The teeth are specially hardened and are ideal for cutting sheet materials, but they cannot be resharpened. |

## Tenon saws

Sometimes called backsaws, tenon saws produce a finer cut for joinery work. A stiff spine along the top of the blade keeps it straight and adds weight to the saw. This weight will cause it to find its own way through the work as you guide it.

When cutting end grain, turn it around for the second cut so that the waste is always on the same side of the saw blade.

**1** Make a small nick in the wood at an angle to start off the saw cut. Sight down the line to establish a good square cut. Concentrate on the direction of the saw.

**2** Slowly increase the length of your stroke and lower the saw with each cut until it is completely horizontal to the wood. Do not grip the saw too tightly.

**3** To make cuts in the end grain, clamp the work or piece of wood upright in a vice and saw down to the shoulder line, stopping exactly at the line.

## Mitre saws

For cutting very fine mouldings and angles, this relatively new type of saw will soon repay its modest investment, especially if you intend to do a lot of framing work. The wide tensioned blade with specially hardened teeth slides within its own carriage, which can be set to any angle between 45 and 90 degrees.

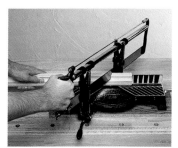

**1** Hold or cramp the wood firmly against the backstop and work the blade back and forth with a smooth cutting action. Very little downward force is required, as the saw operates under its own weight and has its own guide mechanism. Always cut on the waste side of the marked line for perfect results.

## Sharpening saws

A good-quality hand saw will last for years if looked after well; indeed, many woodworkers will say that a saw improves with age. If it needs sharpening, check the set of the teeth first. Each tooth on a saw is a miniature cutting blade that slices through the wood and clears a path for the next one. The teeth are "set" (angled) alternately to each side to prevent the saw blade from binding in the work.

When using a saw file, work systematically along the saw, sharpening each alternate tooth, then work from the other side to complete the process.

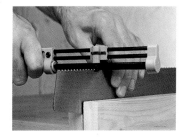

**1** To reset a saw, clamp the blade between two strips of wood to protect and support it. Adjust the gauge of the saw setting tool to suit the number of teeth per inch, and work down the blade, applying the correct amount of set to each alternate tooth in turn.

**2** A saw file is a triangular file with a sliding carriage that fits over the top of the blade. Set the carriage to suit the cutting angle of the teeth, settle the file in the gullet, and slowly draw it back and forth a few times until you see bright steel on the face of the tooth.

# USING POWER SAWS

Portable power saws come into their own when cutting large quantities of wood, especially sheet materials, but they may not be as accurate as hand tools for fine work. Most woodworkers will employ a combination of both to suit each job. As always, follow the manufacturer's guidance for their safe use, and always fit sharp blades. It is false economy, and very dangerous, to work with a cutting tool unless it is set up properly and working efficiently.

### Circular saws

Choose a model with the motor power and type of blade to suit the work. For cutting most sheet materials up to 19mm (¾in) thick, a 1,000W motor and tungsten-carbide-tipped blade, with a diameter of 165–180mm (6½–7in), will be adequate. Heavier work, especially in hardwood, requires a more powerful motor and a greater depth of cut. You will soon burn out the motor if you overload it. Make sure that the spring-loaded safety guard is in working order, and regularly clear it of sawdust as you work. Make a habit of checking the power cord after every use, and attend to any signs of wear immediately.

With practice, you will be able to cut straight lines freehand, but using a guide is safer and more accurate. An adjustable fence is often supplied, but this will be useful for cutting strips only up to about 150mm (6in) wide. For larger sizes, pin a straight-edged batten to the wood as a guide for the saw's sole plate.

### Cutting straight stock from a board

1 Make sure the power saw is disconnected from the power supply, then measure the distance from the edge of the base plate to the blade. To be absolutely accurate when cutting, you should allow for the extra thickness of the tungsten-carbide tips on the blade.

2 Mark the distance away from the cutting line and draw a parallel line along the work. Pin or clamp a straight-edge along this line, then run the sole plate of the saw along it. In some cases, the body of the saw will overhang the base plate, so choose a batten thickness that will not obstruct the saw.

3 Fit the parallel fence to the base plate and saw back in the other direction to reduce the board to the correct width. Make sure it is clamped firmly to the bench. A circular saw will make light work of cutting wood, but be sure not to overload it, and always have the guards in place.

## Making a circular saw jig

If you want to cut large quantities of sheet material, make up a simple sawing jig for quickly setting out square cuts.

Cut two strips of 12mm (½in) plywood as shown and assemble them to form a table on which the circular saw's base plate can travel. Set the upper strip back from the cutting edge by the exact width of the base plate to the left of the saw blade. Fix a cross-batten square across the bottom of the jig. Now place the jig on the panel of sheet material, line it up with the cutting line and run the saw along the line.

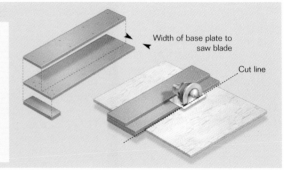

Width of base plate to saw blade

Cut line

## Jigsaws

A jigsaw is one of the most versatile cutting tools you can have in the workshop, being suitable for both straight and curved cuts.

It has a small, reciprocating and narrow blade. It is hand held and easy to use without much setting up. As it is so portable, take particular care to keep the power cord out of the way when working.

If possible, buy a model with a pendulum blade action – this clears the sawdust better and makes a straighter cut in wood. Electronic speed control allows you to slow the cutting action for very delicate work. The variety of jigsaw blades available makes this tool useful for cutting many sheet materials into smaller pieces, including thin sheet metal.

 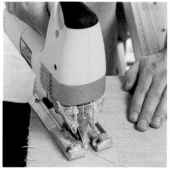 

1 Because the jigsaw blade cuts on the upward stroke, there is a much greater risk of splintering the wood, particularly when cutting across the grain. When working with veneered panels, score along the cut line with a knife and cut just outside the line, then pare down to the cut line with a plane.

2 An alternative is to fit a small, transparent shoe that clips around the blade and presses down on to the surface directly in front of it to keep breakout to a minimum.

3 A useful accessory with some machines is a plastic cover that fits over the sole plate to protect delicate surfaces. If you find that the sole plate is bruising the wood surface too easily, you are probably forcing the saw too much – use a slower speed or fit a new, sharp blade.

## Crosscut saws

Powered crosscut saws, also called mitre saws or "snip-off" saws, make accurate crosscutting of timber (lumber) a simple matter. The best models extend to a capacity of 250mm (10in), allowing extra wide boards to be cut.

Note that the blades are not interchangeable with other circular saws – the plunging action of the saw requires a different tooth profile. It is best to check what type of blades you'll need by reading the manufacturer's instructions.

1 The saw body can be adjusted to any angle, and a compound mitre saw, as shown, will cut two angles simultaneously. It is ideal for framing work and cutting mouldings and coving sections.

2 To save time when making a number of identical components for a piece of work, establish the correct size for the first one. Then clamp a small spacing block to the table to save marking up the rest.

# USING CHISELS

**Always aim to remove as much excess wood as possible from the cut before using your chisel. For example, remove the wood with a saw before cleaning up with a chisel or, when cutting a mortise, drill out as much of the waste as possible and use the chisel to clean and square-up the sides.**

### Chisels

There are two principal types of chisel used for general woodworking and cabinet-making: firmer and bevelled, or bevel-edged. A firmer chisel, with a stout blade and heavy-duty handle designed to accept blows from a mallet, is used for making mortises by chopping down across the tougher end grain of wood. Bevelled chisels may be more familiar, and they have many more uses. The bevelled tip of the blade is weaker and will not stand up to continuous heavy use, but it will suffice for most medium-duty work. This type of chisel comes into its own when used by hand alone for removing small amounts of wood with a gentle paring action.

### Care of chisels

Chisels should always be kept sharp – they can slip away from the work and cause a lot of damage as soon as they lose their edge. Make a habit of sharpening them at the end of every work session (in the same manner as plane blades), and store them safely, either in a box or in a wall-mounted rack that protects the tips. A well-maintained set of chisels should last a lifetime.

1 Scribe the width of the mortise with a mortise gauge and cut across the grain at each end to prevent breakout. Use the firmer chisel, almost vertical with the bevel down, to make a series of deep cuts. Start at the middle and work toward one end, then reverse the chisel for the other end. Clear out any waste as you work – large, wedge-shaped chunks of wood can be chopped out quite easily.

3 To clean up the shoulder of a joint, hold the chisel vertical and steady the blade with your other hand. Lean over it and slice down for a clean cut.

### Tip

Do not leave chisels lying on a bench where the blades can come into contact with metal objects. Fit them with plastic blade guards or keep them in a chisel roll.

2 When you have reached sufficient depth, place the chisel at the very end of the mortise with the bevel facing inward. Strike sharply with the mallet to plunge the blade vertically down and form a good square corner. Push the chisel blade slowly forward to disengage it and true-up (square) the sides at the same time.

4 In the absence of a shoulder plane, a bevelled chisel can be used to pare across the grain of a tenon joint. Use the widest chisel available, and hold it perfectly flat so that it slides evenly over the surface of the wood, removing the minimum amount with each stroke. A paring chisel has an even longer blade and is ideal for this kind of finishing work, but it should never be struck with a mallet.

# USING PLANES

A woodworker will build a collection of planes over time, each having a different use. Planes should have a good-quality "iron" (blade), made of tool steel with a bevelled edge for removing fine shavings of wood. Good-quality planes are sufficiently weighty to avoid "chatter". The size and shape of the sole, or base, and the angle and adjustment of the iron will determine a plane's best function.

### Jack plane

This is used mainly for dressing large areas of sawn or uneven wood. The sole, at 300–380mm (12–15in) long, acts to even out high spots and ridges as you work. Use with a slicing action, angled slightly across the grain, to make a level surface, then make even strokes along the grain to finish off. The try plane, or jointer plane, is longer – up to 610mm (24in) – and is used to true-up (square) the long straight edges of boards before joining.

### Smoothing plane

Ranging in length from 225 to 265mm (9 to 10½in), the smoothing plane is an all-purpose plane for most general carpentry and joinery work. It is an excellent plane to start your collection with.

### Rebate plane

The rebate, or filister, plane has a cutting blade that extends to the full width of the sole, making square-edged rebates (rabbets) simple to achieve. Adjust the side fence and depth stop to suit the size of rebate, then start the cut at the end of the timber (lumber) farthest from you. As the cutter forms the rebate, gradually increase the length of stroke, using your left hand to support the plane and hold it firmly in position.

### Shoulder plane

This miniature rebate plane is good for fine joinery work, as it cuts at a shallow angle, both across the grain and on end grain. The mouth is adjustable to allow the removal of small slivers of wood when paring down for a final fit.

### Block plane

Use the block plane for all kinds of fine finishing. Its blade is set at a shallow angle, allowing the removal of very fine shavings; the bevel on the blade faces upward, rather than down to the wood surface as in most other planes. It is very controllable, being designed for one-handed use.

A sharp and finely set block plane will remove the end grain quite easily. Make up a simple shooting board, as shown, to square the ends of components before jointing. It hooks over the edge of the bench and provides a firm support for the work, while holding the plane body square. Turn the board over for use as a straightforward bench hook.

### Moulding plane

More often found in antique shops these days, old moulding planes, in good condition, can still be useful. The plane iron is held in a hardwood body by a wooden wedge and tapped into place. As with a rebate plane, start shaping the moulding at the farthest end of the piece and work with increasingly longer strokes as the profile is formed.

# USING POWER PLANERS AND ROUTERS

**Power planers are ideal machines for removing large amounts of waste quickly, but they can also be used with some accuracy for fine finishing. Different models on offer vary in size and capacity – look for a minimum depth of cut of 3mm (⅛in) and a dust extraction facility or dust bag to collect the copious shavings produced. Tungsten-carbide-tipped (TCT) disposable blades are best when working with manufactured boards.**

### Electric planers

These can be very aggressive when removing stock, so hold the tool with both hands and keep it moving so that it does not cut for too long in one spot. As with the hand tool, an electric planer can also be used across the grain of wide boards for quick results, provided final finishing is with the grain. Although the electric planer is very fast, the hand-held version rarely gives the quality of finish that can be achieved with a well-set and sharpened bench plane. Check for sharpness and adjustment each time an electric planer is used – and make sure the wood to be planed is held firmly in a vice or clamped down.

1 The depth of cut is controlled by the rotary knob at the front, which doubles as a handle. Push down firmly and evenly on the machine to remove a constant thickness of stock in one pass. The side fence keeps the sole plate square to the edge.

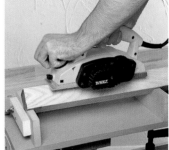

2 Most planers have a V-groove machined in the bottom of the sole plate to permit chamfering. Locate the groove on the square edge of the work to position the cutters at 45 degrees to each adjoining face. The work is in a jig to hold it in position.

### Sharpening plane irons

Remove the lever cap from the plane by raising the lever at the top, then take out the blade assembly. Slacken the screw on the cap iron and swivel the plane iron until it can be lifted over the screw head. Do not allow the sharp end of the iron to contact the cap iron body. Apply a coat of thin oil to the oilstone and rest the bevel of the iron on the stone. Rock it up and down until you feel that the bevel is perfectly flat on the stone. Hold the iron at this angle, then slowly slide it backward and forward. Use the forefingers of your other hand to apply pressure evenly over the width of the iron, and move your arms from the elbows, not the wrists.

Check the bevel by turning it face upward – any slight unevenness will indicate that you need to adjust your grip. Increase pressure with even strokes until the whole face of the bevelled edge has been finely ground and you can feel a small burr running evenly along the back edge of the iron. Turn the iron over and press it flat on to the stone. Remove the burr with a few short strokes.

Keep the iron flat – any slight rounding over on the back face will ruin the cutting edge. Wipe off any excess oil and refit the cap iron. Clean any debris from inside the body of the plane before reassembly, and apply a drop of oil to the moving parts of the adjustment mechanism.

3 Some models allow you to form rebates (rabbets) up to 25mm (1in) deep, using the side fence to control the rebate width. The design of the planer body dictates the maximum rebate capacity, so always check this when buying new equipment to ensure that the tool meets your needs.

## Routers

A router is one of the most versatile power tools available to the home woodworker. It uses high-speed rotary cutters, in a variety of profiles, to remove controlled amounts of material with great accuracy. However, certain safety rules should always be observed when operating a router. The router cutter should be presented to the work in the correct direction, so that the cutting edge bites into the wood. If you get this wrong, the cutter will spin out of control and ruin the work. Take the trouble to double check this every time you use the tool by observing the "clockwise" rule: looking down at the router, the cutter will always turn clockwise into the work. Always clamp the work firmly to prevent accidents, and keep the power cord well out of the way by draping it over your shoulder.

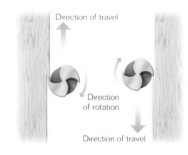

Direction of travel

Direction of rotation

Direction of travel

1 Always clamp the work to the
  bench. Never use the tool single-handed. Grasp it firmly with both hands and push slowly but surely through the wood, letting it cut at its own rate.

2 When using the side fence, a
  vernier scale allows fine adjustment of the cutter position. It is a good idea to keep plenty of offcuts (scraps) to hand for trial runs to ensure that the router is operating correctly.

3 Do not remove too much waste in
  one pass – use the adjustable depth stop to lower the cutter into the work in two or three steps. Remove 6–8mm (¼–⅜in) at a time and you will produce a smoother cut.

## Template follower

A template follower allows the repeated production of identical components by following a master pattern. It is particularly useful for creating curved shapes. Disconnect the power cord when making adjustments. Make sure it is completely seated in its recess.

1 Fit the follower
  attachment to the base of the router using the screws supplied.

2 Measure the distance
  between the cutting edge of the router bit and the outer rim of the follower. The finished work will exceed the template size by this amount. You must allow for this when constructing the template.

3 A trammel point fitted to
  the side bars will simplify forming circular shapes to a fixed radius.

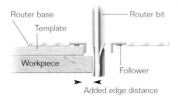

Router base

Template

Router bit

Workpiece

Follower

Added edge distance

# USING POWER DRILLS

**Without doubt, a power drill will be one of the most useful tools in your workshop. It is worth investing in a reasonably powerful model, not so much for heavy-duty use, but to guarantee that the motor will last a long time without working at the limit of its capacity.**

### Drill accessories

If your workshop does not have the space to install a free-standing bench (pillar) drill, a vertical drill stand accessory for your standard power drill is well worth considering.

Many drill bits and accessories depend on precise and controlled operation for accuracy and safety.

### Hole-saws

These make short work of cutting large-diameter holes, but they do have to be mounted in a vertical drill stand. Sizes range from 12mm (½in) up to 100mm (4in). Set the drill to a very low speed when drilling large-diameter holes, and clamp down the work securely.

### Spade bits

Also called a flat bit, these are useful for drilling large holes. Before you start drilling, the point of the bit needs to be engaged with the timber (lumber).

1 The traditional spade bit is much safer and more accurate when used in a drill stand. For a neat hole, set the depth stop so that initially the bit sinks just far enough into the wood for the pointed end to pierce the far side and mark the centre of the hole.

2 Turn the work over and use the small hole to centre the spade bit, then complete the hole. In this manner, you will avoid any breakout in the wood.

### Power drill key features:

- Minimum chuck capacity of 10mm (⅜in); ideally 13mm (½in).
- Detachable side handle for extra grip.
- Keyless chuck, allowing the quick change of drill bits with a simple twisting action.
- Variable speed and reversible action for maximum flexibility.
- Lock-on button for continuous running.
- Automatic clutch or torque control, with variable settings, allowing use as a screwdriver.

### Hinge borers

Many furniture fittings are designed to fit in standard hole sizes – for example, concealed cabinet hinges. The two standard sizes are 25mm (1in) and 35mm (1⅜in), and it is worth acquiring the purpose-made hinge boring bits that produce a neat, flat-bottomed blind hole to suit them.

## Sanding accessories

The rotary power of a drill makes it ideal for many sanding and shaping tasks, without using a special tool. Drum sanders use a small sanding belt fitted on a rubber or foam cylinder in various sizes up to 150mm (6in) in diameter. For smoothing curves or cleaning up the edges of a piece of work these small accessories come easily to hand without the cost of a special tool for the same purpose. If using the drill freehand, always fit the side handle to steady the machine, and work against the motion of the rotating drum or disc to give you greater control.

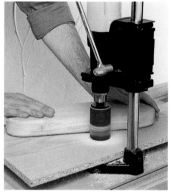

1 Fit a small sanding drum to the drill and pass the work over it, applying gentle pressure. Always wear a dust mask and eye protection when working in this way.

2 You can attach a sanding disc to the drill and use it freehand for shaping curved objects and removing large amounts of surface material extremely quickly.

## Plug cutters

A very useful tool for cabinet-making is the plug cutter. It is fitted into a pillar drill and used to make small wooden pellets or plugs. These are then plugged into holes in the workpiece to conceal fixing screws. Plug cutters are matched to counterbore, or three-in-one, bits in a range of sizes to suit the size of screw, from No. 6 gauge upwards.

1 Use a counterbore or three-in-one drill bit to form the screw hole, sinking the counterbore to a depth of approximately 10mm (⅜in). The tip of the bit, which provides a pilot hole for the screw, is quite fragile, so it is good practice to use a drill stand for this to keep the drill absolutely vertical and avoid breakages.

2 Fit the plug cutter in a drill stand and make a series of small pellets in a matching material. Use stock of suitable thickness (19mm/¾in) and set the cutting depth to about 12mm (½in), leaving all the plugs in place until needed.

3 The easiest way to snap out each pellet is by using a small screwdriver blade or chisel. Apply a drop of wood glue and tap into the screw holes. Match the colour and grain direction of the wood as closely as possible.

4 When the glue is dry and clear, use a very sharp bevelled chisel to pare each pellet flush with the surface of the timber. This will leave it virtually undetectable when finished.

# ASSEMBLY TECHNIQUES

When all the components of your project have been made, you can begin to assemble them. It is always good workshop practice to have a separate area for this operation, so that glued items can be left undisturbed to dry, preferably overnight. A solid bench is essential, and its surface should be perfectly flat. If the assembly bench is warped or uneven, this deformity will be transferred to the item you are making, no matter how accurate the woodwork.

### Drilling

Plan your assembly carefully so that you have enough time to work in stages without rushing the job. A carpenter's brace is a very efficient tool and can sometimes be a quicker option than resorting to a power drill. Auger bits remove large amounts of waste much more accurately in a controlled fashion. Stand directly over the piece of work, using one hand to apply downward force and keep the bit vertical while turning the brace handle with the other hand. Drill pilot holes for any screws, especially in hardwood, countersinking them if required, and clear any debris before fixing the screw.

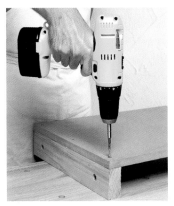

1 Choose a brace with a ratchet drive if possible, as this will allow you to make half a turn at a time and stand close to the bench.

2 Here a counterbore bit drills a pilot for the screw, a clearance hole for the screw shank, and a recess for the head, all in one operation.

3 Always choose a screwdriver bit to suit the screw heads. Do not allow the screwdriver to slip out of the head and ruin a piece of work.

4 Some cordless drills can be used for inserting screws. You can also obtain purpose-designed electric screwdrivers. An adjustable torque setting ensures that you do not strip the head as the screw is tightened, while a magnetic bit holder saves time when working with steel screws.

### Gluing

Before applying any glue to the assembly, always "dry fit" components together and prepare the work. Always seal glue containers after use to prevent the build-up of dried glue in the nozzle. Modern quick-setting PVA woodworking glue should be applied and clamped tight within ten minutes for the strongest bond. Be warned, however: on fine cabinet work intended for a clear finish, the dissolved glue should not be left to soak into the grain, as it may cause discolouration at the final stage. Sometimes it is advisable to leave the glue to set, then carefully cut away the excess with a sharp blade.

1 Apply PVA woodworking glue evenly to the entire joint surface, using a stiff brush to spread it out.

2 Wipe off any excess glue with a damp cloth as soon as a joint has been assembled and clamped.

## Clamping

Apply pressure to a joint as soon as possible after gluing – make a habit of preparing everything you need in advance. Keep a box of small scraps of wood handy and use them to protect the surface of the work. It is a known fact that you can never have too many cramps, and you will soon start collecting a selection of different types and sizes to suit all kinds of assembly technique.

## Adhesives

The traditional woodworker's adhesive was animal glue. While it has been superseded by more modern glues, it is still obtainable and is useful for restoration work and veneering. Small pearls of the material are melted to form a liquid and brushed on to the wood. Unfortunately, the glue is not heat-resistant and can deteriorate, becoming brittle with time.

For most tasks, the standard adhesive is a quick-setting, water-soluble PVA adhesive or wood glue. Generally creamy white in colour, it becomes transparent when dry, leaving an almost invisible glue line. It is non-toxic, non-flammable, safe to use and easy to remove before it dries with a damp cloth. Wood glue can also be yellow in colour. Rapid-drying and waterproof versions are available.

For heavy-duty applications, or exterior use, a more robust glue is recommended. Two-part adhesives are ideal, hardening by curing chemically. They cannot be dissolved or removed when dry. The glue is mixed by adding a liquid hardener to a powder; only mix a small quantity at a time – sufficient for the job in hand. Resorcinol glue is waterproof and heatproof. It is slightly toxic, so wear gloves to protect your hands when using. Another drawback is that it is a dark reddish brown, which makes it very visible on pale coloured wood.

1 G-cramps (C-clamps) come in all sizes, ranging from 25mm (1in) up to 250mm (10in) or more. When buying G-cramps, beware of cheaper types made of low-quality castings – they may shatter as they are tightened. Look for high-grade malleable iron in the specification.

3 Use sash (bar) cramps in pairs to apply pressure evenly. They are ideal for assembling doors and panels that require a parallel clamping action to remain square. Think through the sequence for the clamping process and make sure you have enough cramps to hand.

2 Keep a few quick (spring) cramps handy for fast one-handed clamping. They are not suitable for high-pressure applications, but can be useful for fixing complex assemblies temporarily while making final adjustments. Do not be tempted to release cramps too quickly. Allow time for the glue to dry.

4 Check that a panel is square at the internal corners before applying glue. Accuracy in cutting the shoulders of joints is the key to a square assembly. If the shoulders are slightly out of square, the panel will become permanently deformed when pressure is applied.

### Tip

A good tip for checking the squareness of a panel is to measure the diagonals. If one corner is true, and the diagonals are equal, the panel must be therefore a perfect square or rectangle. Measure both diagonals to make absolutely sure.

# SANDING AND FINISHING

Before applying any finishing coat to your completed work, the wood should be sanded and prepared well. A coat of varnish or polish will show up any blemishes in the surface that were hardly detectable beforehand. Sometimes it is very tempting to rush this part of the process, but there is no substitute for careful and methodical preparation. A power sander will deal with most of the work, but you should always finish off by hand. This gives you the opportunity of checking every part of the assembly and correcting any small defects.

### Using wire wool

Wire, or steel, wool produces an even finer finish than sandpaper. The tiny strands of spun steel fibre burnish the surface of the wood.

The most useful grades range from 0 (coarse) through 00 and 000 to 0000 (very fine). On oily wood, this can leave the surface so smooth that any further finishing is unnecessary. Form a pad from the wire wool when using it, and rub in the direction of the grain. Gently brush along the grain afterwards to remove any fine dust and debris.

1 Form a pad from a small amount of wire (steel) wool and work it along the grain, using smooth, even strokes.

### Using sandpaper

Sandpaper grades are denoted in "grit size". This refers to the size of abrasive particles that are applied in an even coating to the backing paper. Begin with a fairly coarse grade, such as 60 or 80 grit, then use progressively finer grades until the surface is smooth and silky to the touch. Each grade removes the minute scratches left by the previous one. A good range of paper to stock would include 80, 120, 240 and 320 grit for the finest finish; 400 grit is so fine that it is normally used for cutting back the first coat of finish.

1 Use a cork or rubber block on flat surfaces to obtain the right amount of flexibility as you work. You can use a wooden block, but it could tear the sandpaper. Clear the dust away as you work to avoid clogging the paper, particularly on resinous and oily wood.

2 A surform tool is very useful for rounding off the edges of wood, and it is surprisingly accurate. The rows of miniature cutting edges on the blade pare away the surface of the wood with a continuous motion.

3 To finish off a rounded edge, wrap a small square of sandpaper around a section of moulded timber (lumber) of the correct profile (taking care not to tear the sandpaper). Work down through the different grades of sandpaper as normal.

## Using a cabinet scraper

This is a flexible rectangle of high-quality tempered steel, which when used properly makes a versatile cutting tool capable of producing a highly polished finish. Use it before you use abrasive papers, such as garnet paper or silicon carbide, to remove small tears and blemishes.

When you use a cabinet scraper, always with two hands, you should vary the angle of the scraper to fine-tune its cutting action as you push it away from you with smooth strokes.

1 Hold the scraper as shown, flexing the blade between your fingers and thumbs until the cutting edge just begins to bite into the wood surface.

2 You can use other scraper profiles on moulded and curved surfaces, like the gooseneck scraper, which you can turn to suit any concave profile.

## Sharpening a cabinet scraper

A cabinet scraper must be prepared before use and sharpened regularly to maintain its efficiency. The blade is made to scrape rather than cut. The cutting edge must be perfectly flat and square, so it should first be prepared with a file and then polished on an oilstone or grindstone. With the blade fastened in a vice, a hard steel shaft is run along the edge to raise a burr and produce the new cutting edge.

1 The cutting edge of the scraper must be perfectly flat and square before you begin. Clamp it upright in a vice and use a metal file to prepare the edge.

2 Place the edge of the scraper flat on an oilstone and work it back and forth to polish it.

3 Now raise a burr all along the edge by drawing a bar of hardened steel swiftly along and across the square edge. A proprietary burnisher should be used for this, but you can improvise with the shaft of a screwdriver or any similar tool steel. The burr acts as the cutting edge and should be renewed whenever the scraper becomes difficult to work.

Concave, gooseneck and flat cabinet scrapers

# USING POWER SANDERS

Power sanders are most useful for the quick removal of waste stock before finishing by hand. A belt sander is worth considering if you have a lot of heavy-duty work, but does not produce an acceptable finish on its own. For general use, an orbital sander is by far the most versatile power tool to buy. When choosing a power sander, an important feature to look for is an efficient dust-collection facility. This not only reduces the amount of dust in the air, but also increases the working life of the machine and the sandpaper. Even with dust extraction, you should always use eye protection and a dust mask for your own health and safety.

### Belt sanders

A belt sander must be used with great care as the rotating belt removes large amounts of waste and you can easily create deep marks in the work, thus spoiling the piece. Keep the base moving constantly and always flat on the surface without forcing the machine. Its own weight will provide sufficient sanding pressure.

Use a belt sander to deal with uneven ridges in a laminated surface and for scouring off old paint finishes, but never use it for fine sanding and finishing work.

Always use the dust bag supplied with the belt sander, but preferably fit an adaptor to accept a dust extractor. You should empty the bag regularly to prevent the motor from overheating. Always wear a dust mask to prevent inhalation of dust particles, particularly if removing old paint, stains or varnish.

### Sanding belts

These sheets, like sandpaper, come in different grades, but the belts have a cloth backing for longer wear. They range from 40–60 grit (coarse grade) to 180 grit (extra fine). When fitting belts, look for the arrow printed inside, which indicates the direction of rotation.

1 Use the belt sander with a scouring action across the grain to level an uneven surface. The rotary action of the belt will tend to pull the work towards you, so clamp it firmly or use benchstops to prevent it from moving.

2 Using the same grade of belt, change direction to run the sander up and down the grain, removing the sanding marks running across the work. Change to a finer belt and repeat the process until the surface is flat.

### Multi-function sanders

Relatively new is a family of sanders with differently shaped base plates and attachments for sanding difficult profiles. They come with self-adhesive sanding pads, specially shaped to fit the triangular base. While very useful for cutting into corners and mouldings, they are not really suitable for heavy-duty work.

*Right and far right* The pads of these sanders fit easily into the corners of drawers and doors.

## Orbital sanders

As the name implies, an orbital sander moves the sanding pad in a circular motion for a much finer finish than a belt sander. It will still leave small circular marks on the work, however, which can only be removed by hand sanding with a sanding block. As the sandpaper collects more dust, the swirl marks tend to become more obvious, so change the paper regularly and use progressively finer grades, finishing up with 180 or 240 grit paper.

To prevent dust build-up, choose a model with a dust-collection bag that extracts dust from the surface of the wood through holes punched in the base as you work.

Orbital sanders are sold as half-sheet, third-sheet and quarter-sheet models. This allows you to cut a standard-sized sheet of sandpaper – 280 x 230mm (11 x 9in) – to fit the base without waste.

When buying sanding sheets, look for heavy-duty backing paper designed for use with power sanders. Aluminium oxide paper, sometimes called production paper, is by far the most durable and most efficient type.

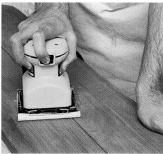

1 Ready-sized sheets of sandpaper are available to fit each particular model, but they are more expensive. However, they do have the advantage of being pre-punched to allow dust extraction from the base. Some models are supplied with a small template for punching your own holes.

2 A small palm sander is ideal for the final finishing grades of paper. Work all over the surface with a series of overlapping circular motions, before finishing off with long strokes parallel to the grain.

3 The orbital sander in use is a much less ferocious cutter than a belt sander, and easier to control. The base plates are often made of foam rubber, which makes them gentle in use and more forgiving to the surface being worked on.

### Go with the grain

Always work "with the grain" when finishing wood – work along the wood fibres and in the direction in which they lie.

Study the edge of the timber (lumber) to obtain a clear picture before you begin. Sometimes the grain will change direction within the length of the same piece, so be prepared to change with it as you work.

On very coarse or uneven wood grain, there may be no easy solution – a block plane (*right*) set for a very fine cut can do the trick if used with a slicing action around difficult areas.

Alternatively, employ a cabinet scraper if you have one – it is well worth mastering the art of this simple tool.

✓ Work with the grain

✗ Not against the grain

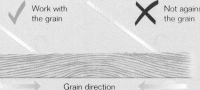

Grain direction

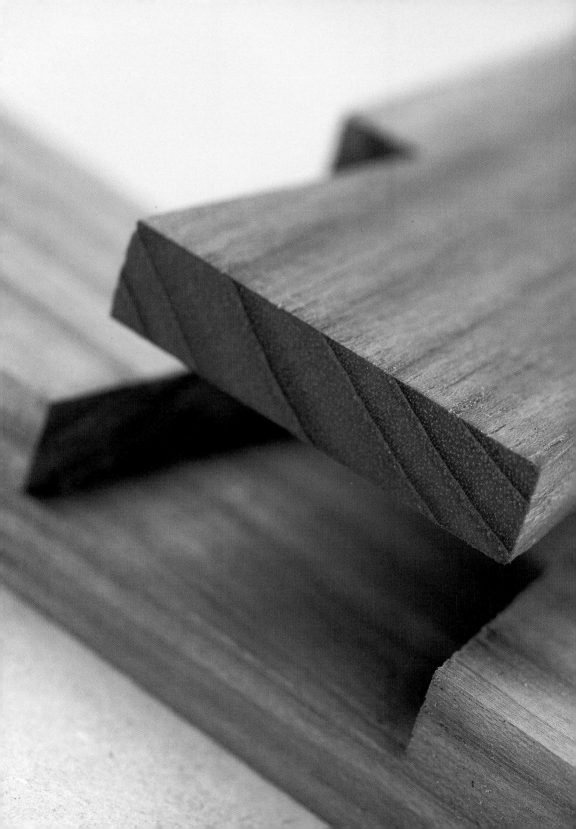

# 6

# MAKING
# JOINTS

**T**he basic techniques of woodworking are all that you need to begin to master the fine art of joinery. Patience, care and attention to detail provide the key to accurate joints; an understanding of how they work will allow you to choose the correct type for a given job. The techniques of joining wood have been developed over centuries, and there is satisfaction to be gained from employing these tried and tested methods. While it can be daunting to look at a long list of different joints with strange names, the following pages will demystify the whole subject. Ranging from the simplest of lap joints to more complex and decorative types, the joints shown cover most applications. As always, practice and good, sharp tools make perfect.

# LAP AND HALVING JOINTS

The simplest and most basic of joints is created where one piece of wood overlaps another. It is not the strongest method of joining two components, and may need reinforcing with extra fixings, but it is a straightforward technique. Where two pieces of the same thickness are to be connected, the strength of the joint can be greatly increased by forming a halving (half) joint.

### Corner lap joint

A typical use would be to form the corners of a drawer or simple box, where the shoulder of the joint adds strength and helps to keep the construction square.

*Right* The finished corner lap joint.

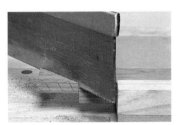

1 Mark out the thickness and depth of the lap with a scribing knife and gauge, then cut along the shoulder line with a tenon saw, keeping to the waste side of the line.

2 Clamp the piece firmly to the bench in a vice or use a G-cramp. Remove the waste wood with a series of small cuts, using a chisel and carpenter's mallet.

3 Pare down the wood to the scribed line with the chisel to complete the joint. Check the fit of the joint and make any fine adjustments. Pin and glue the joint together.

### Mitred halving joint

When glued and pinned from the underside, this more than doubles the strength of a simple mitred corner joint. Note that the end grain is revealed on one edge only.

*Above* The finished mitred halving joint.

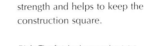

1 Mark out a half lap and the depth of the join on the top half of the joint using a try square and pencil, then remove exactly half the thickness of wood. Pare down to the shoulder with a very sharp bevelled chisel.

2 Mark out the mitre on the top face of the lap and remove the waste with a tenon saw. Lay the finished piece over the lower section and use it as a guide for scribing the other half of the joint.

3 Cut along the shoulder line and remove waste wood by tapping gently with a chisel. Pare away the seat of the joint to make a snug fit. Glue the joint together.

## Cross-halved (half-lap) joint

This is the classic method of joining two intersecting pieces of equal thickness. Cut the shoulders accurately to form a very strong and square connection.

*Above* The completed cross-halved joint.

1 Mark the width of the bottom member on the underside of the top piece, then gauge the depth to half its thickness. Make a series of saw cuts across the waste area.

2 Remove the waste by chopping down sharply with a chisel to snap out small sections of waste at a time. This removes the risk of splitting the timber (lumber).

3 Pare down to the scribed lines using a bevel-edged chisel to ensure a flat and even seat for the joint. Hold the chisel blade perfectly horizontal and work toward the centre.

4 When the top half of the joint fits the bottom piece snugly, use it as a guide for scribing the exact width of the cut-out on the bottom half, then repeat steps 1–3.

## Lapped dovetail joint

An elegant means of creating a very strong joint that prevents one component from pulling away from another. It is useful for connecting rails and cross-members.

*Above* The finished lapped dovetail joint.

1 Cut the top half of the lap first, as for a straightforward lap joint. Use a bevel gauge to mark the dovetail on the top face.

2 Clamp the work in a vice and cut down to the shoulders with a fine tenon saw. Remove the waste and pare down to the lines with a chisel.

3 Lay the finished dovetail over the lower piece to mark out the socket, and cut away the waste. Pare down to the scribed lines carefully with a shoulder plane to make a tight fit. Glue the joint together.

# HOUSING AND BRIDLE JOINTS

Another simple method of joining two pieces of wood where the end of one meets the side of the other is to cut a slot (housing) in the latter for the former. This provides positive location and strength.

### Full housing joint

This is a simple means of joining two parts of a frame at right angles, for example where a cross-rail meets an upright. In this case, the full width of the rail is housed within the cut-out. You can also stop the housing short of the face side of the job.

*Above* The completed full housing joint.

1 The rail must be of a length that allows for the depth of the housing, and its end must be cut square. Use a vernier gauge to check the width of the rail accurately.

3 Use a sanding block, or an offcut (scrap) of wood wrapped with sandpaper (take care not to tear the paper), to trim the housing for a snug fit. Keep it absolutely flat to avoid rounding off the shoulders. You may have to plane the corresponding part of joint to make a good fit.

2 Use the other side of the vernier gauge to set the width of the housing. Scribe and cut the shoulders, then remove any waste to half the thickness of the rail.

### Bare-faced housing joint

When creating a housing joint in a corner, as for a door or window frame, leave an extra amount on the end of the cross-member for maximum strength. The bare-faced tenon on the upright is formed by removing waste from one side only.

1 Cut the shoulder for the tenon on the outer face. This puts the bare face on the inside of the joint to give a fixed internal measurement. Pare the tenon and shoulder to the scribed lines.

2 Set the two pins of a mortise gauge to match the width of the tenon you have made, then adjust the stock so that the housing groove will be positioned correctly.

## Bridle joint

A neat method of joining two components where they meet at a corner. This joint is versatile because it does not have to be a right angle and it is suitable for small sections. The tenon part of the joint is usually one-third of the thickness of the wood.

*Above* The completed corner bridle joint.

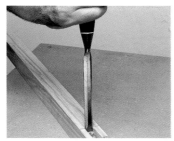

1 Use a mortise gauge to mark out the mortise, making it one-third of the thickness of the wood. Cut down to the required depth and chop out the waste with a chisel.

3 Clamp the tenon member firmly. Cut the shoulders of the joint with a tenon saw and remove the waste. Leave the tenon oversize at this stage for final fitting.

2 Without altering the mortise gauge setting, scribe the tenon to suit the mortise, making sure that you gauge from the face side of the wood. Shade the waste areas with a pencil.

4 Trial fit the joint by sliding both members together on a flat surface. This will indicate any high spots that need removing from the tenon for a flush fit.

3 Scribe the position of the housing with the mortise gauge, then mark the required depth for the tenon. Cut down to the lines with a tenon saw, and chisel out the waste.

*Above* The finished bare-faced housing joint.

# MORTISE AND TENON JOINTS

These are some of the most useful joints you can master. They are the basis for most panelled doors, windows and joinery. The secret of success lies not so much in achieving a good fit for the tenon in the mortise, but rather in the accurate cutting of the shoulders of the tenon, which ensures a square and rigid construction when the joint is drawn up tight.

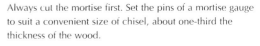

### Basic mortise and tenon

The mortise and tenon joint has been adapted to meet a number of specific jointing needs, particularly to provide additional strength. The main types are shown here, and will prove useful as you develop your jointing skills.

Always cut the mortise first. Set the pins of a mortise gauge to suit a convenient size of chisel, about one-third the thickness of the wood.

1 Set the stock to centralize the mortise, and run the mortise gauge along the face side of the timber (lumber). Set the gauge aside without altering the setting of the pins – it will also be needed to mark out the thickness and the position of the tenon.

2 Drilling a row of holes between the gauged marks is a quick means of removing the majority of the waste. Use a spur-point drill bit (dowel drill bit) to ensure that the holes are kept in line. Make sure the holes are truly vertical – use a drill stand or pillar drill if possible.

3 Chop out most of the remaining waste from the mortise, then begin to pare down to the scribed lines with a broad chisel. Don't be hasty and try to remove too much at a time, otherwise you run the risk of splitting the wood along the grain.

4 Use a small chisel that matches the width of the mortise to chop out the ends. A firmer chisel can be used with a mallet to remove most of the waste. Finish off with a bevelled chisel, as shown, to get right into the corners for a perfectly square mortise.

5 Set out the tenon by marking the shoulder line with a carpenter's pencil on all sides. Use the mortise gauge to scribe the blade of the tenon, again working from the face side. Mark the waste to be removed with a saw and use a knife to scribe the cutting lines for the shoulders.

6 Cut across the grain at the shoulders with a fine-toothed tenon saw, keeping to the waste side of the scribed lines. Take care not to cut too deep, stopping just short of the scribed marks for the tenon blade. It is best to clamp the piece of work in a vice or with G-clamps for a positive hold.

7 Clamp the wood upright in a vice and remove the two outer sections, sometimes called tenon cheeks, again keeping to the waste side of the lines. Making sure that the wood is truly vertical will help you to produce straight cuts and taking time to cut accurately will save later adjustment.

8 Place the wood flat on the bench and pare down to the scribed marks. Use a paring chisel, pressing down on the blade with your forefinger to keep it absolutely horizontal. Try the tenon in the joint as you work, noting where it feels tight and paring gently until you achieve a perfect fit.

## Wedged-through tenon

By far the strongest form of mortise and tenon joint, in which the tenon passes right through the matching component and is locked in place with small wedges.

This method is often used for doors and windows where the frame has to endure a high degree of stress and movement. Gluing the wedges in place ensures that the joint will never come apart, even if the wood shrinks slightly as it dries.

**1** A very slight angle for the wedge is all that's needed to lock the joint. Mark out the waste areas beyond the ends of the mortise, and start the cuts with the tip of a small dovetail saw.

**2** Use a chisel to complete the bevels. Note how the angle has been marked on the outside of the rail to act as a visual guide. Use the same angle when cutting wedges from small offcuts (scraps) of wood.

**3** Apply glue to the joint and fit the pieces together. Slowly tap the wedges into place, alternating from one to the other to draw the joint up square. Leave to set before trimming off the excess.

## Double tenon

Where you are joining a very wide component, such as the middle rail of a door, a continuous mortise would cause too much weakness in the receiving member. You can solve this problem by cutting two tenons side by side. The best door frames usually have mortise and tenon joints and they are frequently used in joinery and cabinet-making.

**1** Form the double mortise in the usual way. If the tenons are 50mm (2in) wide, leave about the same distance between them. Pare the sides of each mortise.

**2** It is more accurate to cut the tenon as a single piece, then remove the section in the middle. Pare down the shoulders. Clean up any waste with a chisel.

**3** Fit the joint together. Both tenons should fit snugly into their mortises. Make sure there is a very small space for glue and then clamp when setting.

## Fox tenon

This variation is similar to the wedged tenon, but is used where the tenon is "blind" and does not pass completely through the receiving member.

It is an elegant and secret joint that will remain locked together. Great accuracy is required, though, because you only get one chance to assemble it. The size of the small "fox" wedges is critical.

**1** Form a stopped mortise and tenon joint, then cut two slots about halfway down the length of the tenon. Note their positions – the idea is to force the edges of the tenon sufficiently outward to grip the inside of the mortise.

**2** Cut two small wedges to such a size that, when the joint is assembled, the bottom of the mortise will drive them home and lock the joint. Set them in the slots, apply glue and fit the pieces together. Clamp them together while the glue dries and sets.

# DOVETAIL JOINTS

The dovetail joint is a fine example of the woodworker's art, combining a sound structural connection with a decorative appearance. You will come across many examples of furniture where dovetails have been used deliberately to display the cabinet-maker's pride in the work.

## Making a basic dowel joint

Accuracy and forethought are called for in setting out the joint correctly. The orientation of the dovetail determines how the components will be assembled.

1 Begin by setting out the "tails" of the joint from which the dovetail joint gets its name. The end of the tail member must be perfectly square, so be sure to use a shooting board and block plane to square up the end grain.

2 With hardwood, an angle of about 7 degrees (or pitch of 1:8) will ensure maximum strength from the joint without weakening the pins. Note how the waste at each end of the joint is roughly half the size of the gaps between the tails.

3 Always mark the waste areas between the tails as you work, because it's easy to become confused at this stage. Use a knife to scribe across the grain and mark the shoulder lines between the tails.

4 Clamp the work upright to make saw cuts for the tails, keeping to the waste side of the lines. Set the wood at an angle so that you hold the saw blade vertical for half the cuts, then reposition it to finish.

5 Use a coping saw to remove the waste from between the tails. Having the waste sections clearly marked out will prevent you from making any mistakes.

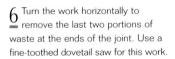

6 Turn the work horizontally to remove the last two portions of waste at the ends of the joint. Use a fine-toothed dovetail saw for this work.

7 Finally, use a bevelled chisel to pare down to the shoulder line and finish the tails. Work gradually towards the line, taking care to make the sides absolutely straight and square.

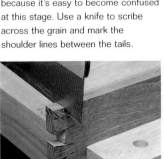

8 When marking out the pins, it helps to hold the work in a vice about 25mm (1in) proud. Highlight the end grain with a piece of chalk, especially on a dark hardwood such as the teak, used here.

9 Use the tails as a guide for marking out the positions of the pins. Place a block of scrap wood beneath the dovetail member so that it is square to and level with the pin member. Shade in the areas to be cut with a pencil.

10 Scribe the cut lines and shoulders for the pins with a knife, mark the waste sections, then remove them with a dovetail saw and chisel. Pare the pins to match the tails until the joint slides together smoothly.

## Varieties of dovetail joint

Over the years, cabinet-makers have developed many varieties of dovetail joint to suit different applications. After you have mastered the basic principle, try some of the other types. The lapped dovetail conceals the end grain of the tails, which are fitted into sockets in the pin member. You might find this in use on the front panel of a drawer. A mitred dovetail is even more challenging – both sections of end grain are concealed by mitred housings. Modern machine-made joints use more permanent adhesives than were available previously, so some of the more artful dovetails have fallen out of use. A comb joint is simple to machine, depending entirely on glue to form the bond, and it can look attractive.

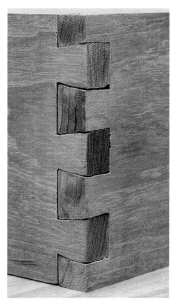

*Above* The completed dovetail joint. The dovetails take their name from their fan shape and the pins form the top and the bottom of the joint and sit in between the tails. Sometimes the pins are smaller in width than the dovetails.

To ensure a good fit, the pins must be scribed accurately and directly off the corresponding part of the dovetail.

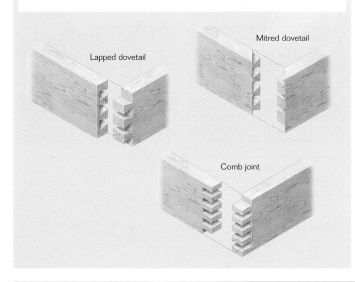

Lapped dovetail

Mitred dovetail

Comb joint

# ROUTERED JOINTS

**A router is a powerful tool that comes into its own for making accurate joints, especially in large panels for carcass assembly. It is particularly useful for repetitive operations that demand a series of identical joints in several components. Accurate setting up and a methodical approach are essential for the best results. Always try out the router on a scrap of wood before starting on the work to ensure that the settings are correct.**

### Housing joints

Routered housing joints are a simple means of locating shelves and dividers in a carcass. The housing is a groove that is precisely cut with a router to accept another piece of timber (lumber) at right angles to it. The strength of the joint depends on a tight and secure fit. The router will cut the shoulders and the base of the housing at the same time.

A stopped housing joint conceals the front edge of the joint from view.

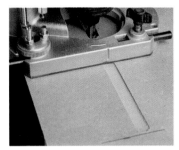

1 Mark the end of the groove at the front edge. Work toward this end if possible, stopping the router cutter just short of the pencil line.

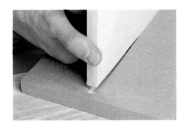

2 To prevent any breakout, use a knife to scribe the square end of the joint.

3 Cut out the rounded portion of waste at the end of the groove with a bevelled chisel.

4 Apply some glue to the bottom of the groove and slot the panel into position.

### Tongued-and-grooved housing

A router is useful for cutting continuous grooves accurately in long lengths of timber (lumber). This technique allows you to form the tongue to fit the groove exactly, whatever the thickness of timber.

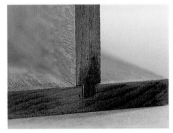

*Above* The finished tongued-and-grooved housing joint.

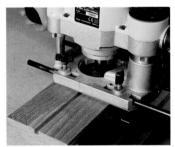

1 Using the side fence of the router as a guide, rout a continuous groove in the first component.

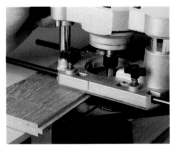

2 Now form the tongue, gradually increasing the depth of cut until it is a perfect fit. Alternatively, you can purchase a matching cutter that forms the tongue in one pass of the router, but it is a lot more expensive and less versatile.

## Dovetailed housing

A dovetail profile cutter makes this self-locking joint easy to fabricate. There is no other practical way to form a long, dovetailed housing. To make a dovetail housing by hand would generally be too difficult and time-consuming.

The housing is of dovetail section. The corresponding part of the joint has a dovetail tongue. This type of joint has great structural strength. The dovetailer cannot be lowered into the work. The depth setting of the groove must be established before you begin working, and completed in one pass of the router.

1 Rout a square-section groove before using the dovetail cutter – this puts much less strain on the router and the cutter blades, as there is a lot of waste to remove.

2 Use a shoulder plane to trim the excess from the dovetail tongue to its finished size.

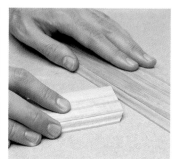

*Right* The finished dovetailed housing joint.

## Scribed joints

Profile cutters in matching pairs allow you to form perfectly fitted scribed joints for making panelled doors and mouldings.

1 When using scribing cutters, the depth setting is critical for a good match, so make sure you have a good supply of extra material of the same thickness to allow a few trial runs.

2 Machine the male portion of the moulding before forming the female half of the scribed joint. Work slowly and steadily to produce a smooth ripple-free finish.

3 The two profiles should match each other exactly. Slide them together on a flat surface to check for perfect alignment.

# DOWEL JOINTS

Beech dowels offer a quick and simple means of strengthening corner joints and aligning two components to prevent them from twisting. Three common sizes are available: 6mm (¼in), 8mm (⅜₆in) and 10mm (⅜in). Choose the diameter to suit the material – as a general rule, do not exceed half the thickness of the timber. There are several easy methods of locating them accurately.

### Centre-point method

Small brass or steel centre-points that match the dowel diameter come in dowelling kits that are available from hardware stores and also include a drill bit and dowels.

*Above* Dowels provide an invisible means of joining two sections of wood.

### Practical tip

The best dowels are slightly fluted to allow the glue to spread through the joint.

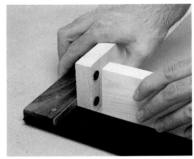

1 Use a dowel drill bit, also called a spur-point bit, to centre each hole accurately. A strip of tape wrapped around the bit makes a simple depth gauge. Hold the drill truly vertical – use a drill stand or pillar drill if you have a lot of holes to drill.

2 Insert the centre-points in the holes and simply push the adjacent component toward them, making sure that it is in its correct position. Use a square to check that the edges are flush.

3 Clamp the second piece in a vice and drill to the correct depth for the dowel.

4 Apply glue to the dowels, insert in the holes and tap the joint together.

### Dowel drilling jig

Slightly more expensive than a centre-point kit, but well worth the investment if you are making a lot of joints, the dowel drilling jig comes in several forms. The type illustrated offers a choice of bushes to take three sizes of dowel drill.

1 Mark the components carefully to ensure the correct orientation in the drilling jig. Clamp the two components together with the jig, making sure that the outer faces are touching.

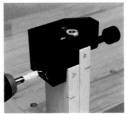

2 Tape the bit to allow for the depth of the drilling bush. Drill the end grain of the first part. Without altering the position of the jig, drill the matching hole(s) in the second part.

3 Apply glue to the dowel and the face of the joint, and simply push together.

# BISCUIT JOINTS

"Biscuit" is the term for a flat wafer of compressed hardwood, usually beech, that acts in the same way as a dowel. However, it must be fitted into a slot cut with a biscuit jointer. Again, they are available in three common sizes: size 0 (16mm/⅝in), size 10 (20mm/¾in) and size 20 (25mm/1in). The biscuits are baked to a low moisture content so that when water-based glue is applied, they swell and make a tight joint – store them in a sealed container to keep them dry.

### Edge joints

The beauty of biscuit jointing is that marking out is easy – simply place the two components together in their intended positions and make a series of pencil marks at suitable intervals.

1 To make a simple plinth, cut the components to size and align them for marking out, ensuring that all the edges are flush.

2 Clamp each side upright in a vice to cut the slot. The reference mark on the jointer automatically centres it on the pencil mark.

3 Cut a slot for the other half of the joint by clamping the piece to the bench. It must be held firmly as you plunge the cutting blade into the wood.

4 To cut slots for biscuits in a mitred corner joint, simply adjust the jointer's scale to 45 degrees and proceed as before. A spacing block is sometimes needed to position the carriage at the correct height.

5 Clear any sawdust from the slots before inserting the biscuits. Coat each with a small amount of glue and tap into place.

6 Apply glue to the faces of the joints and fit the parts together. Apply clamping pressure to pull everything tight – an easy, fast and accurate system.

### Mitred joints

A simple frame with mitred corners can be reinforced with biscuits if the components are thick enough to accommodate them. The versatile jointing machine can save time and improve accuracy in a multitude of applications.

1 A mitre saw will cut the timber (lumber) easily and accurately.

2 Use a try square to align the corners accurately when marking.

3 The oval shape of the biscuit automatically centres the mitred joint as it fits together.

# JOINING BOARDS AND KNOCK-DOWN FITTINGS

**Manufactured sheet materials are available in large sizes, but occasionally it is necessary to join them together neatly. Because they lend themselves to machine-made joints, there are several options to choose from. Knock-down (K-D) fittings are used extensively in the furniture industry for manufacturing self-assembly units. They are useful for furniture that needs to be reassembled.**

## Lap joint

A lap joint is easily made with a router and is useful when matching veneered boards to make decorative panels.

1 Use a router fitted with a fence to form the lap, cutting it to exactly half the thickness of the material.

2 Apply glue and clamp the boards together. When the veneers are well matched, the seam will be almost invisible to the eye.

## Loose-tongue joint

An even stronger bond can be achieved by using a "loose tongue", which acts as a key for the adhesive. This type of joint takes little time to fabricate.

1 Use 6mm (¼in) plywood for a loose tongue. The cross-ply structure is stronger in bending than a long-grained section of hardwood. Apply glue and insert into a routed groove.

2 Firmly clamp the two panels flat to the bench before applying longitudinal pressure to the joint. This will keep it perfectly flat and produce a strong bond.

## Scarf joint

Two plywood panels can be joined with a feather-edged scarf joint, which will provide a large surface area for the glue. When made correctly, this type of joint will allow the completed panel to be formed into a curve without the joint separating or kinking.

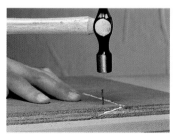

1 This joint can be made easily with hand tools. Make up a simple jig on the workbench to control the angle of the plane.

2 Before clamping the joint together, drive in a few panel pins (brads) to prevent the boards from sliding around. Remove them when the glue has dried.

## Cam fittings

A cam fitting forms a solid connection by a single turn of a screwdriver, which locks a lever arm into place on the mating part of the joint. Such joints allow you to prefabricate a set of components and insert the fittings in the knowledge that they will automatically line up when assembled.

1 Drill a hole in each component for the two halves of the fitting. The exact dimensions for their size and location will be supplied with the fittings. Insert them in the holes.

2 Simply locate the peg of one half of the fitting in the matching hole of the other and turn the cam to lock the joint together.

## Construction screws

These special screws have an extremely coarse thread that is designed to grip the fibres in chipboard panels without splitting them – a common problem when using ordinary wood screws.

## Jointing blocks

This is a modern substitute for the traditional glued wooden block, allowing panels to be dismantled easily. Simply screw the block to each panel.

1 A drilling jig will be supplied with the screws. Drill a clearance hole in the outer panel to suit the shank size of the screw.

2 Using the same jig, drill a pilot hole of smaller diameter into the end of the second panel. A depth stop on the drill bit will allow the depth of the hole to be controlled. Note how the jig locates the hole automatically. Assemble the panels by driving in the screws.

## Panel connectors

When joining large sections of worktop, for example, a positive mechanical connection will hold them tightly together, but still allow the two parts to be dismantled if necessary.

1 Drill a hole in each panel for the connector boss, using a hinge boring bit. Mark out a slot for the bolt, as shown, and cut down with a tenon saw. Remove any waste with a chisel.

2 Align the panels, using dowels or biscuits if desired, and tighten the connecting bolt until the joint is rigid. to the required depth.

# SCRIBING JOINTS

**"Scribing" can be a confusing term. It is often used to describe the marking out of a piece of wood with a sharp knife, but it also specifically refers to the method of transferring the shape of one piece of wood on to another. The latter is a particularly useful technique when working with mouldings of complex profile.**

### Using a profile gauge

A profile gauge incorporates a large number of plastic "fingers" that are free to move independently in the body of the gauge. When pressed against a moulded surface, they duplicate its profile, allowing this to be transferred to another component.

1 Place the moulding on a flat surface, hold the gauge level and press down slowly to achieve an accurate profile.

2 Square across the back of the second piece of moulding to provide a base line, then position the gauge and transfer the contours of the moulding with a pencil.

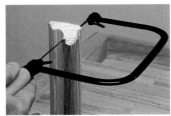

3 Mitre the end of the moulding back to the base line, which gives you a pattern to follow over the moulded surface. Follow this pattern with a coping saw, using the outline on the reverse side to keep the saw straight.

4 Clean up the cut with a gouge until the moulding is a perfect fit. Pare away small shavings at a time to prevent the end grain breaking away.

### Scribing by hand

On less complex shapes, a simple method is to use a scribing block. Any suitable scrap of wood can be used as a spacer to follow the shape.

1 Grip a pencil against the scribing block and run it down the surface to transfer the outline on to the adjoining piece.

2 Cut down the line with a coping saw. The result is a neat fit between the two pieces.

*Left* The finished scribing joint.

# Using Mouldings and Trims

Small sections of decorative moulding can be used to form joints and to add solid wooden edges to manufactured boards and panels. Ready-made mouldings, in a number of different shapes and sizes, are commonly available, and you can usually match solid hardwood trim to the veneered boards used for shelves and carcass work.

## Adding and gluing mouldings

1 Use a length of triangular moulding, sometimes called arris rail, to make a neat connection at an internal corner. This is more discreet than a square section of batten. Match the trim to the material you are working with.

2 Here, the arris moulding has been used to form the corner, leaving both edges of the panels exposed. Complete the joint with a section of scotia glued and pinned into the external corner.

3 If the moulding is thick enough, you can use biscuits to strengthen the joint and hold the moulding flush to one edge. This will provide extra stiffness to a shelf as well as concealing the exposed edge.

4 Finish off with small panel pins (brads), concealing their heads in the moulding detail. Set them in with a nail punch.

## Adding pre-glued veneers

1 Pre-glued edging strip can be obtained in a variety of types to suit veneered boards. It is simply applied by pressing into position with a hot iron. Keep the iron moving to avoid local discolouration.

2 Leave the glue to harden (no more than half an hour is needed), then remove the excess veneer. Wrap some fairly coarse sandpaper around a block of wood and use it with a slow knifing action to cut away the veneer.

# ADVANCED TECHNIQUES

One of the earliest woodworking principles for the novice to grasp is the importance of accuracy in fashioning the raw material, and an essential skill is the ability to produce flat surfaces, straight edges, accurate square corners and perfectly fitted joints. Nevertheless, as any experienced woodworker instinctively understands, wood is an organic material that is never naturally straight or uniform. To exploit the material's potential fully, the craftsperson will progress to exploring the manner in which wood behaves in other ways. From the earliest times, wood has been carved, sculpted, bent and shaped into curved forms. The right tools and techniques make it possible to create a seemingly endless variety of items, from simple wooden bowls to the most intricate of sculptural forms. The following pages show some of the many directions that can be followed to develop your skills as an expert practitioner in the craft of woodworking.

# FORMING CURVES

One of the most attractive qualities of wood is its tactile nature, and many wooden items are made to be handled as well as enjoyed for their visual appeal. When working with wood, there is a natural tendency to soften the sharp edges of an object to break up its outline, making it more comfortable to use at the same time. Whether it is the bow front of a dressing table, the smooth curve around the back of an armchair or simply the rounded edge of a table, few woodworkers can resist the urge to include curved forms in their work. Moreover, there is no limit to the shapes that can be achieved.

### Decorative work

Pierced panels with decorative fretwork make attractive features to include in many designs. A fretsaw or piercing saw can be used freehand to form the most intricate patterns. The very fine blade of a fretsaw is fed through a hole drilled in the centre of this veneered panel. Note that the teeth face toward the handle.

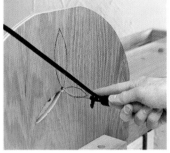

1 Squeeze the free end of the frame inward to attach the saw blade, then release it to tension the blade. The frame of the fretsaw can be up to 305mm (12in) wide, allowing a design to be located some distance from the edge.

2 Clamp the work vertically for the best results and keep the blade horizontal. The cutting action is applied on the pull stroke for greater control and accuracy, and the blade is so narrow that extremely tight curves can be formed.

### Routers

A router is a powerful tool that needs to be kept under control, although it is possible to use it freehand for carving and lettering work if only small amounts of waste are removed. For making smooth curves, especially when you are producing a number of identical shapes from a template, it has no equal.

Alternatively, a trimming cutter could be used to make curves. This has a bearing on the end that matches the size of the cutting blade, allowing the shape and size of the template to be reproduced exactly.

1 To make a circular template, fit a trammel arm to the router base. The trammel pin acts as a pivot point for the router. Slide the pin along the arm to the required radius, press it firmly into position, and move the router to describe an arc. Clamp the work firmly, place a piece of scrap wood beneath the router cutter, or work with the template overhanging the end of the workbench, moving it as required.

2 A template follower is a small circular disc that fits around the cutter and is screwed to the base of the router. A small lip around the edge of the follower slides smoothly on template to reproduce the latter's shape. Note that the finished size of the work is larger than the template. The diameter of the template must be set accordingly.

## Jigsaws

Cutting curves is one of the primary uses of a jigsaw. Ideally, use a saw with a variable speed and work slowly around the shape to be cut, steadying the base plate with your free hand. Always keep fingers clear of the path of the blade. You can obtain "scrolling" saw blades specifically designed for curved work and made to a narrow section to prevent the blade from binding in the cut as it changes direction.

1 In the absence of a scrolling blade, you can resort to this neat solution. Make a series of cuts in from the edge, stopping just short of the line of the curve. Guide the jigsaw just to the waste side of the cutting line, allowing the waste to fall away in small sections and leaving the back of the blade free to turn without binding or overheating.

## Kerfing

Every saw blade leaves a narrow slot behind it as it cuts through the wood. This is called the "kerf" of the blade. Kerfing is the technique of using these small slots to allow a solid piece of wood to bend around a curve.

A series of parallel saw cuts is made on the back face of the wood, being carefully machined to a fixed depth to leave a thin layer of unbroken material at the front. The slots allow the entire piece, no matter how thick it is, to be pulled into shape and glued around a former. If the kerf is of the correct depth, the wood will then bend easily.

This technique was commonly used to make the curved "bullnose" of a stair riser, or the former for the bow front of a veneered cabinet.

1 This example of a kerfed panel was made from 19mm (¾in) plywood, using a circular saw set to a 16mm (⅝in) cutting depth, which left only one or two layers of plywood on the front face. To achieve a radius of 200mm (8in), make a trial cut that distance in from the end of the plywood strip. Adjust the depth of the saw blade if it feels too stiff. When the two edges of the kerf touch, measure how far the plywood has moved, as shown in step 1. This is the exact spacing required between the saw cuts.

2 This operation will be easier with a circular saw table, but it is possible to achieve equally good results with a portable power saw on the workbench. Clamp a straightedge to the end of the panel to guide the baseplate of the saw, and make a series of cuts to cover the required length of the panel. Make sure the cuts are parallel and square to the edge of the work.

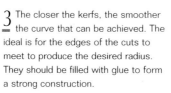

3 The closer the kerfs, the smoother the curve that can be achieved. The ideal is for the edges of the cuts to meet to produce the desired radius. They should be filled with glue to form a strong construction.

# LAMINATING

This is the process of building up a composite form by gluing separate layers, or laminates, together. Because wood is so flexible, all manner of complex structures are made possible by this simple principle. Like a leaf spring, thin strips of wood can be bent around a curved former and glued together to produce a permanent curved shape. It is ideal for fabricating curved work or it can be used to glue blocks of timber on edge to create solid forms. A single large piece of wood, no matter how well seasoned, will be prone to splitting or deformation as it continues to dry out. The problem can be eliminated by laminating small pieces together.

### Laminated corners

A good way to add strength to a shelf or worktop is to trim the front edge with a batten (cleat), fixed on edge to prevent it from sagging. If the shelf is curved at the ends, the laminating technique allows the edge to be trimmed with a continuous length of wood, even though normally the batten may be too thick to bend in one piece.

1 With a circular saw or bandsaw, make a series of longitudinal cuts in the end of the batten, approximately 3mm (⅛in) wide. Then cut a matching number of thin strips from the same material, making them fractionally thinner than the width of the saw cuts to allow for the adhesive. Apply wood glue to both sides of each strip and insert them between the leaves of the batten.

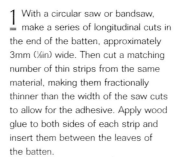

2 With the straight section of the batten fixed to the front of the shelf, apply a layer of glue to the end and gradually and carefully bend it around the curve, using small G-cramps (C-clamps) to prevent the assembly from springing back out of shape. Note how the batten has been cut over-length to provide added leverage while you are bending.

3 Continue the bending process around the end of the shelf. A tip is to cut some small wedges and tap them into place between the frames of the G-cramps and the batten, as shown, to force the laminates into good contact with the curved edge of the shelf. Note how the thin strips have been cut slightly wider than the batten to allow for any slight misalignment.

4 Leave the glued assembly to dry for as long as possible, preferably overnight. Plane the protruding strips flush with the top of the shelf, cut off the projecting end of the batten, sand smooth and round off the edges for a perfect curve. Using PVA adhesive (wood glue), which is transparent when dry, will ensure that the laminates are almost undetectable.

## Making formers

To make a free-form laminated object, first build a former to act as a jig. This example shows how the S-shaped legs of a small chair were made using 3mm (⅛in) strips of softwood. The result was legs that were strong enough to support the chair, but still flexible enough to allow some springiness in the construction.

An offcut (scrap) of kitchen countertop was used to make the baseboard for the former. The plastic facing made the glued assembly easy to remove. As an alternative, use a sheet of plywood coated with wax, or covered with a sheet of newspaper or kitchen film (plastic wrap).

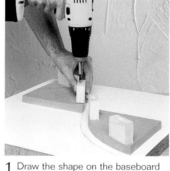

1 Draw the shape on the baseboard and cut curved formers to match. Screw the formers to the baseboard and add a series of wooden blocks to receive the cramps. Carefully space the blocks evenly around the curves.

2 Apply glue to the laminates and insert them into the jig. They will tend to slide around and be difficult to handle, so use a small panel pin (brad) to keep them aligned until the first cramp is fitted.

3 Add further cramps, working from the centre toward the ends. The laminates must be of generous length, as the difference in radius between the inside and the outside of each curve requires the strips to move relative to each other as they bend.

4 To ensure no lateral twist in the final assembly, all the laminates must be in contact with the baseboard. Tap them down with a mallet and block of wood. Tighten each cramp in turn from the centre, to maintain a curve.

## Joining blocks

By gluing together blocks of wood on edge, you can create solid shapes and patterns. Composite blanks for carving are built up in this way. You can make items, such as a butcher's chopping block, from small pieces of solid maple, which is a very hard species of timber (lumber), traditionally used for flooring and chopping blocks.

1 To make the joints as accurate as possible, each piece is fitted individually before laminating. Cut the first piece slightly oversize and use a small offcut (scrap) to mark its exact length. The blocks are simply butt-jointed, so accuracy is essential. Each piece should be a sliding fit in the jig.

2 Continue working around the jig in a clockwise direction, numbering each piece to avoid confusion later. Working from the outside toward the centre in this way ensures that no cumulative discrepancies occur in the overall size of the block and keeps it all square.

# VENEERING

The art of veneering has a long history and demonstrates some of the finest qualities of decorative woodwork. By gluing a thin layer of high-quality wood to a substrate of cheaper, more workable material, the finest finish could be achieved at a lower cost. The same applies today, but often for different reasons, as exotic hardwoods are in short supply. Veneered panels of manufactured boards extend a limited resource and are in common use commercially. They have their uses for constructional work, but the home craftspeople can soon learn traditional veneering techniques, which will open up new avenues of creative woodworking.

### Using veneers

Originally, veneers were cut with a saw, which must have been no easy task. Now they are produced by peeling or slicing the log into thin sheets, no more than 1mm (½in) thick.

Veneers are not only produced from exotic species, but also from any type of wood with an attractive figure or colour, and the best-quality logs are reserved for the process. Of notable value are burr veneers, which display intricate colours and distorted grain that is both visually stunning and difficult to work in solid form.

Veneers are supplied in sheets of varying size and sometimes in rolls. They should be flattened out as soon as possible and stored under a flat sheet of thick plywood in warm, dry conditions until needed. They are extremely delicate, so handle them with care. Keep your working area clean and free of dust.

The base on to which the veneer is glued must be dry, clean and perfectly smooth. Manufactured boards, such as MDF (medium-density fibreboard), make perfect substrates for veneers, as they are stable and uniform in structure. When applying veneer to solid wood or plywood, make sure the grain of the veneer runs at right angles to the grain direction of the board below, to counteract any tendency to move.

### The veneering process

Veneers can be cut easily with a sharp knife or craft knife, but a veneer saw, with no set on its very fine teeth, is worth having. It is designed for use against a straightedge and is less likely than a normal saw to follow the grain or split the veneer. Veneers can be matched and butt-jointed undetectably if cut with perfectly square edges. Small strips for inlays can be produced with a strip cutter, which has two sharp blades mounted in a wooden stock.

### Gluing

The traditional glue for veneering was animal glue, which is still obtainable and preferred by many woodworkers. It is sold as small pearls, and should be mixed and heated with water to dissolve it for use. Always warm the glue in a double boiler to prevent it from overheating. Spread the glue on the substrate while it is still warm. It will soon start to cool and become tacky. Lay the veneer over the glue, cover with a sheet of clean paper and run over it with a smoothing iron, set to a very low temperature. As the glue softens, it is absorbed into the fibres of the wood. Use a veneer hammer to

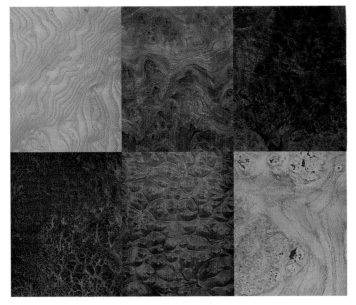

*Left* From left to right, the decorative burr patterns of ash, elm, walnut, (top row) vavona, myrtle and oak (bottom row).

press the veneer down and seal the glue as it dries once more. A veneer hammer should never be used as a regular hammer – it has a wooden head with an inserted strip of brass, which is used to press down on the veneer, using long firm strokes and working from the centre of the panel toward the edge. Iron out any uneven areas or bubbles, and if any air becomes trapped, forming a high spot, make a small slit in the veneer to release it. Use the warm iron to reheat any areas that show signs of lifting.

Local repairs to defects or damaged areas in a veneered surface can be made with a veneer punch. With a sharp blow from a mallet, this will punch through the veneer and create an irregular shape. Also, it produces a patch of identical size from a matching piece of veneer, allowing a repair that is almost undetectable.

The main drawback of using animal glue is that it is not heat-resistant and dries out, becoming brittle with age. A modern contact adhesive can be used, but this is unpleasant to work with and emits a flammable vapour as it dries. Employ a backing sheet of greaseproof paper between the glued substrate and the veneer, pulling it away and firming down the veneer in overlapping strips. Contact adhesive is more permanent than animal glue, but it makes repairs difficult and is almost impossible to remove.

**Matching veneers**

Veneers were often used on large panels to overcome the problem of using solid wood, which had a tendency to shrink or warp over time. They can be used to even greater effect when mixed in contrasting colours to make decorative patterns.

Veneers can be *bookmatched* or *quartered* by selecting leaves of similar grain, cut from the same log, and arranging them in a mirror-image

design. Hold the veneers firmly in place with veneer pins as you position them, and tape across the seams with veneer tape before gluing them down in the normal way. From this process, it is a small step to more complex designs, inlaying thin strips of veneer to create borders and crossbanding. These are produced commercially in a multitude of patterns, incorporating contrasting colours, shapes and grains for ornamentation of great complexity.

*Right* A beautiful veneer-fronted cabinet by furniture designer Tony McMullen. Tiny pieces of veneer were taped together to create a complex, geometric design (*below*).

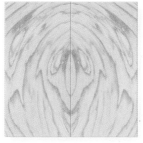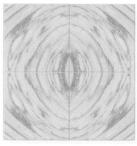

Bookmatched

Quartered

# TURNING

**Woodturning adds a whole new dimension to the art and craft of woodworking. Shaping wood in the round as it spins on a lathe opens up many possibilities, ranging from straightforward spindles and table legs, through bowls and platters, to free sculptural forms. As an occupation for the home woodworker, turning has many attractions. A lathe and a bench will take up less space than a fully equipped workshop, and you can spend a lifetime exploring the potential of the craft.**

### Woodturning lathe

The lathe, uniquely among woodworking machines, requires that the cutting tool is offered up to the work, as opposed to the operator moving the wood on to a cutting blade. Therefore, a different approach is required, and a new discipline and technique for handling the tools must be learned. Although no more dangerous than any other woodworking operation, turning is a skill that must be gained under instruction. The first advice for any would-be turner is to attend a course in woodturning, to study the principles of safe working practice. One-day workshops and weekend training courses are commonplace, so it is not difficult to get started. Any adult education establishment, or even your local toolshop, is a sensible place to make enquiries. Attending a course also gives you a chance to try different lathes and tools before purchasing your own.

The lathe itself is a big investment and should be chosen carefully. As with most tools, the cheapest "beginner's" model may not necessarily be the best option. Even a novice will progress quite swiftly and soon find that a small, lightweight lathe has severe limitations. A robust machine at the lower end of the professional range will be a much wiser investment in the end.

Lathes are denoted according to the distance "between centres", which indicates the longest piece of work that the machine will accommodate. A variable-speed motor provides rotary power to the *headstock*, which turns the work. The *tailstock* supports the other end. Some turners concentrate on bowl making and hollow work, in which case a swivelling head is ideal, allowing large diameters to be worked. A *faceplate* to support the base of the bowl would also be needed. Alternatively, a self-centring chuck is a more versatile option. Whatever the style of turning envisaged, a robust machine with solid mountings and a sturdy tool rest is essential.

### Turning tools

Although traditionally made of carbon steel, turning tools are increasingly being offered in high-speed steel (HSS). While this is more expensive, it keeps an edge for much longer and sharpens more easily.

Good-quality turning chisels are not cheap, and it is best to start off with a core of the essentials, adding to them as your technique develops. Chisels are classified according to the basic operations they perform.

*Left* Turning tools and the woodturning lathe.

*Above* A turned oak bowl by Anthony Bryant.

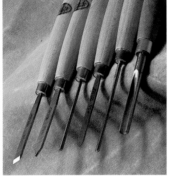

*Top left, from left to right* 25mm (1in) round scraper, 25mm (1in) square scraper, 12mm (½in) round scraper, 12mm (½in) square scraper and 25mm (1in) skew chisel.

*Top centre, from left to right* A diamond parting tool, a standard parting tool and a beading and parting tool.

*Top right* Two standard size roughing gouges and one continental size.

*Far left* Spindle gouges come in varying sizes.

*Left* A small selection of miniature woodturning tools.

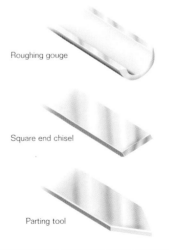

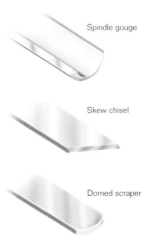

*Domed scraper* – A rigid scraping tool for finishing off the insides of bowls and goblets with a curved profile and flat end. Sizes vary from 12 to 25mm (½ to 1in).

*Parting tool* – A diamond-shaped cutting tool designed for parting off, or removing, the workpiece when finished. It is also commonly used for notching and grooving operations.

*Roughing gouge* – This is a deep U-shaped gouge with a 45 degree outside bevel for the rapid removal of waste. Use it for turning square stock into round. Ideal size: 19mm (¾in).

*Skew chisel* – A very versatile tool with an angled, V-section blade that can be used for smoothing and shaping. The most useful sizes are 12 and 25mm (½ and 1in).

*Spindle gouge* – An all-purpose turning gouge with a shallower bevel than a roughing gouge and a rounded end. The most useful sizes are 6 and 12mm (¼ and ½in) for turning beads and other profiles.

*Square-end chisel* – This is ideal for producing an extremely smooth finish to cylindrical and conical surfaces. The most useful sizes are 19 and 25mm (¾ and 1in).

Roughing gouge

Square end chisel

Parting tool

Spindle gouge

Skew chisel

Domed scraper

# TURNING TECHNIQUES

Acquiring confidence when working the lathe is the first step to developing further techniques for particular projects. Before committing yourself to an important piece of work you should prepare a selection of different sizes of wood, or blanks, and practice the basic skills of reducing square stock to a round section safely and accurately. Turning chisels are very sensitive tools when properly handled. The long handles become an extension of the arm and allow small amounts of presssure to be applied with great precision.

*Above, from left to right* Centre finder, bevel gauge and inside/outside calipers.

### To start turning

Your lathe should be set at the right height to suit your working position, and so that the tool rest is level with your elbow. A well-balanced stance when working is essential – if you stand awkwardly the work soon becomes tiring and there is a great danger of digging the edge of the tool into the workpiece. To start turning, practice turning a square or octagonal length of stock to a round cylinder, which is the first step of most turning projects. Centre the work on the headstock, mount in the lathe, and slide the tailstock to meet it. Clamp it tight and turn it by hand to make sure it revolves evenly, with no obstruction, before starting the lathe.

Take a roughing gouge and position it on the tool rest just away from the work so that it will only remove a small amount of wood. Move the gouge sideways along the rest as it cuts, and roll it slightly in the direction of movement to produce a slicing rather than deep cutting action. Only when you are confident that you have mastered this basic technique should

*Below* Note the angle of the gouge; this causes a slicing rather than a cutting action.

you progress to cutting, scraping and profiling. Always observe the safety points, be patient, and let your skill and feel for the work develop at its own pace.

### Wood for turning

Almost any type of wood can be turned successfully, but the properties of certain species make them favourites. Close, even-grained timber of medium hardness produces the best results. With more expertise, sharp chisels and the correct lathe speed, harder woods with more interesting grain effects can be tackled. The ultimate challenge is highly figured burr wood, which is always sought after for its wild colour and grain effects, making every piece made from it unique.

### Wood species
with good turning properties

Basswood (lime)

Beech

Sycamore

Walnut

Maple

Yew

Ash

Cherry

## Safety points

Even though a lathe has no sharp blades or cutters, like other machinery, it is still a machine that requires great respect. When in motion, the workpiece can catch the end of the working tool and cause serious injury.

- Work carefully and with concentration, keeping your eyes on the work at all times.
- Make sure that safety guards are fitted and that the workpiece is free to turn without obstruction.
- Always use the tool rest to support the tools.
- Offer the cutting tool slowly to the work, moving with the direction of rotation, and working "downhill" on curved and angled surfaces to prevent the tip from digging in.
- Maintain a tidy working area and do not allow debris to collect around you.
- Wear safety goggles or glasses and a dust mask when dealing with fine work.
- Avoid wearing loose clothing, and remove any jewellery.
- Always switch off the lathe to make adjustments and when leaving it, even momentarily.
- Allow the workpiece to stop rotating on its own, without touching it.

*Above right and below left* A beautifully fluid turned oak vase and a bowl turned from burr oak, by Anthony Bryant.
*Below right* A set of dishes, turned by Ian Durrant. Their solid, burnished form shows a quite different approach to turning.

# CARVING

This skilled craft could be considered the most unrestrictive form of creative woodworking. Unlike most disciplines, in which a careful process of assembling separate components to complete a structure is routine, carving involves removing surplus material to reveal the hidden form concealed in a piece of wood. Perhaps the most successful carving is one that achieves a perfect balance between the sculptor's imposed ideas and the innate qualities of the material.

## Types of carving

There is no limit to the scale and variety of what may be achieved by carving in wood; imagination is the only limiting factor. There are different approaches to the process, of course, and completely different styles.

Relief carving is a specialist form of carving whereby the background of a wooden panel is carved away, leaving a two-dimensional form in relief. Delicate floral carvings, in lime or basswood, have a long heritage, reaching their peak in the 17th century with the work of craftsmen such as Grinling Gibbons, the master of fine detail.

At the other end of the scale are pieces of a sculptural nature, carved from laminated composite forms to produce works of breathtaking realism. More abstract work simply lets the material speak for itself, with a little help from an expert hand.

## Wood for carving

As with turning, the best species of wood for carving are close-grained and stable, but because the carver works at his or her own speed, and can choose how to approach every cut, it is true to say that any type of wood will be a candidate for the next subject. Even the most tortuous piece of wild or knotty grain will yield to the correct sharp tool, when approached with care from the right direction.

If possible, choose really well-seasoned wood to avoid the disappointment of cracks appearing as it dries. Work with intricate detail is particularly vulnerable in this respect. It is worth experimenting with polyethylene glycol (PEG), a waxy solution that penetrates the structure of the wood, replacing the water in the cells and stabilizing it. A good craft supplier or toolshop will stock PEG and may also be a good source of small samples of unusual types of wood for carving, cut into small sections called *blanks*. These should have been sealed with a wax coating to keep them stable.

### Wood species with good carving properties

Alder

Basswood (lime)

Jelutong

Mahogany

Ramin

Oak

Walnut

Yellow poplar

*Below left* Part of a highly-worked carved frieze by Kenneth Wilson.

*Below* This hand-carved frame by Ashley Sands incorporates Grinling Gibbons style foliage, grapes and acanthus leaves.

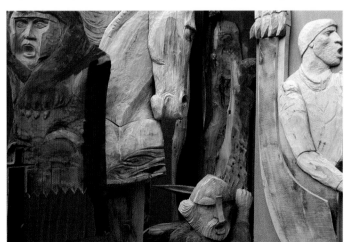

## Carving tools

Tools for carving can range from the humble pocket knife to specially fashioned chisels and gouges with weird and wonderful names, such as *macaroni* and *fluteroni*, *dog-legs* and *fishtails*. The gouge is the basic carver's tool, its outside bevel allowing the wood to be chipped away piece by piece.

A spoon gouge has a cranked, spoon-shaped shaft to deal with deeply recessed work. For roughing out the work, use a *carver's mallet*, made of shock-resistant beech. It has a round head that allows the chisel to approach the work from any angle. The normal range of standard woodworking chisels and shaping tools will come in very useful for the more heavy work before addressing the fine detail.

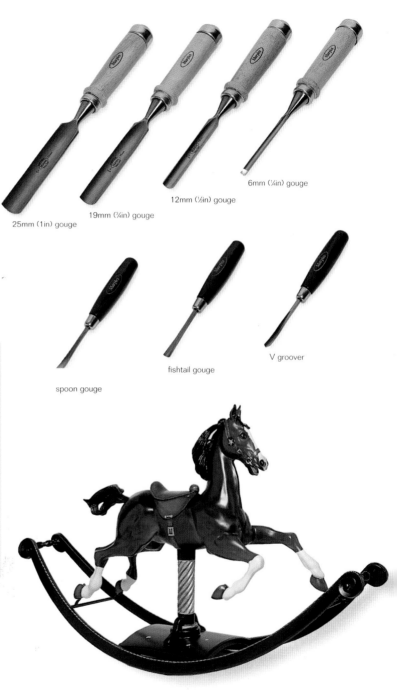

6mm (¼in) gouge

12mm (½in) gouge

19mm (¾in) gouge

25mm (1in) gouge

V groover

fishtail gouge

spoon gouge

### Using gouges

Gouges are commonly used as carving tools, but occasionally they also come in useful when working with curved profiles. Use in the same manner as a straight chisel, with the bevel resting on the surface of the wood to control the depth of cut. Work slowly away from you, using light taps from a small mallet.

*Right* The rocking horse, carved by Bob Cleveland, was made in several stages using pieces of Jelutong laminated together. The fine detail and hand-painted finish make it almost too good to use.

# CARVING TECHNIQUES

Carving work requires the ability to visualize a three-dimensional form on the flat surface of the wood, which takes some practice. It helps to break the subject down into a pattern of overlapping or interlocking planes, dealing with one at a time. On a square piece of stock, draw the shape on all four sides, and work on opposing faces in turn. The cylindrical form of this barley sugar carving presents more of a challenge. The secret lies in the marking out.

**Marking out**

1 It is important to use straight, square stock for good results. Begin by setting out the square capitals or blocks at the top and bottom of the column.

2 Use a fine tenon or dovetail saw to make cuts in at the corners, top and bottom, down to the circumference of the cylinder.

3 Pare away the corners with a spoon gouge until the ends of the column are perfectly round.

4 A spokeshave is the ideal tool for removing large quantities of waste around the centre of the column. Work from the middle of the piece towards each end, as the grain direction allows.

5 Keep turning the workpiece and removing shavings to make a perfect cylinder. With the blade of the spokeshave set for a fine cut, it is possible to work against the grain without encountering many problems.

6 Use masking tape to create a regular spiral around the column. Here, each strip of tape describes half a turn around the column, terminating on the opposite face at the other end. Draw along the margins of each strip with a soft pencil.

## Roughing out

 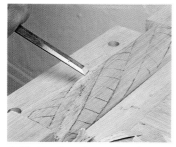 

1 Always mark the area of each twist clearly to establish a reference. In the waste areas in between, work around the column with a bevelled chisel and mallet, cutting across the grain to form a deep channel.

2 Working from the top of each strand toward the waste area, gradually chisel away the margins to define the rounded profile. Direct the cuts down and across the grain. Change direction as required to avoid lifting the fibres of the wood.

3 Once the channels have been defined, it is quite simple to shape each twist, using a spoon gouge along the grain. Complete the roughing out process around the whole piece, leaving it 3mm (⅛in) oversize, before carving the final detail.

## Carving a double twist

This column of four strands was carved out of ash, which is quite hard and positive to work with. Mark out as for the single twist, but give each strand a full turn around the column.

1 After roughing out each strand as shown above, use the gouge to pare away the waste in small flakes. Work patiently. Grip the tool between clenched fingers for greater control.

2 Use a small gouge or V-groove chisel to clear out the waste at the bottom of each strand, working carefully along the grain.

3 Finish off the column with a piece of coarse sandpaper wrapped around a small strip of wood to remove the marks of the carving tools. Fold the sandpaper into a V-shape to reach the smallest crevices.

*Above* The finished double twist spiral.

8

# WOOD FINISHING

**A**pplying a perfect finish to your work may seem to be the last stage in the construction process, but the secret of success is to consider it from the very beginning. From the moment you conceive an idea and determine its design, the finish will influence all your subsequent decisions. Some species of wood are better suited to certain types of finishing materials; conditions of use will dictate the degree of durability and water resistance required.

The orientation of each component and its grain pattern, the types of joint and glue, the tools and techniques used, even the order of work and assembly, will be affected by the demands of the finishing process. Keeping this in mind will help to focus your work, and will require great discipline and forethought. The visual appeal of the material is one of the attractions of woodworking, and the art of finishing is to display that to the best advantage.

# FINISHING EQUIPMENT

There is a wide choice of finishes for your work, from materials that have been tried and tested over hundreds of years to modern products formulated to meet the demands of the furniture industry. Compared to the cost of timber, finishing materials are not that expensive, which allows you to experiment with every project to perfect your techniques and discover the features of each method. For a small outlay, you can assemble the basic equipment to get started, then add to this as you progress.

### Preparation

The key to a good result, as always, lies in careful preparation. When a glossy finish is applied to a surface, small scratches or blemishes will be revealed that previously were barely visible to the naked eye. There is no substitute for a methodical approach, working through progressively finer grades of abrasive paper until you cannot feel any improvement.

A word of warning, though – your fingers can transmit greasy deposits and damp patches to the surface, so keep your hands clean and handle fine items with great care. Pick them up by the edges, or wear disposable gloves. Stack the finished components on clean softwood battens (cleats).

Carry out preparation work well away from the finishing area, and be prepared to move the work back and forth several times as you apply and rub down successive coats. Assemble a good supply of clean rags, wire (steel) wool, abrasive paper and scraping tools. Even used sheets of abrasive paper come in useful, as they lose some of their cutting ability and produce a progressively finer finish.

### Dealing with blemishes

If you find a small blemish in your work at a late stage, all is not lost. There are various filling and stopping compounds, some of which are better than others. Soft interior stopping is fine for tiny cracks, and comes in a range of pre-mixed colours to suit different wood species. You can blend these together or add a drop of wood stain to match the wood's colour and tone, but check first that the stain you

*Above, clockwise from top left* Wire (steel) wool, filler, spatula, soft cloth, sanding block, abrasive papers and cabinet scrapers.

use is compatible with the final finish. Larger holes may need filling with a hard-setting exterior-grade filler. Leave this just proud of the surface, as it tends to shrink as it cures, then sand it flush. Shrinkage is a disadvantage of many fillers, which can shrink further and even fall out of the wood.

### Workshop conditions

A suitable area in which to work is a priority. Sanding activities create dusty conditions, and dust is the enemy of a fine finish. It is best to work in a separate room, well away from the woodworking area. If you do not have this luxury, seal off an area of the main workshop with plastic sheeting or a partition. Organize your work so that you carry out finishing on a separate day, and keep away while each coat is drying.

Most finishing materials depend on the evaporation of solvents as they cure, so the area should be well ventilated, but you should prevent draughts and maintain a controlled temperature to ensure ideal drying conditions. Install good lighting, and position the finishing bench in the centre of the room so that you can move around your work without moving it. Drying racks fixed to the wall will be good for stacking small components.

### Health and safety

Many substances that are used for finishing are flammable or contain ingredients that are hazardous. Keep them in a lockable area, out of the reach of children and preferably out of doors. Always keep containers sealed, and observe the manufacturers' instructions for the safe use of the materials. Do not pour used solvents or thinners into a domestic drainage system – take them to a safe disposal site at your local recycling centre. Old paintbrushes, rags and polishing cloths can also be hazardous – do not leave them lying around or mix them with other waste.

## Brushes

You get what you pay for when buying brushes. Keep a stock of cheap disposable brushes for building up coats of primer and sealer – sometimes the price of thinners for cleaning a brush outweighs the cost of a new one. However, for finish coats, invest in good-quality brushes and keep them separate for different applications to avoid contamination. Clean them every time you use them, wash out in warm soapy water, and store them dry and in a dust-free container. A quality brush improves with age as the bristles become "worked in".

*Right (Top row)* 75mm (3in) disposable brush; 100mm (4in) lacquering brush; 50mm (2in), 38mm (1½in) and 12mm (½in) full-bodied paintbrushes. *(Bottom row)* Polishing mops and a variety of artist's brushes.

## Shellac stopping

More traditional forms of filler, ideal for restoration work, can be obtained from specialist suppliers. Shellac stopping comes in stick form and a useful colour range. It sets quite hard and bonds well to the wood with minimal shrinkage.

1 During restoration of this table top, the removal of an old coat of varnish revealed a large knot. This was not unattractive, but needed to be treated and sealed before the application of a new finish. A cabinet scraper was used first to cut back the fibrous material around the knot.

2 The very centre of the knot had dried out and formed a small hole. The tip of the shellac stick was melted with an old soldering iron, and the small drops were allowed to fill the hole and soak into the wood surrounding the knot.

3 When the filler had hardened, the excess was scraped away with a sharp chisel until it was flush with the surface. More stopping was applied as necessary; several layers would be required for a deep blemish.

4 Wax filler was then rubbed over the areas of rough grain surrounding the knot. This sealed the entire surface and it should prevent further shrinkage of the wood.

5 The table top was smoothed with extra-fine sandpaper (320 grit) on a cork sanding block, using small circular motions at first, followed by working along the grain direction.

6 The entire surface was wiped down with a soft damp cloth, using long strokes parallel to the grain. This removed all final traces of dust and served to raise the grain slightly by adding moisture. When dry, it was rubbed down again with 400 grit paper before finishing.

# STAINING

Stained and polished wood will be familiar to anyone who has seen antique furniture, such as "Jacobean" oak or mahogany from the 19th century. The use of wood stain is less fashionable today, the accent being on letting the natural colour of the material speak for itself. However, the purpose of staining is not always to make the wood appear darker. Creative use of a wood stain can enhance a grain pattern that otherwise would appear bland. With care, you can use very dilute stains to match different components in a construction, or to achieve attractive contrasts of tone. Even quite strong colours can be used to striking effect for a contemporary look on wooden toys and furniture.

### Types of stain

Ready-mixed wood stains are readily available from all good hardware stores and paint suppliers, but care is necessary to ensure that the type of stain is compatible with the finish. All three common types have their advantages and disadvantages.

The colour of wood stain is often labelled according to wood species: pine, mahogany or oak, for example. This can be very misleading, as the result depends on the base colour of the wood to which it is applied. Always test the stain you want to use on an offcut (scrap) of the same piece of wood first and let it dry thoroughly. Apply a coat of the chosen finish over the stain to make sure that there is no reaction between solvents.

*Above* Different types and colours of stain, here being tested on strips of pine.

### Bleaching

Bleaching is a technique that can be used to revive an old piece of wood or correct a patchy appearance. It can even out defects in the wood's appearance before more stain is applied. Always be careful when handling chemicals – wear heavy-duty rubber gloves, overalls and eye protection. Most wood bleach is applied as a two-part treatment. The base coat is washed into the grain, then the activator is added to set up the chemical reaction. Small bubbles appear on the surface and a noticeable colour change should be visible after 15–20 minutes. Rinse with plenty of water, or the required neutralizer, then sand down when dry. Some species of

wood, particularly oily varieties such as teak and rosewood, are not easy to bleach; mahogany, beech and light oak produce better results. Always test bleach on an offcut or concealed area of the workpiece before committing yourself.

### Fuming

Fuming is another application of chemistry to the art of finishing. Wood with a high acid content, oak in particular, will react with ammonia gas and turn a deep rich brown. Not being a surface stain, the colour is fixed in the material. The process is particularly useful for treating an entire piece of furniture that has many detailed parts, which would make applying stain difficult. Ordinary household bleach contains ammonia, although more consistent results can

be obtained from a stronger solution. You can build a simple fuming chamber by constructing a light framework that is large enough to contain the object, then covering it with thin plywood or hardboard. Seal all the joints with plastic tape, then place the item inside with a wide, shallow container of ammonia solution. Handle the container with great care, making sure you do not splash the liquid on to any exposed skin. Wear gloves, goggles and protective clothing, and work in a well-ventilated area, preferably outdoors in a sheltered spot. Seal the chamber and leave for at least 24 hours. The amount of darkening depends on the exposure time allowed.

### Applying wood stain

Wear a pair of disposable latex gloves to protect your hands, particularly when working with a solvent-based stain. This also prevents the workpiece from being marked by the oils in your hands when you move it. Shake the container well, and if you have mixed up your own blend, make sure that you have prepared enough to complete the job.

1 Use a small brush to test the colour or to apply small patches of stain to even out any pale areas of the wood. Dilute the stain when treating the end grain of timber, which is more absorbent and will take too much stain, leading to a darker finish.

2 With a soft cloth or ready-made staining pad, apply the stain with quick circular motions, keeping the pad fully charged. For an even coat, the wood should absorb as much stain as possible while it is still wet.

3 Before the stain has completely dried, rub the pad along the surface with long strokes up and down the grain to remove any excess colour.

### Touching up

You can use a small watercolour brush to match the grain pattern of highly figured wood. Here, a small piece of veneer has lifted after the staining process.

1 Add a drop of stain to a small amount of stopping that matches the lighter background. Apply this to the damaged area with a spatula or modelling knife.

2 Rub down the repair very gently and dab with a light stain to blend it in. When dry, mix up a darker stain and copy the grain pattern with a fine-tipped brush.

3 The completed repair becomes almost undetectable when the finish coat is applied.

## Wood stains

### Water-based stains

**Pros:** Low in cost, safe to use and contain no harmful solvents. They are non-toxic and taint-free, and suitable for wooden toys, food utensils, storage units or items where safety is paramount.

**Cons:** These can produce uneven or patchy results, are slow drying and have poor penetration on oily and resinous woods. Not always colour-fast and can fade in strong sunlight. They will raise the grain of some woods, especially softwoods.

### Solvent-based stains

**Pros:** These are quick drying; they use methylated spirit as a solvent. They will not raise the grain and can be inter-mixed successfully, or mixed with shellac sealer or polish to add body to further coats. Light-fast stains have a long life.

**Cons:** These require fast work to prevent blotchy results and variations in finish due to overlapping. They are not compatible with cellulose lacquers.

### Oil-based stains

**Pros:** These come in a range of pre-mixed strong colours and are easy to apply evenly. Only one coat is required: further applications of stain tend to lift the first coat.

**Cons:** These are difficult to dilute or mix to create your own colours. They are not compatible with white spirit-based finish coats or wax polish. They give mixed results on close-grained wood.

# VARNISH, PAINT AND LACQUER

For a hard wearing and waterproof finish, a coat of clear varnish takes some beating. Traditional, oil-based varnish is not ideal for finishing wood, as the resins in the varnish give an orange cast to the film and can obscure the natural colours of the wood.

Of the more modern varnishes, polyurethane is easier to apply and produces a clearer result. It requires white spirit (turpentine) as a solvent and is safe to use with the normal precautions. Acrylic varnish is water-based, less toxic and quick drying, but it is less hard wearing in the long run.

Lacquers tend to be much thinner and require a build-up of several coats to be effective. The best results are obtained by spray application, which is not always a practical proposition for the home woodworker. Cellulose solvents for lacquer are quite unpleasant and flammable at lower temperatures.

## Preparation

Varnish needs a good key to the wood surface to prevent blistering and peeling. On oily wood, apply a coat of shellac sanding sealer beforehand, as this will improve adhesion. Alternatively, apply a priming coat of varnish diluted with 50 per cent white spirit (turpentine), allowing it to soak well into the grain of the wood. Leave to dry for 24 hours before rubbing down lightly with fine sandpaper.

## Paint

While the benefits of a natural wood finish are undeniable, good paintwork also has its place. The brushing technique is much the same as for clear varnish and demands the same care in preparation. On very resinous and coarse-grained wood, apply a priming coat of shellac sanding sealer before painting to prevent patchy drying and cracking of the paint film. Continue with primer and several undercoats until the surface is smooth before applying the topcoat. Although paint is opaque, it will not necessarily mask unsightly blemishes.

Painted furniture and other woodwork is a subject in its own right, offering a wide choice of paint effects to explore. You can experiment with acrylic paints and glazes, which bond well to wood and can be used to good effect as tinted backgrounds with all manner of decorative touches.

Always seal the wood with a topcoat of clear lacquer to protect the finished paintwork.

## Common finishing faults and their causes

### Patchy areas in the finish coat

Uneven sanding of the surface during preparation

Oil or grease contamination

### Ridges or ripples

Varnish drying too quickly as you join up the brush strokes – work on a smaller area at a time; check that the room temperature is not too high

### "Orange peel" effect – small pinholes in a rough surface

Varnish applied too thickly in each coat

Uneven drying

### "Bloom" – milky-white colour in the film

Presence of moisture on the surface or in the brush

Damp atmosphere or cold draughts

### Crazing – small surface cracks developing in the glaze

Applying coats too rapidly without leaving time to dry

Using incorrect solvents that react with a stain or sealing coat

*Top right* The carcass of this display case was made from medium-density fibreboard, which was painted after assembly.

*Left* This table was finished with several coats of clear lacquer, rubbing down carefully between each coat for a mirror finish.

## Varnishing technique

Use a good-quality brush with a full head of bristles, making sure that it is clean. Small flecks of dust or dried varnish in the brush will tend to loosen as you work and ruin the job. Pour a quantity of varnish, sufficient for one coat, into a small container and reseal the tin at once to prevent a skin from forming. Dip the brush no more than halfway into the varnish and avoid overloading it. Drips and runs are the most common causes of a poor finish.

1 If treating a complex piece of work, such as this panelled door, always begin with the fine detail. Use a small brush to work along the edges of mouldings and panelling, brushing out any build-up in the corners.

2 Change to a larger brush for the wider areas of panelling, using long strokes. Hold the brush at an angle to the surface and work quickly, but carefully. Pay attention to the V-grooves, which can trap small runs of varnish.

3 Support the work on small clean battens (cleats) to lift it clear of the finishing table. This allows treatment of the outer edges. Try not to overload the brush here – too much varnish will creep down and collect on the underside.

4 Move to the main members of the panel, treating the cross-rails first. Brush along the grain.

5 Finish off by brushing up and down the vertical stiles of the door, picking up the brush strokes at the ends of the rails and brushing out well along the grain. When dry, turn the door over and coat the other side in the same way before rubbing down.

6 Use 000 grade fine wire (steel) wool to remove any nibs of varnish on mouldings and edges. Brush the debris well clear to remove small fragments of wire wool, which easily become trapped in the corners.

7 Rub down all the flat surfaces with 320 grit silicon carbide paper until the first coat of varnish is silky smooth. For a quality finish, repeat the entire operation four or five times, building up a really flat and well-keyed surface.

8 Apply the final coat with a fine-haired polishing mop. If the surface is really smooth, this requires no effort and can be carried out very quickly, avoiding any streaks and ridges, for a mirror finish.

# FINISHING WITH WAX AND OIL

Wax has been used as a treatment for finishing wood for centuries, and it is still very much in favour. Whereas a coat of varnish has to bond to the wood and provide a separate protective layer, wax sinks into the surface and produces a deep, lustrous finish that improves with age. Less skill is required for its application, and it is easy to refresh and renew. Oil is even more straightforward to use, and some modern formulations have the advantage of being slightly more durable and heat-resistant. No special equipment is needed to apply wax or oil, other than a soft cloth and fine wire (steel) wool.

### Types of wax

Pure beeswax is a natural product that provides a wonderful finish for fine furniture. However, it is less durable than other types and can soften in warm temperatures.

The most common wax for wood is carnauba wax. It is much harder than pure beeswax – a mixture of the two can be successful. It is more resistant to wear, but more difficult to apply.

Beware of using silicone-based "wax polish" as a natural wood treatment. It is quick to apply and produces a glossy finish, but when this wears off, the result is patchy and dull. It attracts a build-up of dust and dirt, and is difficult to refresh. Silicone is not compatible with any other type of finish and is impossible to remove.

Furniture wax can be obtained ready coloured to suit different wood types. It will not act as a stain on its own, but over time will build up a deep lustrous colour within the wood surface. It can be applied safely over a spirit wood stain, but can cause problems with oil-based stain. On soft wood with open grain, it helps to seal the wood beforehand. When you are working on very dense, close-grained wood, warm the wax beforehand over a low heat, such as above a radiator. Finish off by rubbing along the grain and leave it for an hour or two to settle.

*Left, clockwise from top left* There are many different types and colours of wax for polishing woodwork and furniture: liming wax, carnauba wax, teak oil, soft cloth, wax filler sticks, beeswax, solid beeswax.

1 Apply a thin coat of sanding sealer or clear shellac. This provides a stable base for the wax, but does not prevent it from sinking deep into the grain. When dry, rub down very lightly with worn pieces of fine sandpaper and brush off.

2 Apply the wax with a ball of fine wire (steel) wool. The wax lubricates the cutting action and prevents too much abrasion, while being forced deep into the wood fibres. Use a strong circular motion to work the wax well in. The harder you work, the more friction is created, which softens the wax further.

3 Form a polishing pad from a soft duster and buff the wax vigorously. Add two or three more thin coats as the wax settles, then continue to build up the finish. To refresh a polished wax finish, first wash with warm soapy water to remove any debris. If the finish is really soiled, clean it with fine wire wool moistened with white spirit (turpentine). Add another coat of wax.

## Liming wax

A limed finish can be very attractive, particularly on oak and other wood with a strong grain figure. The white liming paste penetrates the grain and provides pleasing highlights. Over time, the lime continues to react with the acid content of the wood to produce a deep lustre.

*Above* A coat of liming wax accentuates the grain of the wood beautifully.

**1** Apply a coat of sanding sealer. When it is dry, work the liming wax into the grain with fine wire (steel) wool. Use a circular motion, as you would for normal wax, but do not finish off along the grain. This would tend to lift the wax from the grain.

**2** Wipe the excess wax away with firm strokes directly across the grain. Use a soft mutton cloth with a coarse weave for the best result. Leave to dry for about four hours, then buff with a soft cloth. Seal with clear lacquer, or add more clear wax for a silky finish.

## Oil treatment

Oil is a natural waterproofer and, as such, is the perfect finish for outdoor furniture, especially on oily woods such as teak. It will outlast any varnish treatment, without the risk of water penetrating the film and causing it to lift, which is a common problem with exterior varnish. The correct oil will dry to form a protective film, but can be cut back and enriched by adding another coat at any time.

Linseed oil is not an ideal choice, as it remains soft and attracts the build-up of dust. Boiled linseed oil will form a protective crust, but is not heat-resistant and can become tacky in warm weather. Teak oil and Danish oil contain mineral extracts that help to preserve wood. They are more durable and are the best choice. One word of caution: oil is sometimes used to finish wooden culinary utensils and salad bowls. Clearly, metallic-based oils are not suitable for such items, so use thin vegetable oil instead.

**1** Application of an oil finish could not be easier. Remove all traces of dust from the surface and work in the oil with fine wire (steel) wool. Allow it to soak in and, if uneven patches are visible, keep applying more until the wood achieves a uniform colour.

**2** Finish off with long strokes up and down the grain, using a very soft cloth to work in the oil well. Leave it to dry overnight.

# FRENCH POLISHING

**French polish is a general term that applies to many different products and techniques. However, all share the same basic raw material: shellac dissolved in methylated spirits (rubbing alcohol).**

### Shellac

This is derived from a sticky resin produced by small insects in the Indian subcontinent. Successive layers of shellac will bond together to form a deep protective coating that is not too brittle with a translucent quality and rich colour. The colour will vary with the method of preparation.

### Common types of shellac

*Button polish:* more orange or golden in colour; the purest form of shellac.
*French polish:* a light to medium brown tone suitable for most finishes.
*Garnet polish:* a much darker richer brown for dark wood.
*Shellac sealer:* a useful product for building up or sealing the substrate before applying polish, or for use as a binder for stains and fillers.
*White or pale polish:* bleached shellac ideal for pale wood.

There is a great deal of mystique attached to French polishing, and certainly the best practitioners of the

art deserve the utmost admiration. The deep, rich quality of a well-polished piece of furniture is unmistakable, and difficult to reproduce by other means. "Instant" French polish treatments, which promise similar results in one coat, are not worth using. There is no substitute for good old-fashioned hard

*Above, clockwise from top left* Clear sealer, button, French and garnet polish, polishing mop, artist's brushes, cotton wadding, cloth.

work to achieve a fine finish. Try the technique on a spare piece of wood to get the hang of it – you will soon learn the basic principles.

### Filling the grain

As you might expect, careful preparation is essential. For a mirror-smooth finish, most polishers like to fill the grain first to create a truly flat surface for the polishing process. On coarse-grained wood, this is essential, as the shellac sinks into the open pores and sometimes shrinks. Ready-mixed filling paste is sold as grain filler, and is not to be confused with wood filler or stopping. If the wood is to be stained, do this before the filling process, and stain the paste to match the final colour.

1 Press the paste into the surface with a broad-bladed filling knife. Work across the grain to prevent the filler from being pulled out.

2 Leave the filler for 24 hours to dry thoroughly, then rub down with 400 grit silicon carbide paper to remove excess paste from the surface.

3 Finish by wiping across, then along the grain with mutton cloth, moistened with a drop of methylated spirit to collect all traces of dust.

## Applying the polish

French polish depends on friction to build up the coats of shellac, so it is applied with a polishing pad, or "rubber", rather than a brush. Plain unmedicated cotton wool (cotton balls), or upholsterers' wadding (batting), and clean, lint-free cotton cloth are all you need to make one.

There is no fixed size for a rubber pad – to some extent, it depends on the size of the work to be polished, and on the size of your hand. The base of the rubber pad must be completely smooth and free of creases and wrinkles. Make sure you always work on a dust-free surface.

1 Place a square of wadding in the centre of a square of cloth that is twice the size. Fold the front edge of the cloth over the wadding.

2 Fold the two front corners over to hold the wadding in place and form a point. Make sure the base of the rubber is free of dust.

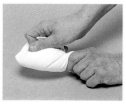

3 Twist the "tail" of the rubber pad around the back of the wadding to form a pear-shaped pad that is comfortable to hold.

4 Charge the rubber pad with polish by unfolding it and pouring a small quantity into the centre. The idea is to use the wadding as a reservoir to feed the face of the rubber with polish as you work. Never apply polish directly to the face of the rubber pad.

5 Apply a base coat of the polish, working swiftly up and down the grain and squeezing out more polish as you proceed. Keep the rubber pad moving at all times, using long overlapping strokes to spread the polish around and fill the grain.

6 Leave the polish to dry for half an hour and begin the "body up" process. Add more layers of polish, using figure-of-eight motions to cover the surface. When the rubber begins to stick or drag, leave the polish overnight to dry. Store the rubber in an airtight jar.

7 The base coat will sink into the grain as it dries. Rub down with fine abrasive paper to remove any nibs from the surface, and brush away all fine particles. Do this away from the finishing area, which must be completely dust free from now on.

8 Build up further coats, working for half an hour at a time and allowing four or five hours between sessions for the polish to harden. As more is applied, you will find that the rubber pad begins to "pull" the surface as it softens the layer beneath. Lubricate by applying a dab of raw linseed oil to the face of the rubber.

9 You will soon see a high gloss forming as the polish is built up. Dull areas indicate too much oil. If this happens, leave to dry, then work over the surface again with a clean rubber pad charged with fresh polish. Use longer strokes, applying more pressure to harden the polish. This is called "stiffing up".

10 The final task is "spiriting off". This removes all traces of oil, a fresh rubber pad being charged with finishing spirit, or diluted polish, and applied with a light touch. Use long strokes, gliding the rubber on at one end and off at the other to avoid dragging. Leave the finish to harden for 48 hours before handling.

# 9

# PROJECTS

**T**he previous chapters of this book provide an introduction to the raw material and the essential tools and techniques of woodworking. However, that information will go to waste if you do not put it into practice. All of the following projects were produced specifically for this book, in order to give you a flying start in the principles of design and construction. Whatever your level of expertise, there is sure to be something here to catch the eye and engage the imagination, which is all you need to get started. You can follow the plans and instructions in detail or simply use them as an aid in designing your own version to a different size or style. The nature of woodworking is that it is a continual journey of discovery and experience, and no two creations are ever the same. With each successful project, your confidence will grow, your technical skills will increase and, no doubt, you will obtain more satisfaction from the results.

# WINE RACK

### Materials

- 760 x 600mm (30 x 24in) of 12mm (½in) birch plywood

THIS SIMPLE PROJECT WILL PROVIDE practice in handling a few basic tools and learning one of the most important skills in woodwork – cutting straight and accurately to form simple halving (half) joints. It is made from birch-faced plywood, which can be attractive in its own right, and is finished with clear lacquer to seal it.

### Construction

There are six components to this project, and only two different panel sizes. The only critical dimension is the width of each compartment, which must suit your chosen wine bottle – 90mm (3½in) is a typical size.

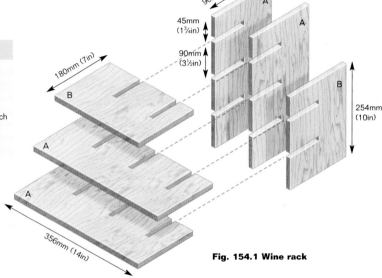

Fig. 154.1 Wine rack

90mm (3½in)
45mm (1¾in)
90mm (3½in)
180mm (7in)
254mm (10in)
356mm (14in)
A
B

**1** Cut the panels to size (see diagram above) with a panel (crosscut) saw or jigsaw, making sure that all are square. When cutting across the end grain of plywood, you will obtain a much neater finish by scoring along the cut line with a knife to prevent the saw from splintering the outer layer of ply.

**2** Firmly clamp each panel upright in a vice and trim down to the scored lines with a smoothing plane to produce neat, square edges all round. Finish off with medium sandpaper wrapped around a sanding block, using long, smooth strokes to keep the edges straight and square.

**3** Set out the lines for each slot as shown, using the dimensions given in the diagram. Draw along each side of a small offcut (scrap) of plywood to establish the correct slot width without measuring each time. Use the first panel as a template for marking out the others.

4 Clamp each panel vertically and cut downward carefully, keeping to the waste side of each line. A sharp panel saw will be more controllable than a power saw for making accurate cuts of this kind.

5 Use a mallet and a 12mm (½in) chisel to tap down at the ends of the slots. Each slot should extend to half the width of the panel so that the two halves of the joint slide together and leave the edges of the panels flush.

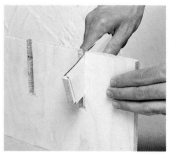

6 Wrap a strip of medium-grade sandpaper around a suitable offcut of wood and clean up the slots where necessary. The width of each slot must provide a good sliding fit for the 12mm (½in) plywood.

7 You will find it much easier to apply a finish to the components before assembling them. Clean up the panels with medium and fine sandpaper, then brush on a thin coat of varnish or clear sealer.

8 Slot the components together to join the rack. A dab of PVA wood glue may be needed on the inside of each joint, but if you have finished the slots well, it should not be necessary.

# PICTURE FRAME

## Materials

- 1.5m (5ft) of 50 x 25mm (2 x 1in) hardwood
- 355 x 280mm (14 x 11in) of 3mm (⅛in) hardboard for the backing
- PVA wood glue
- Panel pins (brads)
- Retaining clips
- Fixing attachment

VISIT ANY PICTURE FRAMING SHOP and you can take your pick from literally hundreds of different frames and mouldings. There is nothing to stop you making your own, however. Some pictures will look better if displayed in a deep box frame. This one was made from white oak with a clear lacquered finish.

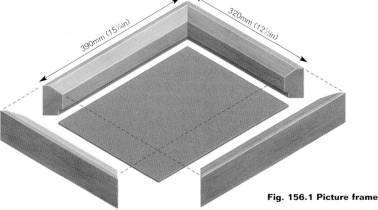

390mm (15¼in)

320mm (12½in)

**Fig. 156.1 Picture frame**

30°

50mm (2in)

6mm (¼in)

6mm (¼in)

25mm (1in)

**Fig. 156.2 Section**

### Practical tip

To calculate the internal dimensions of the frame, the size of the picture should be measured off along the inner edge of the rebate (rabbet), then 6mm (¼in) subtracted from each end to determine the measurement along the inner face of the wood. Finally, add on a small margin for clearance.

### Construction

This design has a chamfered profile to give the box frame added depth. You can improvise any variation to suit your own taste. A section of the profile used for this frame is shown in figure 156.2. The depth of the rebate is determined by the thickness of glass and backing board, plus the picture and its mount.

Cut the hardboard backing to size, then have a piece of glass cut to exactly the same size. Slip the glass into place. Fit small brass clips to act as retainers for the backing and check everything for a good fit before mounting the picture.

1 Cut the four frame members roughly to length before forming the rebate (rabbet). Leave them over-length at this stage. Use a plough (bullnose) or rebate plane to cut the rebate to a suitable depth in the bottom edge.

2 Turn the work over and plane a chamfer on the inner edge. Set a bevel gauge to 30 degrees, mark the angle at each end, and use a small block plane to trim accurately down to the line.

3 Check the angle of the chamfer
with the bevel gauge as you work,
particularly at the ends where the
corners will meet.

4 Make a 45 degree mitre cut at one
end of each frame member with a
mitre saw. Calculate your internal
measurements as instructed.

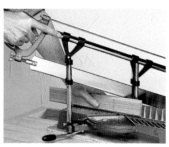

5 Mark this measurement on the inner
face and square a line across the
face. Align the mitre saw with this line
and cut each piece to the right length.

6 Use mitre (frame) cramps to hold
the assembly together while you
check that the mitres are a good fit.
Make any adjustments with a block
plane, apply glue to each face and
reassemble, tightening the clamps.

7 Fasten each corner with a couple of
panel pins (brads) to lock them
together. In a very hard wood such as
oak, it is advisable to drill short pilot
holes to avoid splitting the delicate
mitre joints.

8 Before the glue has set, fit a web
clamp around the frame. This helps
keep the assembly square. Tighten the
ratchet clamp with a spanner (wrench),
check the frame with a try square and
leave for the glue to dry.

9 When the glue has set, clean up
the edges of the frame and sand
smooth all round by hand. Apply the
finish and fittings of your choice.

# CD Rack

THE IDEA FOR THIS COMPACT DISK storage system came about because a piece of cherry wood, with distinctive figure in the grain, and a short offcut (scrap) of waney-edged yew with an interesting shape was leftover in the workshop. You can use any type of wood, of course, possibly something left over from another job. With a little imagination, you can turn short lengths of wood into all manner of items.

## Materials

- 760mm (30in) of 125 x 25mm (5 x 1in) hardwood for the rack
- 760mm (30in) of 25 x 12mm (1 x ½in) hardwood for the sides
- 280mm (11in) of 150 x 19mm (6 x ¾in) hardwood for the base
- PVA wood glue
- Brass panel pins (brads)

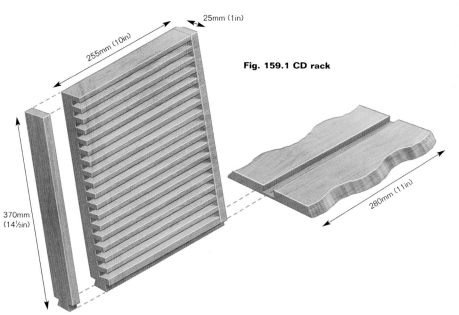

**Fig. 159.1 CD rack**

255mm (10in)

25mm (1in)

370mm (14½in)

280mm (11in)

## Construction

The design is simplicity itself – it uses the cantilever principle to support the weight of the CDs. A width of 255mm (10in) will allow two columns to be stacked side by side. The rack can be any height you like, provided the base is wide enough to make it stable. As a guide, ensure that the top of the rack, inclined at 10 degrees, is vertically above the back edge of the base. The diagram shows how to set out the ingenious dovetailed housing joint that holds the unit together.

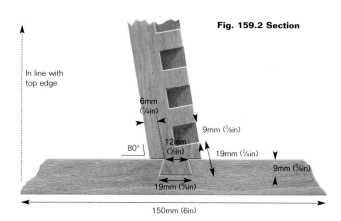

**Fig. 159.2 Section**

In line with top edge

6mm (¼in)

9mm (⅜in)

80°

12mm (½in)

19mm (¾in)

9mm (⅜in)

19mm (¾in)

150mm (6in)

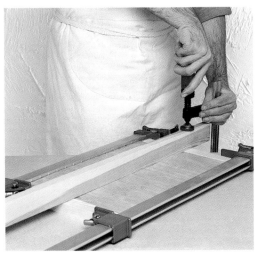

1 Cut the 125 x 25mm (5 x 1in) hardwood into two pieces 370mm (14½in) long for the main portion of the rack. Plane the edges square, glue and clamp them together. Simple butt joints are sufficient. To make sure that the board remains absolutely flat, clamp a stout batten over the top of the assembly before finally tightening the sash cramps.

2 Use a 9mm (⅜in) diameter router bit (to match the thickness of a CD cover) to rout a slot 19mm (¾in) up from the bottom edge, using the router fence as a guide. Then make a routing jig to do the rest by screwing a small strip of 9mm (⅜in) wide hardwood to the router base, exactly 9mm (⅜in) from the cutter's edge.

3 It is a simple matter to run the hardwood strip along each slot to position the next groove correctly. Continue in this way to the end of the board. Make sure the work is firmly clamped to the bench when doing this, or use a bench stop.

4 Use a dovetail cutter to rout the housing groove in the base. To deal with a waney edge, pin a straight-edged piece of plywood to the underside and run the router fence along it. Screw it down to the work surface so that it cannot move.

5 Cut the tails on the two side pieces with a fine dovetail saw. Use a bevel gauge to set the shoulders at an angle of 10 degrees, as shown in figure 159.2. Then make a small template to mark the shape of the tails to suit the profile of the dovetail groove.

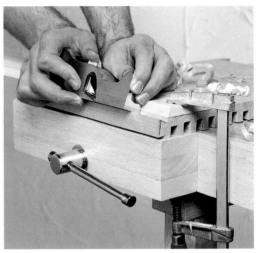

6 Use the same template to mark out the bottom edge of the main upright. Scribe the shoulders along its length with a marking gauge, and clamp a straightedge along the shoulder line to guide the tenon saw. Keep the saw blade perfectly level to ensure the shoulders are straight and parallel.

7 To form the tail on the upright, plane the required angle on a scrap piece of wood to make an accurate guide for a small shoulder plane. Use a paring chisel to remove the waste from the corners. The angles are different on each face because of the sloping profile, and should match those on the two side pieces.

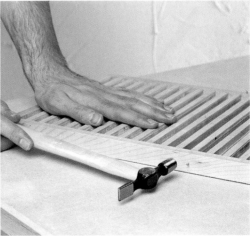

8 Plane the bottom edge of the tail to the required angle to complete the joint, paring it down until the tail has a good sliding fit in the housing. Before fitting the side pieces, you should clean up each groove with a small sanding block.

9 Pin and glue the side pieces to the upright, using small brass panel pins (brads). Align the dovetails accurately and position the pins to avoid the slots. Apply glue to the dovetailed housing in the base and slide the rack into place. When the glue is dry, apply the desired finish.

# MIRROR FRAME

It is remarkable how a plain mirror can be enhanced by adding a narrow bevel around the edge of the glass. This bevel-edged frame, which is built to generous proportions out of thick material, creates an even more striking effect. It was made from solid ash, which has a strongly figured grain, and it is simply finished with a coat of clear pale polish.

### Materials

- Sufficient 75 x 30mm (3 x 1¼in) hardwood to surround the chosen mirror
- 4 25mm (1in) barrel nuts
- fixing attachment

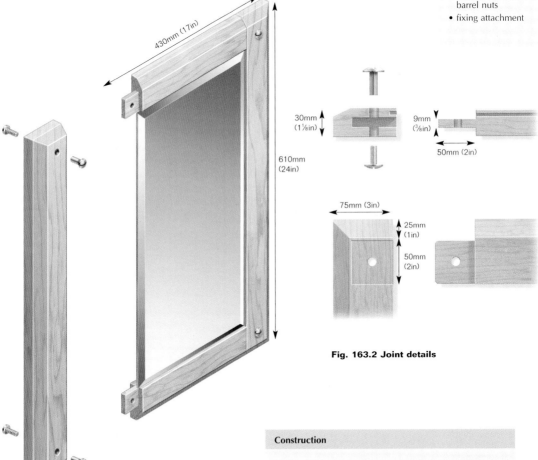

430mm (17in)

610mm (24in)

30mm (1⅛in)

9mm (⅜in)

50mm (2in)

75mm (3in)

25mm (1in)

50mm (2in)

**Fig. 163.2 Joint details**

**Fig. 163.1 Mirror frame**

## Construction

The frame is made with mortise and tenon joints, and uses a clever device called a barrel nut to connect them. This is a sleeved nut, which is inserted through the cheeks of the mortise and the blade of the tenon to lock them together. Should the worst happen and the mirror have to be replaced, simply remove the bolts, tap out the barrels and the frame will come apart easily.

1 Cut the frame members to length to suit the mirror. Set out the mortise and tenons according to the dimensions given in figure 163.2. Deduct 6mm (¼in) all round from the overall size of the mirror to determine the internal size of the frame. Chop out the mortise to a depth of 50mm (2in) and clean up the corners with a bevelled chisel.

2 Cut a 25mm (1in) haunch to each tenon with a tenon saw so that the blade is 50mm (2in) square. Pare down the tenon to be a loose sliding fit in the mortise – it should not be too tight. Nip the corners off the tenon to prevent it from fouling the bottom corners of the mortise.

3 Cut a slot on the internal edge of each component to receive the mirror. The exact dimension will depend on the thickness of the mirror glass and the size of the bevelled edge. This frame required a slot only 3mm (⅛in) wide and 6mm (¼in) deep, which was carefully cut on a circular saw bench.

4 Plane a 25mm (1in) bevel on the outer edge of each frame member. The ends of the upright members, often known as stiles, will also require matching bevels. It is better to leave these until the next step, after the joint is fitted together, in order to achieve a good match.

5 Before assembling the frame, drill an 8mm (⁵⁄₁₆in) diameter through-hole in the centre of each mortise. Clear the waste, insert the tenon and use the same drill bit to mark the centre of the hole on the blade. While the joint is still fitted together, mark the bevel required on the ends of the stiles. Finish the corner detail with a sharp block plane.

6 Take the frame apart again to drill matching holes in the tenons. For a really perfect fit, they should be offset slightly toward the shoulder. This will draw the joint up tight when the barrel nut is inserted. Use a bradawl to offset the centre point by 1.5mm (¹⁄₁₆in). Make sure the hole is drilled straight and square.

7 It is a good idea to assemble the frame first without the mirror so that you can check that everything fits perfectly. Tap two of the barrel nuts into place; you should find that the rails are drawn up tight on to their shoulders. Remove one side of the frame, slip the mirror into place and reassemble the frame.

8 Insert the male portion of the connector from the back of the frame into the threaded sleeve and tighten with a wide-bladed screwdriver. You now have a completely secure frame assembly that can be dismantled easily if you have to remove the mirror glass for any reason. Choose a suitable fixing attachment for the weight of the mirror frame.

# MAGAZINE RACK

THIS FOLDING RACK TAKES little time to construct and uses a few basic techniques. There are no joints to make, and no expensive tools are required; all you need are the basics of accurate marking out, cutting and fitting together. The materials are easy to obtain and are ready to use without further preparation. The interlocking design allows the rack to be opened up or folded flat and stowed away, with no need for clips or catches.

### Materials

- 4.2m (14ft) of 75 x 12mm (3 x ½in) planed softwood for the slats
- 2.7m (9ft) of 50 x 25mm (2 x 1in) planed softwood for the legs
- 6mm (¼in) MDF (medium-density fibreboard for the template
- 16 25mm (1in) brass wood screws
- 2 50mm (2in) brass wood screws
- Panel pin (brad)
- 2 65mm (2½in) coachbolts (carriage bolts), nuts and washers
- Thin cord

**Fig. 167.1 Magazine rack**

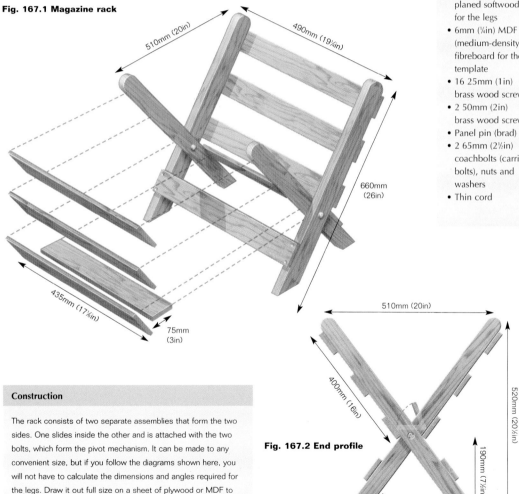

510mm (20in)

490mm (19¼in)

660mm (26in)

435mm (17⅛in)

75mm (3in)

510mm (20in)

400mm (16in)

520mm (20½in)

190mm (7½in)

52.5°

345mm (13½in)

**Fig. 167.2 End profile**

### Construction

The rack consists of two separate assemblies that form the two sides. One slides inside the other and is attached with the two bolts, which form the pivot mechanism. It can be made to any convenient size, but if you follow the diagrams shown here, you will not have to calculate the dimensions and angles required for the legs. Draw it out full size on a sheet of plywood or MDF to create a template for marking out.

1 Cut the legs and the slats to their overall length. The slats for the inner frame are 55mm (2⅛in) shorter than those used for the outer frame, allowing them to easily slide within the latter. Cut a rounded profile at the top of each leg if desired, using the first as a pattern for the others so that they will be uniform.

2 Lay each pair of legs in turn over the template you have drawn out on a sheet of MDF (medium-density fibreboard) and mark the positions of the slats and pivot point. Support the upper leg with a small offcut (scrap) of wood to keep it level. Drill a small pilot hole through the pivot point of each leg at this stage.

3 Assemble the inner frame. Insert one screw at each end of the top slat, then use a try square to adjust the assembly before you proceed. It is essential that the frames are absolutely square. Make sure the ends of the slats do not protrude over the sides of the frame.

4 Add the third slat, then turn the frame over to attach the bottom slat. The final assembly will be easier if you omit the second slat at this stage; it can be added when the rack is bolted together. Three slats are sufficient at this stage to keep the assembly square.

5 Use the inner frame as a building jig for the outer frame. Position the components carefully, making sure that the pivot holes are in line. Insert a small panel pin (brad) to keep the legs aligned in the correct position as you work. Note how the angled ends of the legs face in opposite directions.

6 Use two small offcuts of 12mm (½in) wood at each side to support the outer legs at the correct level. Screw the top and third slats in place, checking they are square as before. All four legs should be parallel to allow the assembly to move freely.

7 Turn the assembly over to fit the bottom slat. At this stage, the two frames should enclose each other, but they can still be slid apart if required. Now is a good time to clean up any rough edges with medium-grade sandpaper before proceeding. You could also apply a coat of clear sealer or varnish.

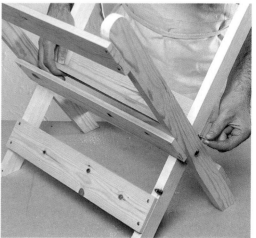

8 Drill through the legs for the coachbolts (carriage bolts), using the pilot holes to guide the drill bit. Fit a coachbolt to each side, inserting a large washer between the moving parts to reduce the amount of friction. Fit the nuts on the inside but do not over-tighten them or you will distort the framework. Note how the bottom slat on the outer frame will act as a stop to hold the rack in the open position.

9 Insert the bottom piece, which acts as a floor for the rack. Cut it to fit between the legs of the inner frame and attach with two long brass screws. It should pivot easily, allowing the rack to be folded flat for storage. Put in the remaining two slats. Add a couple of lengths of thin cord between the bottom slats as a final touch to secure the legs in their open position.

# BOOKSHELF

MANUFACTURED BOARDS WITH VENEERED FACES, sometimes called decorative boards, can make quick work of any project. However, the exposed edges of veneered plywood and MDF, or medium-density fibreboard, are vulnerable to damage and not at all attractive. To overcome this drawback, you can buy ready-made solid wood trim to match most common types of veneer, or you can make your own if you have the right tools. This bookshelf was made from boards veneered with American white oak, edged with darker oak trim to provide a contrast.

## Materials

- 760 x 610mm (30 x 24in) of 12mm (½in) veneered plywood or MDF (medium-density fibreboard)
- 2.7m (9ft) of 19mm (¾in) angled moulding for edge trim
- PVA wood glue
- Panel pins (brads)

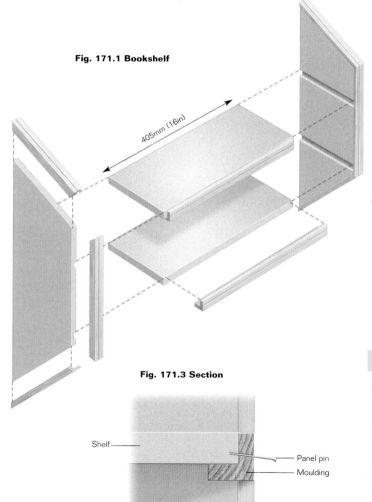

**Fig. 171.1 Bookshelf**

405mm (16in)

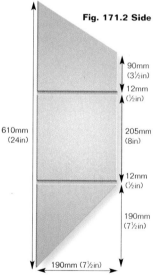

**Fig. 171.2 Side**

90mm (3½in)
12mm (½in)
205mm (8in)
12mm (½in)
190mm (7½in)

610mm (24in)

190mm (7½in)

**Fig. 171.3 Section**

Shelf

Panel pin

Moulding

## Construction

The dimensions of this small shelf unit are provided as a guide only. You can alter them to suit your own books or any other items you may wish to display. A suitable height for most paperbacks is 205–255mm (8–10in). Bear in mind that 12mm (½in) boards will sag under heavy loads if you make the shelves too wide.

1 Set out the profile on one end of the unit, cut it out and use it as a pattern for the other end to ensure that they are a perfect match. Scribe the angled cuts across the grain with a sharp knife to avoid tearing the grain of the thin veneers. Cut just outside the line with a jigsaw, if you have one, or sharp panel (crosscut) saw.

2 Clamp the angled ends in a vice so that they are horizontal, then plane them down to the scribed lines with a block plane. Work with the grain angled away from you to avoid damaging the veneer. The block plane, with a finely set, sharp blade, is the ideal tool for working this material.

3 Form the housings for the shelves with a router, running it along a straightedge pinned to the inner face. A good way to ensure accuracy is to clamp the two ends together tightly and cut the grooves in one operation. Pin a strip of scrap wood to the board edge to prevent breakout at the end of the groove.

4 The boards can vary in thickness depending on the type of veneer. It is not always possible to match the size of board exactly to the diameter of the router cutter. If necessary, plane small rebates (rabbets) on the underside of each shelf until it fits the grooves perfectly. This also improves the strength of the glued joint.

5 Apply glue to the housings and slot the unit together. It is good practice to use the glue sparingly. Any excess will have to be removed completely to prevent discoloration of the veneer at the finishing stage. Wipe off with a slightly damp cloth, and avoid rubbing glue into the grain.

6 Sash cramps are ideal for holding the assembly steady while pinning the shelves in place. Small panel pins (brads) are sufficient for a small unit such as this. Check that all corners are square and leave to set overnight. Note the small scraps of wood used to protect the veneer.

7 Cut two lengths of angled moulding to trim the front edges of the shelves. The moulding shown has a small shadow line, or "quirk", running along its length. This is designed to help conceal the heads of the panel pins when punched down with a nail set (see figure 171.3).

8 The same moulding is used to trim the end panels. Mitre the ends at the corners with a small tenon saw or adjustable mitre saw. To determine the correct angle for the mitred corners, place a short section of moulding in position and use it to mark pencil lines on the end panel, parallel to the front edges. Draw a line from the corner to the point of intersection to bisect the angle exactly. Then use this as a guide for setting an adjustable bevel gauge.

9 Apply PVA wood glue to the front edges of the end panels and pin the mouldings in place. Notice how the minimum of glue has been used. This is to prevent any excess from being squeezed on to the veneer surface when the pins are punched in with the nail set (punch). When the glue has dried, apply coloured stopping to each pinhole with a small spatula or modelling tool before sanding smooth all over, ready for finishing.

# Bar Stool

THREE DISCS OF WOOD and three lengths of round-section dowel are all it takes to make this kitchen or bar stool. The simplicity of construction is reflected in the uncluttered design, reminiscent of Shaker style. Southern yellow pine, which has a distinctive grain figure and a deep colour to the annual rings, has been used here. It has the advantage of being commonly available in wider boards, allowing each round section to be made in one piece.

## Materials

- 1m (39in) of 305 x 25mm (12 x 1in) softwood for the seat and stretcher
- 2.45m (8ft) of 32mm (1¼in) diameter softwood dowel
- 6mm (¼in) plywood or MDF (medium-density fibreboard) for template
- PVA wood glue
- 3 6mm (¼in) beech dowels

## Construction

All three discs are the same diameter and are cut from one piece of board. The legs are splayed for extra stability, and instructions are given for making a jig for drilling the angled holes. Having set up to do this, you may consider making several stools at once for a matching set.

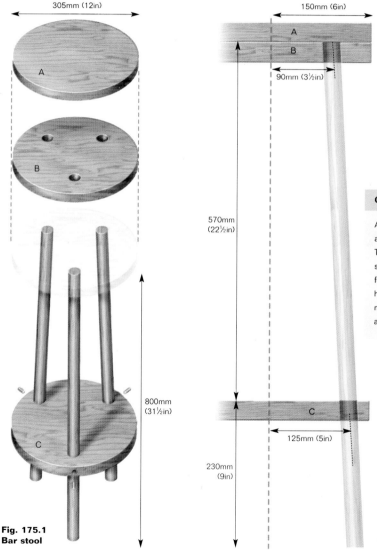

305mm (12in)

150mm (6in)

90mm (3½in)

570mm (22½in)

800mm (31½in)

125mm (5in)

230mm (9in)

A

B

C

**Fig. 175.1 Bar stool**

**Fig. 175.2 Section**

**Fig. 176.1 Making a drilling jig**

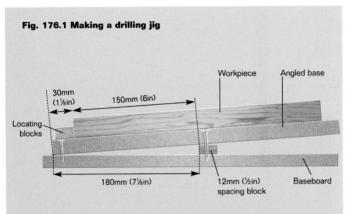

Workpiece | Angled base
30mm (1⅛in)
150mm (6in)
Locating blocks
180mm (7⅛in)
12mm (½in) spacing block
Baseboard

To drill the angled holes in the discs, make a drilling jig. First, cut a base board to fit under the drill stand, then screw a second board to it at an angle. You don't need to calculate the angle; simply screw a 12mm (½in) thick spacing block exactly 180mm (7⅛in) in from the front edge of the angled base. Provided you line up the centre of each disc with the centre of the jig, the holes will be set at the correct angle. Pin a couple of locating blocks to the angled base to position the disc accurately.

1 Make a 305mm (12in) diameter
— template from 6mm (¼in) MDF (medium-density fibreboard) and draw three radial lines at 120 degree intervals to divide it into equal segments. With a pair of compasses, mark the centres of the leg positions for the top and bottom discs, and drill a small pilot hole at each point. See figure 175.2 for the dimensions required.

2 Cut three discs from the board
— with a jigsaw, making them oversize by about 6mm (¼in). Mark the discs A, B and C, as in the diagram. Pin the template to each piece in turn and use a template cutter fitted to the router to trim the edges to the finished size. Before removing the template from B and C, use a punch to mark the centres of the holes for the legs.

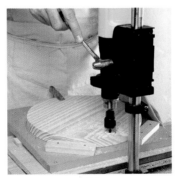

3 Fit a hole saw of the correct
— diameter in the drill stand and slide the drilling jig into place. Insert disc C in the jig and adjust it until the drill bit is centred exactly over one of the hole positions. Clamp the jig so that it cannot move and drill the hole. Repeat for the other two holes.

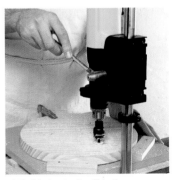

4 Drill holes in disc B in the same
— way – you will have to move the jig further toward the drill stand to allow for the holes being nearer the centre of the disc, but the angle remains the same.

5 Cut the legs to length and make a small wedge-shaped slot, 19mm (¾in) deep, in the top of each. Note the pencil line that identifies the outside of each leg to orient it correctly. This ensures that the angles at the bottom of the legs sit flat on the floor and keep the stool level.

6 Place disc B upside down on the workbench. Insert the legs into disc C and slide it to its position 230mm (9in) from the ends. Before gluing, locate the tops of the legs into disc B to hold them at the correct angle. Apply glue to the holes in disc C and tap it into place, making sure that it is level. Drill a 6mm (¼in) hole into each leg and glue in a small beech dowel to secure the disc.

7 Leave the lower part of the assembly for the glue to dry before proceeding. When it is quite firm, carefully pull the legs away from the top disc one at a time, apply glue and tap them back into place. Keep the pencil line on each facing outward to prevent the legs from twisting out of position.

8 Turn the stool over and insert three small wedges, made from offcuts (scraps) of softwood, into the tops of the legs to lock them in place, as shown. Apply a generous amount of glue and tap the wedges firmly home. Allow the glue to dry, then plane flush with a block plane, set for a fine cut.

9 Finally, glue disc A to the top of the stool to complete the job. Two or three panel pins (brads) will prevent it from sliding around as the clamps are tightened. Note how the pattern of the growth rings has been reversed. This not only creates an attractive visual effect, but also serves to stabilize the two pieces by balancing any tendency to shrink or expand.

# OCCASIONAL TABLE

No matter how fashions change, a low, neat table always makes a useful addition to the living space, and this one is a classic of its kind. With its well-proportioned, delicate frame supporting the bold, oval top, it combines clean, contemporary looks with all the best in traditional woodworking. White ash was used to make this example, and it was clear finished to bring out the honey colour of the wood.

**Fig. 179.1 Occasional table**

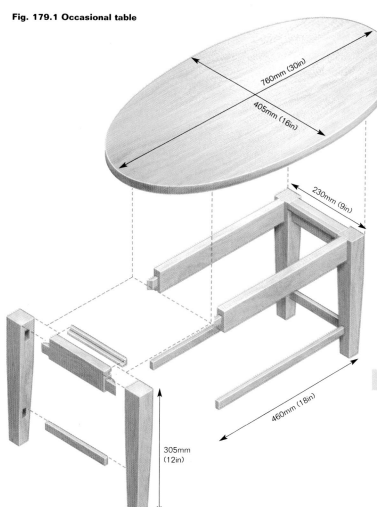

760mm (30in)

405mm (16in)

230mm (9in)

460mm (18in)

305mm
(12in)

### Materials

- 1.6m (63in) of
  205 x 25mm
  (8 x 1in) hardwood
  for the top
- 1.25m (48in) of
  38 x 38mm
  (1½ x 1½in)
  hardwood for
  the legs
- 1.4m (55in) of
  50 x 19mm
  (2 x ¾in)
  hardwood for
  the top rails
- 1.4m (55in) of
  25 x 12mm
  (1 x ½in)
  hardwood for
  the lower rails
- 6mm (¼in) MDF
  (medium-density
  fibreboard) for the
  template
- PVA wood glue
- Biscuits for
  jointing
- 38mm (1½in) brass
  wood screws
- Panel pins (brads)

### Construction

The frame for this table provides a good exercise in classic carpentry, with fine detail to the tenon joints and a slight taper to the legs to add visual balance. The shape of the top was chosen, in part, to make the best of the attractive figure of the wood grain. Setting out the oval is simple with a neat geometrical device – a loop of string and two panel pins.

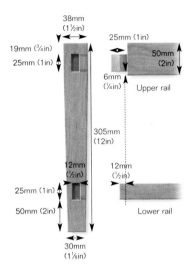

**Fig. 180.1 Leg detail**

1 The size of the top determines the proportions of the frame below, so start by setting out an oval shape to suit your pieces of wood. Cut a template panel so that it is slightly larger than the overall size of the top, and insert two panel pins (brads) on the centre line as shown. A loop of string placed over the pins will allow a pencil to describe a perfect ellipse. Practice with the length of string until you achieve a profile that looks right.

2 Cut two top boards to a suitable length, plane their edges square and insert biscuits in the edges prior to gluing them together. Position the biscuits in such a way that they will not be exposed when cutting the top to its final shape. Clamp the boards with sash cramps and leave to set while you make the frame.

3 Set out the mortises for the legs by following the dimensions in the diagram. The taper begins 50mm (2in) below the top of the leg so that the shoulders of the upper rails can be cut square. Note that the mortise for each lower rail is more of a socket, being the full size of the rail itself; no shoulders are required.

4 Pare the tenons on the upper rails with a wide bevelled chisel or shoulder plane. Accuracy is vital for this assembly to ensure that all mating parts make good contact for the adhesive. Even the small shoulders at the sides of the tenons play a part in keeping the frame square and rigid.

5 The tenons intersect inside the mortise at the top of each leg. Cut a mitre on the end of each tenon and check each corner in turn so that there is a snug fit. Mark up the rails and legs in their respective positions before moving on to fashion the tapers on the legs.

6 Scribe guidelines around the foot of each leg with a marking gauge. Use a straightedge to form the outline of the taper on two opposing faces and plane carefully down to the lines. Work from the top of each leg, with the grain, down toward the tapered ends.

7 On the faces you have just planed, mark the same taper profile for the remaining two sides and repeat the operation. Note the wedge in the vice that clamps the tapered leg in position. The tapered ends should be 30mm (1⅛in) square when you have finished.

8 The two short rails are grooved to receive the rebated (rabbeted) blocks that connect the frame to the top. Use a plough (bullnose) plane to form the 9 x 9mm (⅜ x ⅜in) housing, then fashion two fixing blocks from an offcut (scrap) of 19 x 19mm (¾ x ¾in) hardwood.

9 Assemble the frame, upside down, on a flat surface to ensure that it is square and level. Glue, cramp and leave to dry while you work on the table top. Cut out the oval shape of the template with a jigsaw and smooth the edges. Pin it to the underside of the top, and use a router with a template follower to transfer the shape.

10 Plane the table top flat, sand it smooth and, if desired, rout a profile around the edge. Drill and countersink the small fixing blocks for 38mm (1½in) brass wood screws and fix the frame to the top. There is no need to use glue – this type of attachment method allows the solid top to shrink or expand slightly without disturbing the frame assembly.

# STORAGE CHEST

THIS IS A CLASSIC STORAGE CHEST with traditional lines, which can be used as a linen chest in the bedroom, or perhaps as a window seat or toy chest. The clean design, with discreet brass fittings (trims), makes it equally suitable for contemporary and period-style interiors. The chest was made from reclaimed pine floorboards, which have a deep orange colour that is rare in new-grown softwoods. A clear wax finish brings out the full character of the grain.

### Materials

- 11m (36ft) of 150 x 25mm (6 x 1in) softwood
- 6.7m (22ft) of 50 x 25mm (2 x 1in) softwood
- 915 x 380mm (36 x 15in) of 6mm (¼in) MDF (medium-density fibreboard)
- 915mm (36in) brass piano hinge
- PVA wood glue
- Biscuits for jointing
- 25mm (1in) panel pins (brads)
- 38mm (1½in) countersunk wood screws
- 2 brass lid stays
- 2 brass drop handles

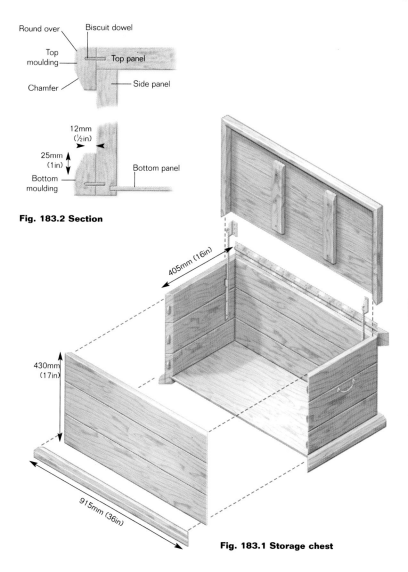

**Fig. 183.2 Section**

*Labels in Fig. 183.2:* Round over, Biscuit dowel, Top moulding, Top panel, Chamfer, Side panel, 12mm (½in), 25mm (1in), Bottom moulding, Bottom panel

*Labels in Fig. 183.1:* 405mm (16in), 430mm (17in), 915mm (36in)

**Fig. 183.1 Storage chest**

### Construction

This design relies on the gluing together of pine boards to make wide panels, the edges being butt jointed and reinforced with biscuits to align them. You will find a mitre saw invaluable for cutting all the joints for the sides and ends.

1 Cut all the boards roughly to length and plane the long edges square for butt joints. Align the boards with a try square and straightedge to set out mitre cuts at each end. Make pencil marks at about 300mm (11¾in) intervals for the biscuits.

2 You may find that the mitre saw is not quite accurate enough to produce a perfect joint every time. Make a mitred shooting board, as shown, so that you can true (square) the ends of each piece with a block plane, set for a fine cut.

3 Rout a 6mm (¼in) groove in the bottom board of each panel to receive the base panel. The easiest way to clean up the groove is with a sheet of medium-grade sandpaper wrapped around a thin strip of plywood.

4 Insert biscuits and glue up each panel in turn. The biscuits will help keep the faces of the boards flush and level, as well as adding strength to the edge joint. Make sure the mitred ends are aligned perfectly, tidying them up with a block plane if necessary.

5 Use a biscuit jointer, set at 45 degrees, to cut slots in the mitred faces at the corners. Insert the biscuits and glue the box together with PVA wood glue. Slide the bottom panel into place before putting on the last side of the box. Clamp and leave to dry.

6 Cut the material roughly to length for the top and bottom mouldings, then plane a chamfer on one face of each piece. Figure 183.2 shows the dimensions used for this chest, but you can vary them to suit your taste. Check the angle with a bevel gauge.

7 Mitre the ends of the bottom mouldings so that they fit the external dimensions of the base. Use more biscuits to hold them flush with the bottom edges. Lock each joint with 25mm (1in) panel pins (brads).

8 Glue and clamp three boards for the lid. To make it stay flat, alternate the orientation of each board's growth rings. Cramp from above and below to equalize the pressure on the joints.

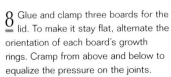

9 Apply a rounded edge to the top mouldings, then mitre the corners and fit to the front and sides of the lid. Omit the back edge at this stage.

10 Sand down the top of the lid and smooth the edges. The back edge is visible, showing how the ends of the mouldings are mitred.

11 Before fitting the lid, make up two battens to fit on the underside. These stiffen the top, keep it flat, and allow the chest to be used as a seat.

12 Chamfer the edges of each batten with a plane, and make matching cuts at the ends, using a dovetail or tenon saw. Glue and screw the battens to the inside of the lid. Note that they should be located at least 32mm (1¼ in) in from the back edge.

13 The final length of top moulding is fitted to the chest, not to the lid. Use a rebate (rabbet) plane to cut a shallow rebate for the brass piano hinge. It must be deep enough to accommodate the thickness of both leaves of the hinge – no more than 1.5mm (¹⁄₁₆in).

14 Mitre the ends of the moulding to fit the back of the lid, and screw it to the chest so that it projects above the top edge to match the thickness of the lid. Double check that the hinge rebate lies parallel to the edge.

15 Screw the piano hinge along the back edge of the lid, using small countersunk screws, then put the lid in place, slotting the lower hinge leaf into the rebate. Attach it with a couple of screws at each end first, then check for smooth opening and closing before adding the rest.

16 Attach the brass stays. Adjust the sliding arm of each stay so that the lid is held in a position just beyond the vertical to prevent straining the hinge. Finally, attach the drop handles to each end of the chest.

# THREE-LEGGED CHAIR

THIS THREE-LEGGED CHAIR is made in a traditional Windsor fashion, the seat acting as a mounting structure for the two front legs, which are wedged and glued. The back leg is attached by a tenon so it can extend above the seat to form the back. This form of chair was common in the medieval period, although all the elements would have been turned and the seat would have been a triangle.

## Materials

- 700mm (27½in) of 100 x 40mm (4 x 1½in) beech for the back leg
- 850mm (33½in) of 40 x 40mm (1½ x 1½in) beech for the front legs
- 210mm (8¼in) of 40 x 40mm (1½ x 1½in) beech for the back rest
- 2 330mm (13in) lengths of 135 x 40mm (5¼ x 1½in) beech for the seat
- 390mm (15¼in) of 60 x 40mm (2¼ x 1½in) beech for the seat
- Plywood for the template
- PVA wood glue
- Biscuits for jointing
- Small dowel

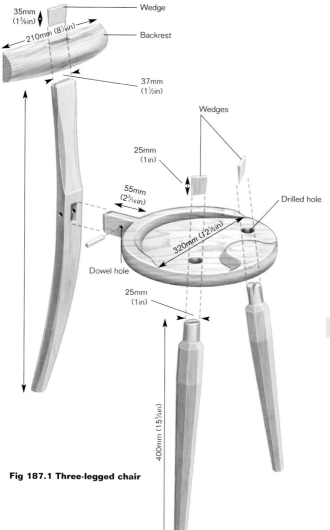

**Fig 187.1 Three-legged chair**

Wedge
Backrest
35mm (1⅜in)
210mm (8¼in)
37mm (1½in)
Wedges
25mm (1in)
55mm (2³⁄₁₆in)
Drilled hole
320mm (12½in)
Dowel hole
25mm (1in)
400mm (15¾in)

## Construction

This chair relies on one of the most common joints, the mortise and tenon. Two of the joints are round and wedged but work on the same principle as the rectangular variety.

1 The seat is formed from three pieces of wood. Plane a face side and edge on each of these boards, prior to cutting them to length. Square edges are essential for jointing the boards if the seat is to be flat.

2 Cut the prepared boards to size and form a tenon on the end of the centre section, which will fit into the mortise in the back leg. The central square strip in the seat makes cutting this joint easier.

3 Join the boards together with PVA wood glue and biscuits, using sash cramps to hold them while the glue sets. Leave to set overnight as the joint is stronger if fully cured before removing the cramps.

4 Make a plywood template to match the profile of the back leg, then mark and cut out the leg from a planed piece of wood.

5 Cut out the seat shape with a jig saw and drill the angled holes for the front legs. Either make a drilling jig, or cut the angle on a scrap piece of wood and stand this next to each hole position so that the drill can be held at the same angle, as shown here.

6 Plane the front leg blank into a hexagonal section before cutting it in half to form the two legs. Allow enough timber for the saw cuts.

7 Plane a taper on each front leg, as shown in the diagram, working from opposing sides to form a square at the base.

8 Use a V-block to hold the leg firmly in place while you remove the corners to complete the tapered hexagonal section.

**9** Make an angled cut with a tenon saw in the top of the leg to match the angle of the hole drilled in the seat. Using a chisel, form a 25mm (1in) round peg to fit the hole. Cut the mortise in the back leg to fit the seat tenon.

**10** Use a spokeshave to form the chamfers on the back leg. Shape the leg in the same way as the front legs to create a tapering hexagonal section, taking care to leave the cheeks of the mortise square.

**11** Having already cut the mortise in the backrest for the back leg, plane the backrest to shape, rounding off the front face. Create a taper on the back of the rest, as shown, using a block plane.

**12** Using a shallow gouge, start carving out a concave shape in the seat blank.

**13** Continue in this way until you are satisfied with the shape; be careful not to remove too much material around the points where the legs join. Round the edge of the seat with a spokeshave.

**14** Drill a small dowel hole through the back leg mortise, insert the seat tenon and mark the position of the hole on it. Remove the tenon and drill the hole slightly off-centre, toward the seat. Attach the leg using a small dowel. When the dowel is driven home, it will pull the joint together.

**15** Make a saw cut into the peg at the top of each front leg, apply glue and insert the peg into its hole in the seat. Secure the leg by driving a small wooden wedge into the cut in the peg. Secure the backrest to the top of the back leg in the same way. Remove any excess material when the glue has dried.

# DISPLAY CASE

A COLLECTION OF INTERESTING OR PRECIOUS ARTEFACTS can be seen to best advantage if displayed in a purpose-made cabinet. Whatever you may want to show off, you can keep everything safe behind the sleek glass doors of this custom-built case. It is a simple pine box with a separate insert of pigeon-hole compartments, which can be removed for easy cleaning.

## Materials

- 3.8m (12ft 6in) of 205 x 25mm (8 x 1in) softwood
- 1m (39in) of 38 x 38mm (1½ x 1½in) softwood for the corner blocks
- 1,050 x 775mm (41 x 30½in) of 6mm (¼in) MDF (medium-density fibreboard) for the back panel
- 1.65 x 1.25m (65 x 48in) of 12mm (½in) MDF for the inserts
- Glass doors cut to size
- Glass door hinges and magnetic catches
- PVA wood glue
- Biscuits for jointing
- 50mm (2in) countersunk wood screws
- Panel pins (brads)

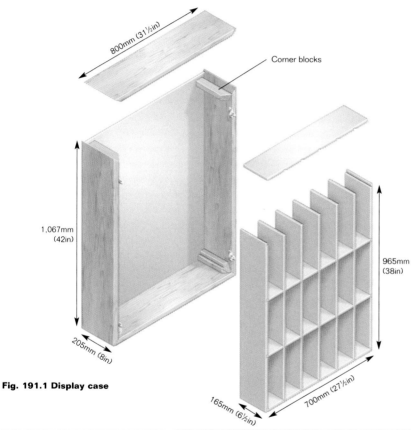

800mm (31½in)

Corner blocks

1,067mm (42in)

205mm (8in)

965mm (38in)

165mm (6½in)

700mm (27½in)

**Fig. 191.1 Display case**

## Construction

This cabinet can be made to any size. This one was based around 18 compartments, each measuring 300 x 100mm (11¾ x 4in). Make a scale drawing of the ideal arrangement of compartments and calculate the external size of the box from this. This design features a 25mm (1in) gap between the insert and the outer box.

## Fig. 191.2 Making the insert

The shelf insert is made from MDF and then painted to provide a contrast with the natural wood finish of the cabinet. The sides, top and bottom of the insert are rebated (rabbeted) 6mm (¼in) deep to receive the inner dividers, which are slotted to interlock and simplify assembly. The top and bottom are also rebated into the sides, making all the horizontal components the same length.

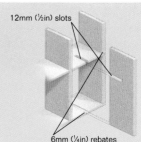

12mm (½in) slots

6mm (¼in) rebates

## Fig. 192.1 Ordering the doors

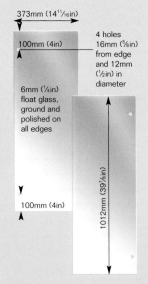

373mm (14¹¹⁄₁₆in)

100mm (4in)

4 holes
16mm (⅝in)
from edge
and 12mm
(½in) in
diameter

6mm (¼in)
float glass,
ground and
polished on
all edges

1012mm (39⅞in)

100mm (4in)

Measure the internal dimensions of the box and calculate the size of glass required for the doors. Subtract 1.5mm (¹⁄₁₆in) all round for clearance and a similar amount where the doors meet in the centre. The hinges used required small holes to be drilled in the glass – definitely a job for a specialist. Take a sketch to your glazier when you order the doors.

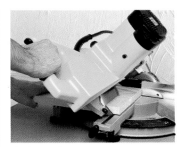

1 Cut the four sides to length, using a power crosscut saw to form the mitres in the softwood. This particular saw has sliding bars on the body that enables it to be extended in order to cut wide boards.

3 The corner joints are aligned using biscuits. This biscuit jointer has an adjustable front fence that makes it very easy to set the required angle, a feature to look for when buying.

5 Depending on the type of hinge being used, you may need to chisel a small recess for each hinge mounting plate. Glass door hinges are specialized items, so be sure to obtain them before you start the job.

2 A mitred shooting board is used to tidy up the face of each joint to ensure perfectly square corners. The end of the shooting board must be planed to a 45 degree angle to guide the sole plate of the block plane.

4 Use a router or rebate (rabbet) plane to cut a 6mm (¼in) deep by 12mm (½in) wide rebate along the back edges of the box to receive the recessed back panel.

6 Prepare four corner blocks from a length of 38 x 38mm (1½ x 1½in) batten. Cut a 12 x 12mm (½ x ½in) rebate along one edge and cut four pieces with angled ends. The overall length of each block is 150mm (6in).

7 Apply glue to the mitred ends of the boards, insert the biscuits and clamp the box together, face down on the bench. Use small offcuts (scraps) of rebated corner block to protect the corners under the cramp heads.

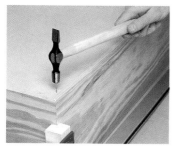

**8** Check that the box is square, then lay the MDF (medium-density fibreboard) back panel into its rebate. Attach it in place with panel pins (brads). The panel will help keep the box square when you turn it over.

**9** Install the corner blocks to ensure the box is square – vital for a good fit for the glass doors. The bevel at the front of each block guides the insert into position, making the block less apparent when the cabinet is complete.

**10** To make the insert, cut the MDF into strips, 165mm (6½in) wide, then cut them to their respective lengths. Mark out all the rebates and slots on all parts, clamping them in pairs so that they match perfectly.

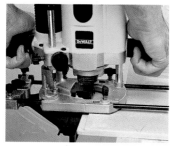

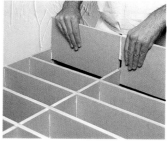

**11** Set the depth stop of the router to cut 6mm (¼in) deep rebates and grooves in the outer panels. Use a fence when making the edge cuts. Clamp a straightedge to the work when forming the remaining housing joints.

**12** Create the slots in the dividers by routing halfway across the width of the piece. You should square the end of each slot with a 12mm (½in) bevelled chisel.

**13** Assemble the box using glue and panel pins. Slide each divider into place – the construction will become quite rigid as each bit is added. Check that all is square, wipe off any excess glue with a damp cloth and leave to dry.

**14** Before attaching the insert, add the hinges to match the hole positions in the glass doors. This type of hinge is best for glass doors and provides a positive fixing through glass.

**15** The chrome-plated clips on the doors act as striker plates for the magnetic touch latch. This device springs the door open with a light touch, so no handles are needed.

**16** Offer the insert into position to ensure that it is a good sliding fit before painting. Tap it all the way in. Remove and apply the finish of your choice before fitting the doors.

# BEDSIDE CABINET

THIS SMALL CABINET is made of American white oak veneer with a liming wax finish to produce a smart, contemporary look. Solid wood trim and edging are easily applied to match the oak-veneered door and panels. The distinctive grain pattern of the oak is enhanced by the pale colour, while the lustrous wax finish suits the soft, comfortable feel of the bedroom.

## Materials

- 1.5 x 1m (60 x 39in) of 12mm (½in) veneered MDF (medium-density fibreboard)
- 305 x 305mm (12 x 12in) of 6mm (¼in) MDF for the template
- 1.5m (60in) of 19 x 19mm (¾ x ¾in) hardwood moulding for the top
- 4m (13ft) of 12 x 6mm (½ x ¼in) hardwood edge trim
- Pre-glued veneer edging strip
- 2 brass hinges
- Ball catch
- Door handle
- 4 brass shelf supports
- PVA wood glue
- 19mm (¾in) panel pins (brads)
- 12mm (½in) countersunk brass wood screws

## Construction

The distinctive profile of the cabinet sides incorporates a simple curve that forms the legs at the bottom and a matching handle detail at the top. Pre-glued strips of veneer simplify the process of applying edging to the shape. The top of the cabinet is finished with an angled moulding, which forms a shallow recess on the top to prevent stray items from rolling off. With a router and a few basic hand tools, this project can be constructed with ease.

**Fig. 195.2 Profile**

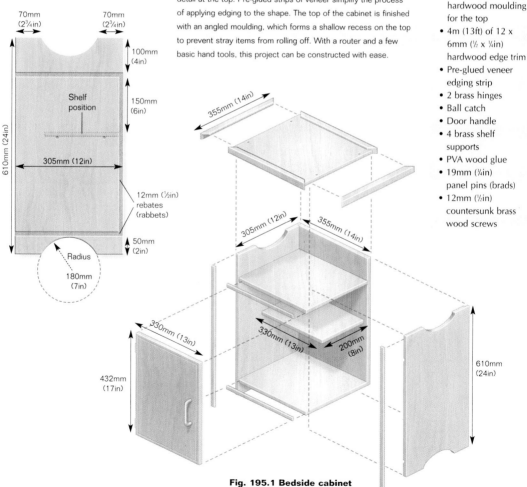

**Fig. 195.1 Bedside cabinet**

1 Cut the two side panels to their overall size, using a router with a 12mm (½in) cutter to rebate (rabbet) them for the shelves and back panel. Set out the rebates according to the dimensions given in figure 195.2. Cut out the back panel and rebate at top and bottom for the horizontal panels.

2 Make a template using 6mm (¼in) MDF to the radius shown. Line up the centre line of the template with the centre of the panel and transfer the shape to each end. Remove any waste with a jigsaw, set to a slow speed to avoid forcing the blade through the work.

3 Smooth down the curves with a pad of sandpaper, taking care not to round over the edges of the cutout. The edging strip requires a perfectly flat surface when it is applied. Use a rotary sanding drum if you have one.

4 Using the tip of a warm iron, press the pre-glued strip into place so that it follows the curve. Keep the iron moving at all times to avoid overheating the delicate material. Leave for at least 15 minutes for the glue to set.

5 Trim off the excess veneer with a long, flat blade, pressed flat on the surface of the panel. This helps to prevent splinters from being picked up by the blade. Use a slow knifing action in long strokes to remove the small slivers of veneer.

6 Drill four small holes, 6mm (¼in) deep, for the support pegs of the removable shelf before assembling the cabinet. Note the masking tape on the drill bit, which acts as a depth gauge. Then sand down all the internal surfaces.

7 Assemble the cabinet face down on a flat worksurface. Apply glue to the rebates and slot in the horizontal panels. Push the back panel firmly into position to square the assembly.

8 Use 19mm (¾in) panel pins (brads) to attach the joints. Check the cabinet is square and that all front edges are flush. Wipe off excess glue with a damp cloth and allow to dry.

9 Cut short lengths of 6mm (¼in) hardwood edge trim to fit the front edges of the horizontal panels. Glue and pin them in place, taking care not to position the pins too close to the ends to prevent the material from splitting. A small pilot hole may be required for the pins.

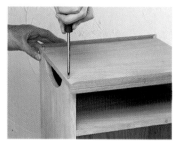

10 Mitre four pieces of moulding to edge the top panel. Fit the front and back sections of moulding to the panel, gluing and pinning them as for the front trim. Centre the top on the cabinet and attach, using four narrow-gauge screws; they will be hidden by the remaining lengths of moulding.

11 Glue and pin the two side mouldings in position. Punch down all the heads, apply stopping to the pin holes and sand down ready for finishing. Take care when sanding veneered edges. Use a hand sanding block rather than a power sander.

12 Measure up and cut the door to size from a matching panel of veneered board, making it just over 6mm (¼in) smaller all round to allow for the edge trim. Mitre the ends of the trim pieces and glue them in place, then sand to a fine finish.

13 Flush hinges of the type shown require no recesses for the leaves. The barrel of the hinge pin lodges against the front edge of the side panel and automatically aligns the door. Fit with 12mm (½in) countersunk brass screws.

14 Screw the wooden handle of your choice to the door before fitting the catch. This allows you to control the closing action more easily and avoid straining the hinges. Now fit the brass ball catch just behind the handle.

15 A quick and easy way to align the tip of the ball catch is to apply a dab of ink to the base, and close the door on to it to make a small mark.

16 Make the removable shelf. Finish the front edge with a length of edging strip. Insert the shelf supports and offer the shelf into position. Coat the cabinet inside with clear lacquer.

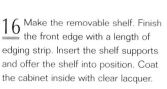

# COMPUTER CABINET

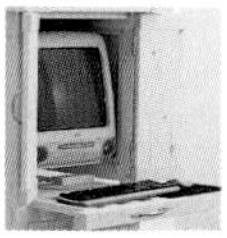

THIS CABINET IS DESIGNED TO hold the basic requirements for home computing – monitor, hard drive and printer. The plans can be adjusted as required to fit the size of your personal computer equipment. Readily available materials have been used throughout.

**Fig. 199.1 Detail of pull-out shelf**

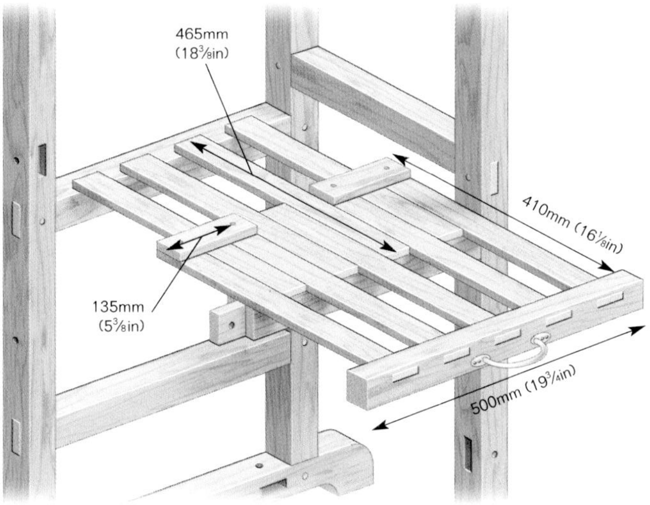


## Construction

The cupboard is built using mortise and tenon joints throughout, secured with square pegs that pull the joints together with the aid of offset holes drilled in each mortise and tenon. These are achieved by drilling the mortise first, fitting the tenon and marking the position of the hole, then removing the tenon and drilling the hole slightly closer to its shoulder.

## Materials

Unless specified otherwise, all wood is planed softwood

- 2 700mm (27½in) lengths of 70 x 45mm (2¾ x 1¾in) for the foot rails
- 4 1.06m (41¾in) lengths of 45 x 45mm (1¾ x 1¾in) for the uprights
- 8 510mm (20in) lengths of 45 x 45mm (1¾ x 1¾in) for the cross-rails A
- 3 510mm (20in) lengths of 45 x 20mm (1¾ x ¾in) for the cross-rails B
- 5 350mm (13¾in) lengths of 45 x 20mm (1¾ x ¾in) for the drawer rails C
- 4 465mm (18⅜in) lengths of 45 x 20mm (1¾ x ¾in) for the drawer members
- 2 510mm (20in) lengths of 45 x 20mm (1¾ x ¾in) for the shelf supports
- 510mm (20in) of 45 x 45mm (1¾ x 1¾in) for the drawer front
- 8 410mm (16⅛in) lengths of 19 x 19mm (¾ x ¾in) for side board supports
- 4 380mm (15in) lengths of 19 x 19mm (¾ x ¾in) for side board supports
- 2 135mm (5⅜in) lengths of 19 x 19mm (¾ x ¾in) for drawer connectors
- 225mm (8⅞in) of 19 x 19mm (¾ x ¾in) for drawer connector
- 4 410mm (16⅛in) lengths of 45 x 19mm (1¾ x ¾in) for shelf ends
- 4 205mm (8in) lengths of 45 x 19mm (1¾ x ¾in) for door ends
- 2 600mm (23½in) lengths of 90 x 19mm (3½ x ¾in) for top ends
- 3.2m (10ft 6in) of 10 x 10mm (⅜ x ⅜in) for pegs
- 22m (72ft) of 90 x 15mm (3½ x ⅝in) tongued-and-grooved cladding boards for cladding sides, top, doors and shelves
- PVA wood glue
- Galvanized fittings
- Castors
- 16 40mm (1½in) screws
- Panel pins (brads)

**Fig. 200.1 Computer cabinet**

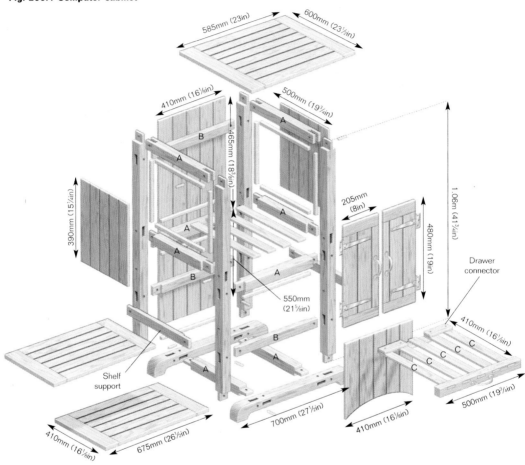

Labels in figure: 585mm (23in); 600mm (23½in); 410mm (16⅛in); 500mm (19¾in); 465mm (18¾in); 390mm (15¼in); B; A; A; A; B; 205mm (8in); 480mm (19in); 1.06m (41¾in); Drawer connector; 550mm (21⅝in); B; A; Shelf support; 410mm (16⅛in); C C C C C C; 410mm (16⅛in); 700mm (27½in); 410mm (16⅛in); 500mm (19¾in); 410mm (16⅛in); 675mm (26½in)

1 Cut the softwood sections to length as required for the frame, and mark out all mortise and tenon joints.

2 Start by cutting the profile of the bottom rails with a jigsaw and planing chamfers on all edges to finish off. Cut all the mortise and tenon joints.

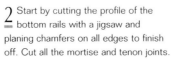

3 Assemble the base frame, pulling the joints together by driving square pegs into round holes drilled through the cheeks and blades of the mortise and tenon joints. Clean off any excess glue.

4 Drill peg holes in the uprights, making sure you keep the drill at 90 degrees to the workpiece and have a piece of waste wood underneath to drill into.

5 Assemble the front and rear frames of the cabinet by gluing and pegging the joints. Wipe away excess glue with a damp cloth before it dries. Check the frames for squareness by measuring the diagonals.

6 Fit the side rails to the rear frame. Make sure you label the rails to get them in the correct order, as three of the rails are slimmer so that they allow the cladding to sit on top of them.

7 Join the front to the back. Lay the assembled frame with side rails on a bench and then joint the assembled front to the back. Check the frame for squareness by standing it on a flat surface and check the angles with a try square.

8 Attach the base frame and then attach it to the main frame. Add the top rails. It may be easier to work on the floor to join all the components together. Glue and nail to the cross rails.

9 Where the sides and back are to be panelled with tongued-and-grooved cladding boards, you need to attach battens to which they can be nailed. These battens must be set back by the board thickness from the face side.

10 Pin and glue tongued-and-grooved cladding boards on to the back, driving the pins through the tongues of the boards and setting them with a nail set (punch). You will have to cut the outside boards down to fit.

11 Cut the cladding boards to size and attach them to the sides and front. Note at the front, the ends of the boards are cut to produce a curved edge to the panel to allow toe space.

12 Start to assemble the pull-out shelf, gluing and pegging the joints in the same way as before. Trim the pegs flush with the surface of the wood with a tenon saw. Finish off with a chisel.

13 Assemble the three central slats of the drawer, as shown, using the other slats as spacers so that the shelf will slide. Make sure that the fit is not too tight or it will be difficult to slide the shelf into position.

14 Turn the drawer over and join the two outer slats together. It is constructed in this manner so that the slats are not pinched and will not bind. Finish by attaching the "loose" slats to the cabinet with screws. Make sure that they are fitted parallel so they will not bind when the shelf is pulled out.

15 Cut shoulders on the ends of the tongued-and-grooved cladding boards that will form the top, shelves and doors. These shoulders will locate in a groove cut in each end piece, which helps to keep the boards flat. Use sash cramps when gluing these to the boards. Mark out the position of the hinges and handles on the finished doors.

16 Fit the top by gluing and pegging. Assemble the doors and attach the hinges and handles. Fit the shelf so that it will take the monitor using three pieces of tongue-and-groove. Complete the cabinet by adding castors and other fittings as required. The finish used on this cabinet was linseed oil mixed with white colouring.

# BUTCHER'S BLOCK

No WELL-EQUIPPED KITCHEN would be complete without a good, solid butcher's block to provide a self-contained workstation for chopping and preparing ingredients. Here, laminating is used to make the chopping block from solid, hardwearing maple. This project incorporates the worktop into a sturdy freestanding table unit. It includes an optional drawer for your chopping and cutting utensils.

## Construction

The table legs are made from large-section timber (lumber), and the rails are equally sturdy, being tenoned into the legs to provide a strong support for the chopping surface. This assembly has a painted finish and a coat of hardwearing clear lacquer for hygiene and durability. The knots were treated with a shellac sealer so that they would cause no problems in the finished table.

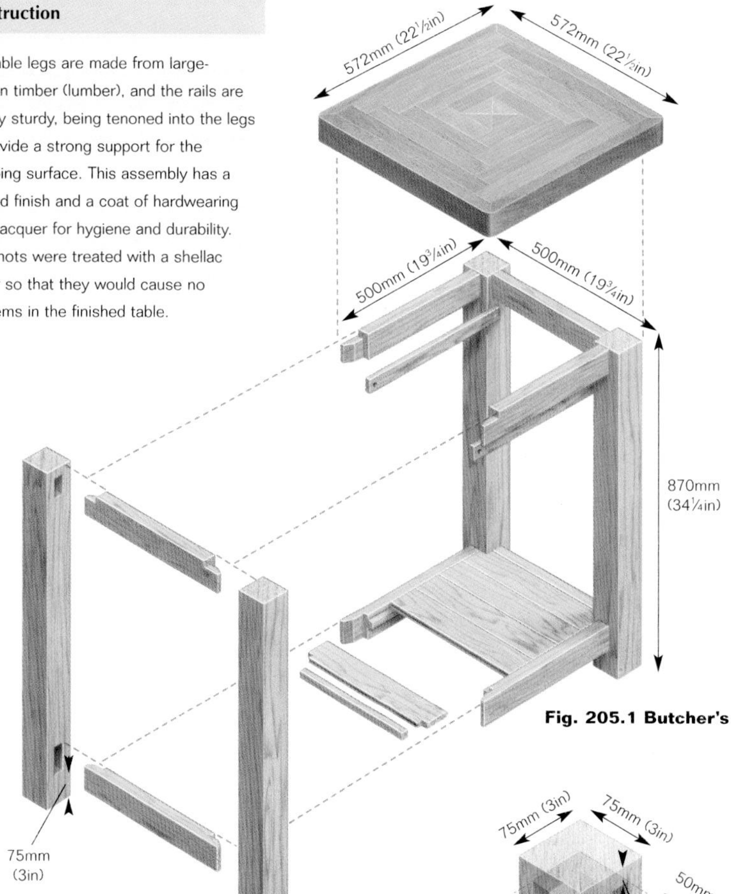

572mm (22¹/₂in)
572mm (22¹/₂in)
500mm (19³/₄in)
500mm (19³/₄in)
870mm (34¹/₄in)
75mm (3in)

**Fig. 205.1 Butcher's block**

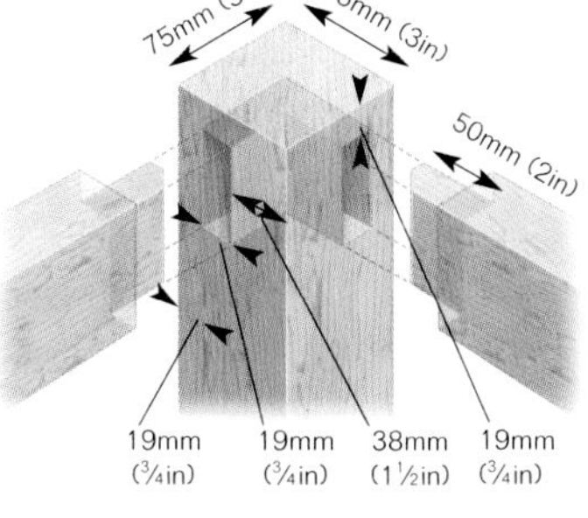

75mm (3in)  75mm (3in)  50mm (2in)

19mm (³/₄in)  19mm (³/₄in)  38mm (1¹/₂in)  19mm (³/₄in)

**Fig. 205.2 Detail of leg and rail joints**

### Materials

- 3.6m (12ft) of 75 x 75mm (3 x 3in) softwood for the legs
- 3.7m (12ft 2in) of 75 x 38mm (3 x 1¹/₂in) softwood for the rails
- 2m (6ft 6in) of 75 x 12mm (3 x ¹/₂in) tongued-and-grooved cladding boards for the shelf
- 1.6m (63in) of 19 x 19mm (³/₄ x ³/₄in) softwood for the shelf battens
- 2.4m (8ft) of 25 x 12mm (1 x ¹/₂in) softwood for the drawer runners
- 400mm (15³/₄in) of 125 x 19mm (5 x ³/₄in) softwood for the drawer front
- 400 x 400mm (15³/₄ x 15³/₄in) of 12mm (¹/₂in) plywood for the drawer sides
- 400 x 400mm (15³/₄ x 15³/₄in) of 6mm (¹/₂in) plywood for the drawer bottom
- 7.3m (24ft) of 50 x 35mm (2 x 1⅜in) hardwood for the top
- PVA wood glue
- 38mm (1¹/₂in) lost-head nails
- 6mm (¹/₄in) dowels
- 38mm (1¹/₂in) countersunk wood screws
- 25mm (1in) round-head wood screws
- 4 metal corner brackets
- Draw handle

## Construction

The drawer is simply butt jointed together with dowels to strengthen the corners. Apply glue to the dowels and insert them into the drawer sides. Slide the bottom panel into place and tap the assembly together. Clamp the corners and leave to dry, after which the front panel can be glued and screwed to the carcass.

**Fig. 206.1 Drawer**

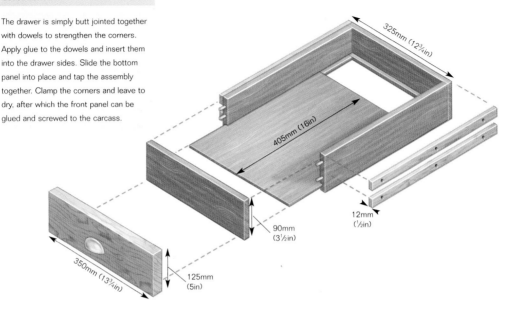

325mm (12¾in)

405mm (16in)

12mm (½in)

90mm (3½in)

350mm (13¾in)

125mm (5in)

1 To make the body of the block, cut the legs to length and make sure that their ends are absolutely square for a stable structure. Set out the mortises for the rails according to the dimensions in the accompanying diagram. Clamp the legs together in pairs to allow accurate marking out. Note that the mortises for the top rails are set back from the top edges, or "relished" (revealed), by 19mm (¾in).

2 Cut the mortises, cleaning out the corners with a bevelled chisel. The tenons of each adjacent pair of rails meet in the centre of the leg, at the bottom of the blind mortises, so make sure that they are deep enough and that all the waste is removed.

3 The tenons are "bare-faced" in that the shoulder is formed on only one side of the tenon. This has the effect of moving the inner face of the rail inward while centralizing the mortise in the leg for maximum strength.

4 Mitre the ends of the tenons where they will intersect, paring them down until they both fit together perfectly inside each corner joint. This allows longer tenons and provides a stronger glue bond. The lower rails are treated in the same way, but as they are located 75mm (3in) from the ends of the legs, no "relish" is required.

5 Begin assembling the components by gluing and clamping the legs and rails together in pairs. Set up two sash cramps (clamps) on the workbench to tighten the joints of each sub-assembly. Note the small offcuts (scraps) of wood that protect the soft timber from bruising under the cramp heads.

6 Complete the construction with the legs inverted on a flat surface to keep the unit square. Slide the two leg assemblies on to the remaining rails, remembering to glue the mating surfaces of the mitred tenons where they meet inside each leg.

7 Apply sash cramps and lock the tenons in place with 38mm (1½in) lost-head nails at the inner corners of the legs. Punch the nail heads just below the surface. Check that the assembly is square, wipe off excess glue and allow to dry overnight.

8 Cut four shelf support battens from 19 x 19mm (¾ x ¾in) softwood and screw them to the lower rails as shown. Set them down from the top of the rails by the thickness of the shelf and clamp in place while attaching.

9 Cut the shelf material to size from 75 x 12mm (3 x ½in) tongued-and-grooved cladding boards. You will need to plane down the end boards to achieve the correct width for the shelf. Making it in boards allows you to fit each side in turn and cut notches to clear the legs.

10 Assemble the shelf. The boards can be sprung into place by fitting the last tongue into its groove and pushing firmly downward. The result is a perfectly fitting, strong assembly with no gaps.

11 If you want to make the optional drawer, refer to the diagram for details of its construction. Cut four lengths of 12mm (½in) plywood, 90mm (3½in) wide, for the drawer ends and sides. Then use a router with a 6mm (¼in) bit to groove them for the bottom panel. Fit centre-points to mark the ends for the dowel joints.

12 Screw the bearers for the drawer runners to the legs, using a small spacing block to position them. For 25 x 12mm (1 x ½in) runners, you should leave a gap of about 30mm (1⅛in). Drill the correct size clearance holes for the screws, countersinking the heads, to prevent the ends of the runners from splitting.

13 Finish assembling the draw, then fit the top runners to it, flush with the top edges of the drawer tray, and offer it up to the block to check for smooth operation. Then add the lower runners – these should be 25mm (1in) apart. The assembly is now ready for sanding and painting with the finish of your choice. Finally attach a handle to the drawer front.

14 The top of the block is made by laminating small components of maple together to make a herringbone pattern. All the components were prepared from quarter-sawn stock, the growth rings running vertically to the face of the block. To maintain the geometry of the design, the external size is determined by the building jig, made from straight lengths of maple screwed to a baseboard. Make sure the corners are perfectly square.

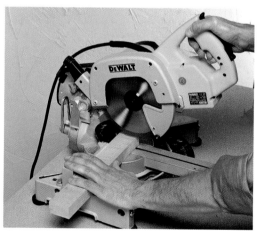

15 To make the joints as accurate as possible, each piece is fitted individually before laminating. Cut the first piece slightly oversize and use a small offcut (scrap) to mark its exact length. The blocks are simply butt-jointed, so accuracy is essential. Each piece should be a sliding fit in the jig.

16 A powered crosscut saw, is a quick means of cutting accurate square ends on each component. This machine can remove the smallest sliver of wood, so cut outside the line initially and slide the work fractionally toward the blade to make a second, or even third, cut at the exact length.

**17** Continue working around the jig in a clockwise direction, numbering each piece to avoid confusion later when you start to laminate the blocks into position. Working from the outside toward the centre in this way ensures that no cumulative discrepancies occur in the overall size of the block and keeps it all square.

**18** The centre of the block is formed by four triangular pieces. Mark the mitres with a mitre square and a sharp scribing knife for accuracy. The final central piece should be a really tight fit to lock everything together.

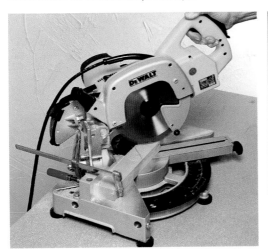

**19** Making a mitre cut on a small length of wood will be safer if it is clamped to the saw table. Make the first cut, swing the saw body through ninety degrees, slide the wood along to align it, clamp it in position and make the second cut.

**20** With all the components now fitted and numbered, start laminating, again from the outside toward the centre. Apply a thin film of glue to each piece and assemble the block, making sure that each piece is put into its correct place.

21 Tap the final piece of timber into position and wipe the excess glue from the surface with a damp cloth. If any hairline gaps remain, work some more glue into them and then give the piece a final wipe.

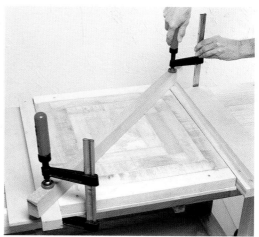

22 Tap the individual blocks firmly on to the baseboard and clamp a stout, straight-edged batten over the assembly to keep it flat as it dries. It is important to make sure the workbench underneath the board is also completely flat.

23 After at least 12 hours, remove the board from the jig and sand it down. Maple is so hard that a belt sander will probably be needed to create a flush surface, followed by a small orbital sander for a fine, smooth finish.

24 Place the top of the laminated block face-down on the workbench, align and position the leg assembly and attach the top with the corner brackets and round-head wood screws to create a sturdy fixing.

# BOOKCASE

THIS BOOKCASE HAS A TOUCH OF THE CLASSICAL. With its solid proportions, clean-cut mouldings and fluted columns, this bookcase will make a stylish addition to any part of the home. The basic carcass is a straightforward box made of veneered MDF (medium-density fibreboard), with solid wood trim providing the extra detail. The example shown here was made from American cherry wood, left in its natural colour for the interior, but stained and polished on the outside to bring out the deep, rich figure of the grain.

## Construction

The versatility of a router comes into its own for mounting the bookcase strip and fashioning the columns and mouldings, as well as making quick work of the carcass. The three types of router cutter illustrated below were used for this example, but you can vary the style of decorative detail.

**Fig. 213.2 Router cutters**

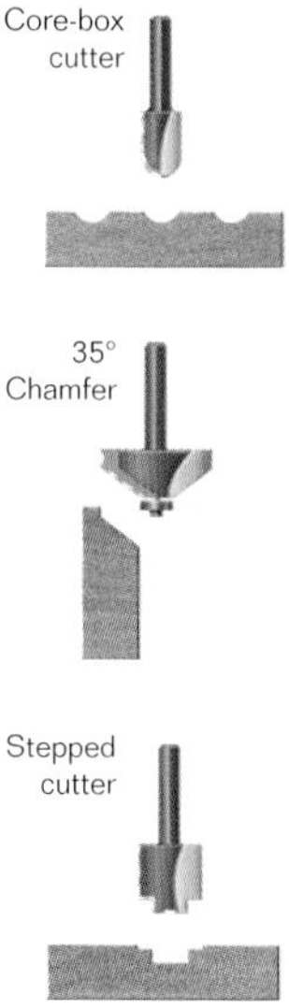

Core-box
cutter

35°
Chamfer

Stepped
cutter

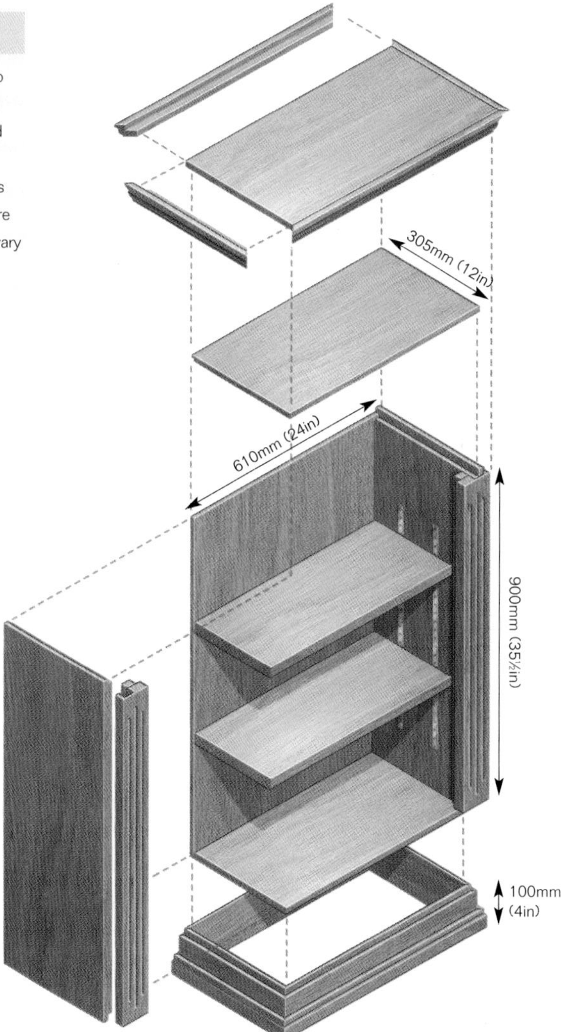

## Materials

- 2.45 x 1m (8 x 3ft) of 12mm (½in) veneered MDF (medium-density fibreboard) for the carcass
- 1250 x 250mm (48 x 10in) of 25mm (1in) veneered MDF for the shelves
- 2.1m (7ft) of 100 x 25mm (4 x 1in) hardwood for the plinth
- 2.1m (7ft) of 50 x 19mm (2 x ¾in) hardwood for the bottom mouldings
- 2.1m (7ft) of 25 x 25mm (1 x 1in) hardwood for the top mouldings
- 1.8m (6ft) of 75 x 25mm (3 x 1in) hardwood for the columns
- 1.8m (6ft) of 19 x 19mm (¾ x ¾in) hardwood for the battens
- 1.2m (4ft) of 25 x 10mm (1 x ⅜in) hardwood for the shelf trim
- 2.45m (8ft) of brass bookcase strip and shelf clips
- Small countersunk brass screws
- Biscuits for jointing
- PVA wood glue

305mm (12in)

610mm (24in)

900mm (35½in)

100mm
(4in)

**Fig. 213.1 Bookcase**

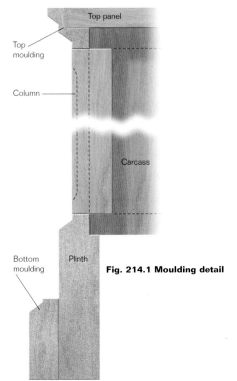

**Fig. 214.1 Moulding detail**

Labels: Top panel, Top moulding, Column, Carcass, Bottom moulding, Plinth

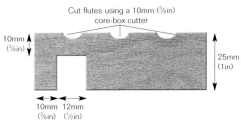

Cut flutes using a 10mm (⅜in) core-box cutter

10mm (⅜in)

25mm (1in)

10mm (⅜in)   12mm (½in)

**Fig. 214.2 Column detail**

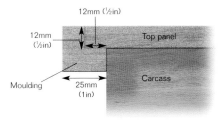

12mm (½in)

12mm (½in)

Top panel

Moulding

25mm (1in)

Carcass

**Fig. 214.3 Top moulding detail**

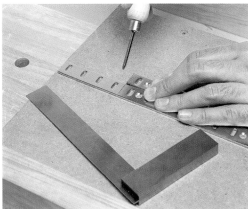

1 The carcass for the bookcase is easily made. Cut the main components to size from the sheet of veneered MDF (medium-density fibreboard), and form edge rebates (rabbets) in the two sides to receive the ends and back panel. Clean them up with a sanding block, taking care not to damage the delicate veneer facing.

2 Before assembling the box, the recessed bookcase strips should be fitted to the sides. Cut the brass strip into four lengths, making sure that the slots for the shelf clips will align correctly. If the strips are not identical, the shelves will not sit level. The best course is to cut one strip to size and use it as a pattern for the others.

3 Mark out the positions of the strips on each side with a carpenter's pencil, using a try square to locate them. For maximum stability, each strip should be set back from the edge of the shelf by approximately 38mm (1½in). The strips do not need to continue to the full height of the bookcase, unless you want a very shallow top shelf.

4 Rout the grooves for the inset strips, squaring the ends with a bevelled chisel. Two grooves are required for each strip – one should be equal in width to the strip itself, and another slightly deeper and wide enough to provide clearance for the hooks of the shelf clips. You can do this with two separate cutters, or invest in a special stepped cutter (shown in figure 213.2), which completes the operation in one pass.

5 It is a good idea to sand down the inner surfaces of all the panels at this stage, so that they are ready for finishing. Then fit the brass strips, using small countersunk brass screws. Make sure the slots are correctly aligned, and that the top end of each strip is fitted toward the top of the bookcase.

6 Glue and screw the carcass together, checking that it is square. Make sure that the screwheads are countersunk well below the surface. The design of the unit ensures that the screws along the edges will be concealed by the top and bottom mouldings. Leave to dry.

7 Cut four lengths of 100 x 25mm (4 x 1in) hardwood for the plinth and form a 12mm (½in) wide by 6mm (¼in) deep rebate (rabbet) along one edge of each to receive the bottom of the bookcase carcass. Mitre the ends and insert biscuits to reinforce and aid the alignment of the joints.

8 Glue the plinth together, strengthening the corners by adding small glued blocks. Wipe away any excess glue. Note that the internal dimensions of the rebate around the inner edge of the plinth should match the external size of the cabinet, which simply slots into position.

**9** Fit the plinth over the bottom of the cabinet and secure it with small wooden blocks and screws. There is no need to glue them, as the plinth will be removed later to add the decorative moulding before sanding and finishing. It needs to be fitted at this stage to assist in aligning the fluted columns.

**10** Make the columns according to the dimensions given in the diagram. Cut a 12mm (½in) housing in the back to locate each column on the front edges of the carcass, and use a core-box cutter to add the fluting to the front face (see figure 213.2). Use a small cylinder of sandpaper to remove any marks left by the cutter in the rounded flutes.

**11** Screw a 19mm (¾in) batten flush with the inner edge of the housing of each column to provide a secure attachment to the carcass without any visible fixings.

**12** Apply glue to the front edges of the bookcase and tap the columns into place. They should fit exactly between the top and bottom of the carcass, stiffening the sides and giving a solid, well-proportioned appearance to the whole assembly.

**13** Cut the panel for the top of the bookcase and glue on the edge profile. The latter is made from 25 x 25mm (1 x 1in) stock, rebated to suit the panel, as in figure 214.3. Mitre the ends and clamp around the edges, making sure that it is perfectly flush with the surface of the panel for a smooth finish.

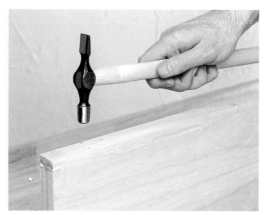

14 Check that the top panel is a good fit over the carcass – note how it locates over the top edges of the box, concealing the screws along the sides. Now you can add the moulding detail around the edges. Profile the top moulding using a 35 degree chamfer cutter (see figure 213.2). Sand, stain and polish the top and mouldings before finally attaching it to the carcass with screws from the inside. Use the same chamfer cutter to profile the plinth and bottom moulding.

15 Make two shelves for the unit, using 25mm (1in) board for extra strength. They should be slightly shorter than the internal width of the cabinet by about 1.5mm (1/16in), which will allow enough clearance for them to be tilted sideways for fitting. Glue and pin small strips of hardwood along the front edges to finish them off neatly.

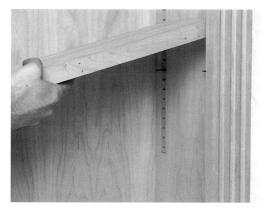

16 Insert the shelf clips into the recessed brass strips and fit the shelves.

### Practical tip

To avoid having to buy a small quantity of 25mm (1in) veneered board, you can use offcuts (scraps) from the sheet of 12mm (½in) material and laminate them together.

# CORNER CABINET

THIS ELEGANT CORNER CABINET, with its limed beech finish and patterned glass doors, would make an attractive feature in the bathroom. Of relatively small dimensions, it uses literally every corner of space to provide a versatile storage unit. The front of the cabinet projects just a few inches from the wall to break up the visual line of the corner.

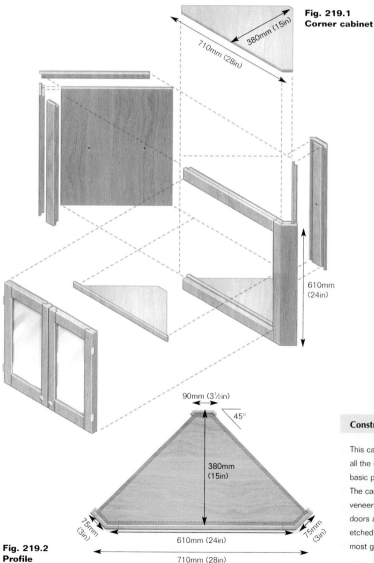

**Fig. 219.1
Corner cabinet**

380mm (15in)

710mm (28in)

610mm (24in)

90mm (3½in)

45°

380mm (15in)

610mm (24in)

75mm (3in)

75mm (3in)

710mm (28in)

**Fig. 219.2
Profile**

## Materials

All materials are hardwood, unless specified otherwise:

- 1.25m (48in) of 75 x 25mm (3 x 1in)
- 3.3m (10ft 10in) of 38 x 25mm (1½ x 1in)
- 2.45m (8ft) of 50 x 25mm (2 x 1in)
- 1.25m (48in) of 50 x 10mm (2 x ⅜in)
- 610mm (24in) of 90 x 25mm (3½ x 1in)
- 3m (10ft) of 12 x 12mm (½ x ½in) glazing bead
- 1.25 x 1.25m (48 x 48in) of 12mm (½in) veneered MDF (medium-density fibreboard)
- Biscuits for jointing
- PVA wood glue
- 25mm (1in) and 38mm (1½in) wood screws
- 25mm (1in) panel pins (brads)
- Patterned glass for glazed doors
- Shelf supports
- 4 brass hinges
- 2 magnetic catches
- 2 door knobs

## Construction

This cabinet is not as complex as it may appear – all the upright components are fitted around the basic profile, which determines the final shape. The carcass is made from 12mm (½in) ash-veneered MDF and solid beech was used for the doors and main frame members. Engraved or etched glass for the doors can be obtained from most glaziers, who will cut it to size.

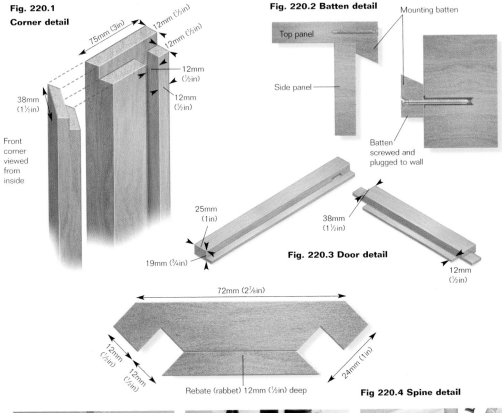

**Fig. 220.1**
**Corner detail**

75mm (3in)

12mm (½in)

12mm (½in)

12mm (½in)

12mm (½in)

38mm (1½in)

Front corner viewed from inside

**Fig. 220.2 Batten detail**

Mounting batten

Top panel

Side panel

Batten screwed and plugged to wall

25mm (1in)

38mm (1½in)

**Fig. 220.3 Door detail**

19mm (¾in)

12mm (½in)

72mm (2⅞in)

12mm (½in)

12mm (½in)

24mm (1in)

Rebate (rabbet) 12mm (½in) deep

**Fig 220.4 Spine detail**

1 Make a template for the basic profile, using the pattern shown in figure 219.2. The top and bottom panels, which determine the shape, are 12mm (½in) smaller all round than the external dimensions of the cabinet. Pin the template to the veneered board and cut out both panels with a jigsaw, making them slightly oversize.

2 Use a router fitted with a template cutter to finish the shape of the top and bottom panels. For the best visual effect, the grain direction of the veneer should run from side to side across the cabinet. The small pin-holes can be filled later with light-coloured wood stopping (wood filler).

3 Cut all the vertical members to the same overall length, and plane the edges of the front pieces of wood to an angle of 67.5 degrees from the outside face. When joined, these form the required internal angle of 135 degrees at the front corners.

4 All the vertical members need rebates (rabbets) at the ends for the top and bottom panels. In addition, rout 12mm (½in) housing grooves in the outer corner pieces to receive the side panels. Figure 220.1 provides a clear view of the corner detail.

5 Join the angled faces of the corner members together with biscuits. Set the angled fence of the biscuit jointer to 67.5 degrees. The biscuits not only strengthen the glued joints, but also serve to align the front edges and prevent the components from sliding apart when clamped together during the gluing process.

6 Use the bottom panel of the cabinet as a template for assembling the corner joint. Apply glue, insert the biscuits and slide the two parts together. Note how the housing groove for the side panel is aligned with the outside edge.

7 Cut the cross rails to fit between the corner uprights, rebate them to fit over the top and bottom panels and glue in place. Each is locked in position with a strip of 10mm (⅜in) hardwood that also acts as a stop for the doors. It keeps the front of the cabinet square, too.

8 Insert a side panel into the groove in one corner post, and align the top and bottom panels with a couple of 25mm (1in) panel pins (brads). If you keep the edges flush, the cabinet will automatically conform to the desired shape as it is assembled.

9 The rear spine member locks the side panels together and stiffens the whole structure. Cut its housing grooves according to the dimensions given in figure 220.4. Rebate (rabbet) the top and bottom, and slot into position. Add the second side by sliding it into place in its housing grooves in the front and back members.

10 With the second side panel in place, apply tension to the whole assembly with a pair of web cramps. These will tighten all the joints and pull the cabinet into shape. Insert more panel pins to hold the top and bottom panels in position. Check that the front is square and leave the cramps in tension as the glue dries.

11 Add short battens to the top and bottom edges of the side panels. Notch the ends of the battens to clear the corner posts, as shown, and, if wished, plane bevels on the upper pair to make a neat system for mounting the cabinet. Figure 220.2 shows how the cabinet can be simply lifted into place and hooked on to a matching pair of battens screwed to the wall.

12 Use what remains of the veneered material to make a triangular shelf for the cabinet. Set it back by 50mm (2in) from the front frame, which will allow it to be tilted and offered into position. Glue and pin a strip of wood along the front of the shelf to trim the edge.

13 To make the doors, use 38mm (1½in) stock for the stiles, and 50mm (2in) for the horizontal rails. Set out and cut the 25 x 10mm (1 x ⅜in) mortises as shown, then form 19mm (¾in) deep by 12mm (½in) wide rebates in the rear faces for the glass and beads.

**14** Cut the matching tenons and rebate the rails in the same way. Note that the 25mm (1in) tenons have unequal stepped shoulders to accommodate the rebates in the stiles. Pare down to fit with a bevelled chisel. See figure 220.3.

**15** Glue and assemble the two doors, clamping them together flat on the bench. The joints are so small that no wedges should be required to secure the tenons if they are a good fit. When the glue has dried, remove the projecting horns with a small tenon saw.

**16** Measure the size of glass required for the doors and order the two panes from your local supplier. If using decorative etched glass, be sure to mention that they must be a matched pair with symmetrical patterns. Cut the glazing bead into lengths to hold the glass in place, but hang and fit the doors before inserting the glass.

**17** Mount the brass hinges on the doors, in line with the inner edges of the rails. The offset pins make it easy to locate the hinges accurately.

**Practical tip**

White liming wax accentuates the delicate flecked figure of the beech wood, preserves its pale colour and protects it from the humid conditions of a bathroom.

**18** These miniature magnetic catches are very discreet and ideal for lightweight doors of this type. Each magnetic barrel is simply inserted into a hole drilled in the bottom rail of the frame. The small striking plate is tapped into position in the end of the door stile.

**19** Finally, add two matching knobs to the doors. Sand down and apply a coat of sealer, then liming wax or your chosen finish, before fitting the glass into the doors. Cut small glazing beads and fit using small panel pins, taking care to protect the glass as you do so.

# Dining Table

A COMPACT DINING TABLE OF striking appearance, this unique design is a composition of great subtlety and balance. The top displays the rustic quality of elm, with its swirling grain pattern and tight knot clusters. The supporting framework is made of straight-grained teak. Clear carnauba wax is the only finish required to bring out the character of the wood.

## Materials

- 4.6m (15ft) of 230 x 25mm (9 x 1in) hardwood for the top
- 3m (10ft) of 75 x 75mm (3 x 3in) hardwood for the legs
- 2.1m (7ft) of 75 x 25mm (3 x 1in) hardwood for the rails
- 4m (13ft) of 50 x 25mm (2 x 1in) hardwood for the top frame
- PVA wood glue

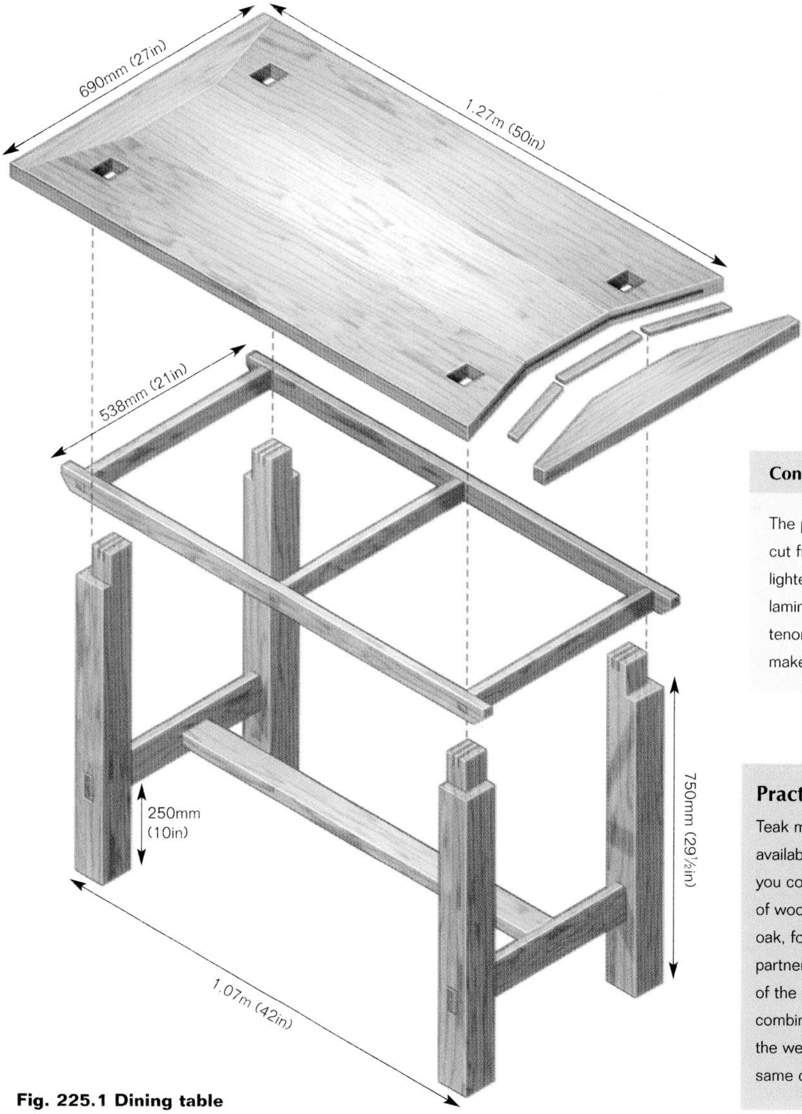

690mm (27in)

1.27m (50in)

538mm (21in)

250mm (10in)

750mm (29½in)

1.07m (42in)

**Fig. 225.1 Dining table**

## Construction

The pieces for the table top are cut from two elm boards, one of lighter tone than the other, neatly laminated together. The legs are tenoned through the table top to make a bold geometrical pattern.

## Practical tip

Teak may not always be readily available, nor affordable, in which case you could substitute a different type of wood of contrasting colour – dark oak, for example, makes a natural partner for elm. The attractiveness of the design is derived from the combination of the two species. Even the wedges for the tenons use the same contrast to highlight the effect.

**Fig. 226.1 Top detail**

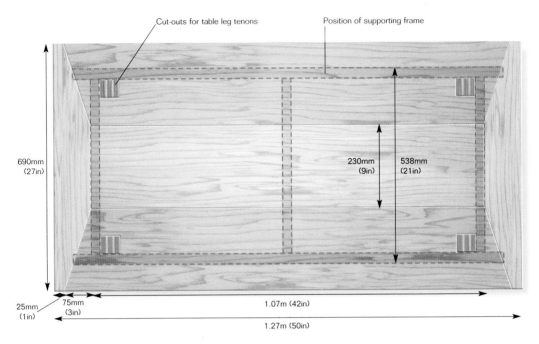

Cut-outs for table leg tenons

Position of supporting frame

690mm (27in)

230mm (9in)

538mm (21in)

25mm (1in)

75mm (3in)

1.07m (42in)

1.27m (50in)

1 The "fishtail" design of the table top is not only attractive, but also serves to lock the ends of the boards together and keep the top flat. The five components are edge-jointed, using loose tongues made of 6mm (¼in) hardwood offcuts (scraps). Cut the three main boards to the sizes shown in figure 226.1 above.

2 It is best to laminate the top in two separate stages. First glue and clamp the three long boards together, making sure that the angled ends are aligned correctly. Use two straight-edged battens (cleats) to clamp assembly flat on the bench while the glue dries.

3 Make an angled template as an aid to shaping the end sections. Pare down the edges if necessary to accommodate any discrepancy in the assembly. Position the template so that the most suitable and attractive portions of wood will be used to complete the table top. Mark out the end pieces and cut them to size.

4 Plane the edges of the end pieces so that they are absolutely square, and pare them down carefully to fit the table top. When they fit perfectly, rout the 6mm (¼in) grooves for the loose tongues. Stop the grooves short of the ends by 25mm (1in).

5 Apply glue, insert the hardwood tongues in the grooves and clamp the ends in place. Note how the grooves stop short of the ends to avoid weakening the corners. Set the top aside for the glue to dry while you work on the table frame and legs. Use weights or cramps to keep it as flat as possible.

6 Make the legs in pairs to suit each end of the table. Clamp each pair together, as shown, and set out the mortises for the lower rails. The mortises are sized at 68 x 19mm (2¾ x ¾in). This is slightly smaller than the rails, leaving a 3mm (⅛in) shoulder around each tenon.

7 At the outer face of each table leg, angle the sides of the mortise to receive the locking wedges. As the wedges have a decorative aspect, they can be generous in size, adding 6mm (¼in) to each end of the mortise.

8 Pare the tenons down to a good fit and dry assemble the legs, making sure that the shoulders sit squarely. Then set out the mortises for the horizontal stretcher bar in the centres of the rails.

9 The mortises for the stretcher are the same size as those for the rails, allowing a similar amount for the wedges. Good accurate joints are required for this assembly to ensure a rigid base for the table.

10 Assemble the stretcher to the rails and set aside. Then make the supporting frame for the top. Mark up all the components carefully to avoid confusion at the construction stage – each leg must be fitted individually to the table top.

11 The supporting frame is mortised and tenoned together, having three cross rails to span the laminated top and hold it flat, so make absolutely sure that the frame is not twisted. No wedges are used for these smaller tenons – they are simply glued and clamped together.

12 The longitudinal bearers of the frame extend beyond the outer cross rails, to provide full support for the table ends. Cut small bevels on the ends of each bearer to remove the bottom corners. Then glue and clamp the frame together, making sure that it is square.

13 The tenon at the top of each leg measures 50 x 50mm (2 x 2in) in section, being bare-faced on the inner edge. The shoulders locate under the supporting frame members. Add the thickness of the table top to the depth of the frame members to establish the length of the tenons.

14 Centralize the assembled supporting frame on the underside of the table top. Attach it in position with a couple of screws at each corner, then place each leg in turn in its corner of the frame as shown. Mark the positions of the mortises on the top, then remove the frame, marking it first so that you can replace it in the same position.

**15** Use a try square to transfer the mortise positions to the upper face of the top and scribe around the edges of the cut-outs. Use a spade bit or auger mounted in a drill to remove the bulk of the waste, then pare down the sides so that the tenons are a sliding fit.

**16** Clamp each leg upright and cut two small slots in the top of the tenon for the wedges. The slots should be no more than 25mm (1in) deep – the thickness of the table top – in order to avoid weakening the tenons more than necessarily.

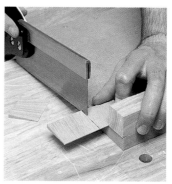

**17** Fashion a wedge-shaped section of wood from an offcut (scrap) of the table top material, using a bandsaw or circular saw to achieve a sharp feather edge. Note the grain direction. Using a hand saw, cut the strip into eight 50mm (2in) wedges.

**18** Make 12 smaller wedges to fit the cross rail and stretcher tenons in the same way. Glue each pair of legs and corresponding cross rail in turn, keeping them flat and free from any twisting. Clamp them so that the assembly is square, insert the small wedges and tap them in.

**19** Stand the two ends upright on a flat surface. Slip the support frame over the tops of the legs to position them correctly, then insert the connecting stretcher between the rails. Place the table top over the tenons, square up the legs and tap in the wedges. Leave both sections to dry before proceeding to the next step. Leave the top in position to keep the assembly square while the glue dries, then remove it for the final attachment.

**20** Apply glue to the tenons at the tops of the legs, replace the table top and hammer in the wedges, using a small block of wood to protect the ends and keep them straight. Note the direction of the slots in the tenons – this prevents the wedges from applying pressure to the longitudinal grain of the table top. When the glue is dry, cut the excess from the wedges and sand the tops of the legs flush with the surface.

# SETTLE

"SETTLE" IS AN OLD NAME for a wooden seat with a high back and raised arm rests. This version reflects the early origins of the concept by using wedged-through tenons, one of the earliest carpentry techniques, dating from medieval times. It departs from tradition, however, in the gently curved profile of the ends, which give a more contemporary feel to the whole design. The example shown was made from wide boards of sweet chestnut, a much neglected wood often mistaken for oak, with its attractive grain figure and delicate pale brown colour.

## Materials

- 3.3m (11ft) of 305 x 2 mm (12 x 1in) hardwood for the ends
- 3.3m (11ft) of 150 x 25mm (6 x 1in) hardwood for the seat
- 4.9m (16ft) of 125 x 25mm (5 x 1in) hardwood for the back and arm rests
- 1m (3ft) of 50 x 25mm (2 x 1 in) softwood batten for the seat braces
- 1,100 x 610mm (43 x 24in) of 6mm (¼in) plywood or MDF (medium-density fibreboard) for the template
- PVA wood glue
- 8mm (⅜in) wooden dowels

## Practical tip

Position the seat slightly lower if you want to add an upholstered cushion, maintaining the overall height above the floor of 460mm (18in).

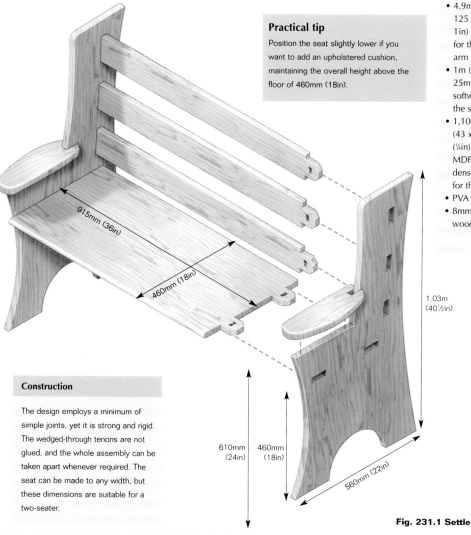

915mm (36in)

460mm (18in)

1.03m (40½in)

610mm (24in)   460mm (18in)   560mm (22in)

**Fig. 231.1 Settle**

## Construction

The design employs a minimum of simple joints, yet it is strong and rigid. The wedged-through tenons are not glued, and the whole assembly can be taken apart whenever required. The seat can be made to any width, but these dimensions are suitable for a two-seater.

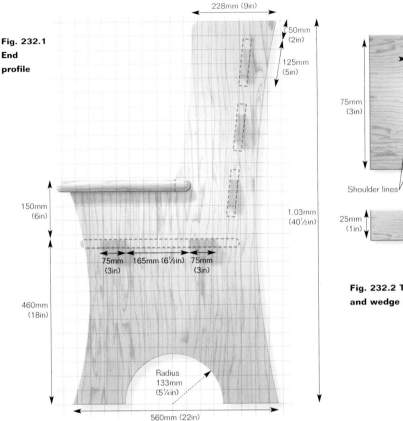

**Fig. 232.1**
**End**
**profile**

228mm (9in)

50mm (2in)

125mm (5in)

1.03mm (40½in)

150mm (6in)

75mm (3in)   165mm (6½in)   75mm (3in)

460mm (18in)

Radius 133mm (5¼in)

560mm (22in)

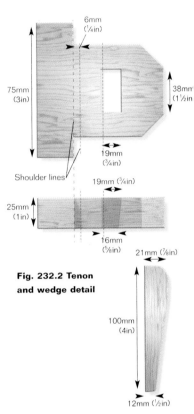

6mm (¼in)

75mm (3in)

38mm (1½in)

19mm (¾in)

Shoulder lines

19mm (¾in)

25mm (1in)

16mm (⅝in)

21mm (⅞in)

**Fig. 232.2 Tenon and wedge detail**

100mm (4in)

12mm (½in)

1 Make a full-sized template for the end profile from 6mm (¼in) plywood or MDF. Use the scale drawing provided (figure 232.1), plotting the outline on a scaled-up grid to transfer the shape accurately. Mark and cut out the mortise positions in the template at the same time.

2 Begin by edge jointing all the components for the seat and the ends. Rout grooves in the edges of the boards and clamp them together with loose tongues for extra strength. Note the straight batten clamped over the work to keep it flat as the sash cramps are tightened.

3 The arm rests are laminated from a double thickness of wood. Make a template of suitable shape, cutting a 50 x 25mm (2 x 1in) locating slot in it. Cut out and shape four pieces, using a router fitted with a follower cutter. Square off the ends of the locating slots.

4 Glue the arm rest pairs together and set aside for the glue to dry before shaping. Note the small block of wood inserted into the slot to keep the two pieces aligned. Remove the excess glue, sand smooth and round off the edges.

5 Cut the ends roughly to shape, slightly oversize, and pin the template to each in turn. Mark through the template to transfer the positions of the cut-outs for the tenons on to the workpiece so that both ends are identical.

6 Use a router fitted with a follower cutter to trim the ends to their final shape. The bearing on the end of the cutter follows the curved template beneath the work, which should be clamped firmly to the bench.

7 To make the cut-outs, drill a hole at each end of the slot and join them with a jigsaw to remove the waste. Cut just inside the line. Pin the template to the reverse of the work and then use the router to trim the slot to size, as in the previous step.

8 Square the ends of each slot with a bevelled chisel. A good tight fit to suit the thickness of the tenons will ensure a rigid construction when the latter are wedged in place. Ease the slots with a piece of sandpaper and a wooden block of the right size until a good sliding fit is achieved.

9 The seat is housed in a groove for maximum support. Clamp a straightedge to the inner face of each end to guide the router, aligning the groove exactly with the slots. A depth of 6mm (¼in) is sufficient for the housing. When the wedges on the seat are drawn up tight, the seat should fit securely in the housings.

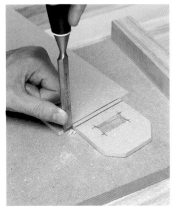

**10** Rout a similar 6mm (¼in) deep groove in the underside of each armrest to fit over the ends. Square off the end of the groove with a chisel to suit the exact length of the side location. Then radius the edges and sand smooth.

**11** Drill two holes for 8mm (⁵⁄₁₆in) dowels in the edge of each end that supports the arm rest. Insert the dowel centre-points and slot the arm rest over the end piece, pressing down to mark the corresponding hole positions on the underside of the arm rest. Drill the holes.

**12** Make a template for the tenons, using the diagram (figure 232.2) as a guide. Note the alternative shoulder lines that allow the same template to be used for both seat and back rails, the former being longer by 6mm (¼in). For the rails, the shoulders are flush to the inside face of the sides.

**13** Cut the tenons on the ends of the back rails, and mark out the small slots for the wedges. Set the shoulder lines 915mm (36in) apart on each rail to the internal width of the seat. Trim the corners of the tenons, as shown, and sand them smooth.

**14** Use the same template to mark out the tenons on the seat, but note how the shoulders are set forward by 6mm (¼in) to allow for the housing groove that receives the seat. Scribe along the shoulder lines and cut the ends carefully to shape with a jigsaw,

**15** Drill out the slots for the wedges and remove the waste. Make each slot 16mm (⅝in) wide, then use a chisel to form the small bevel shown in the diagram. Mark the bevel on the side of the tenon as a guide to keep the chisel at the correct angle.

**16** Make ten wedges from offcuts (scraps) of wood, following the dimensions given. The angle of each wedge should fit the slot in its tenon exactly. Shape one wedge first, check for accuracy, then use it as a pattern for the others.

**17** Before assembly, glue and screw two 50 x 25mm (2 x 1in) battens to the underside of the seat to stiffen it and help prevent any deformation of the edge-jointed sections. The battens are 25mm (1in) shorter than the width of the seat at each end.

**18** Assemble the settle, easing each tenon into its slot and inserting the wedges temporarily to hold it together while you add the components. An assistant is useful at this stage to support the other end of the seat and rails.

**19** Insert the rails with the slots facing forward, as shown, and tap all the wedges home. Because the slots are inset slightly from the outer faces of the seat ends, the wedging action will tighten the whole assembly until it is completely rigid.

**20** Finally, attach the arm rests, locating them with the dowels and tapping them firmly into place. Use a block of scrap wood to protect the surface.

# CONSERVATORY BENCH

THIS PROJECT WOULD LOOK PERFECTLY AT HOME in a conservatory or garden room. Its slatted construction allows plenty of light to pass through and around it, while keeping the weight down so that it is easily moved. For all that, it is remarkably strong, and being of generous length, it could even be used as a day bed if provided with a few loose cushions. It is made of iroko, a naturally hard and durable wood, so it would be equally suitable for use outdoors as a garden bench during the summer.

### Materials

- 3.6m (12ft) of 50 x 50mm (2 x 2in) hardwood for the legs
- 10.7m (35ft) of 75 x 22mm (3 x ⅞in) hardwood for the rails
- 2.45m (8ft) of 65 x 19mm (2½ x ¾in) hardwood for the large slats
- 14.7m (48ft) of 19 x 19mm (¾ x ¾in) hardwood for the small slats
- 4m (13ft) of 38 x 25mm (1½ x 1in) hardwood for the seat battens
- 1.4m x 900mm (55 x 35in) of 12mm (½in) birch plywood for the seat
- 8 100mm (4in) bolts and cross-dowels
- PVA wood glue
- 8mm (⁵⁄₁₆in) wooden dowels
- 25mm (1in) and 38mm (1½in) wood screws

**Fig. 237.1 Conservatory bench**

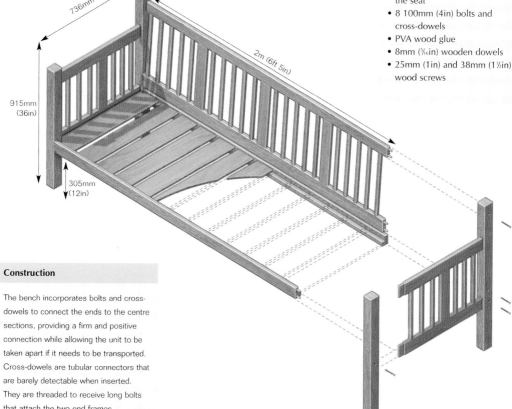

736mm (29in)

915mm (36in)

305mm (12in)

2m (6ft 5in)

### Construction

The bench incorporates bolts and cross-dowels to connect the ends to the centre sections, providing a firm and positive connection while allowing the unit to be taken apart if it needs to be transported. Cross-dowels are tubular connectors that are barely detectable when inserted. They are threaded to receive long bolts that attach the two end frames.

**Fig. 238.1 End profile**

50mm (2in)

50mm (2in)

75mm (3in)

482mm (19in)

915mm (36in)

25mm (1in)

75mm (3in)

305mm (12in)

19mm (¾in)  65mm (2½in)  19mm (¾in)

50mm (2in)  50mm (2in)

736mm (29in)

1 Make the end frames first. Cut the legs to length, and scribe 12mm (½in) wide mortises with a mortise gauge as shown. Do this with the front and back legs clamped together, flush at the bottom. The diagram (figure 238.1) gives the dimensions required to set out the end frames.

2 Cut the mortises 32mm (1¼in) deep to leave enough room for the connecting bolts. Pare the ends and sides of each mortise true and square, making sure that the bottom is free of obstructions.

3 Set out the tenons on the cross rails, then clamp the rails together in pairs to mark out the mortises for the vertical slats. The wider, central slat is positioned first, then the smaller slats are placed at equal intervals along the rail.

4 Cut the tenons on the rails, and pare down with a shoulder plane for a good square fit in the mortises. Note that the shoulders only run along the wide faces of each rail. The mortise is the full height of the rail in this case.

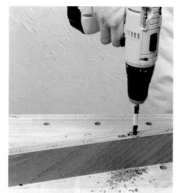

5 Cut all the mortises in the rails. You can drill to a depth of 32mm (1¼in) and chisel them out, as shown, but there are a lot of them, so if you have a drill stand or, even better, a mortise attachment for a power drill, it's well worth setting up to do this.

6 Cut the tenons on all the slats and pare them to fit, clamping them together so that you can true up (square) all the shoulders in one operation. This ensures that all will be drawn up tight when the frame is glued together.

7 Before assembling the frame, sand all the surfaces that will be difficult to clean up later – it saves a lot of time and trouble.

**Practical tip**

This project is made up in stages from several sub-assemblies. As each one is completed it can be easier to finish and apply a coat of sealer before constructing the finished bench.

8 Glue all the slats and fit them to the rails to make a sub-assembly that can be connected to the legs in one operation. It should not be necessary to wait for the glue to dry in this instance; the assembly should be rigid enough to proceed to the next step.

9 Clamp each frame together with a pair of sash cramps, keeping them flat on the bench to prevent any twisting. Wipe off any excess glue and continue with the slatted back section of the bench while the glue dries. Lay one frame on top of the other to make sure they are identical in size.

10 Clamp the bottom rail in a vice and insert all the vertical slats. If you have worked accurately and methodically, all the narrow slats and all the wider slats should be interchangeable. Double check each one before applying glue, however, in case it should need easing slightly.

11 Attach the top rail, starting at one end of the assembly and then gradually working your way along. You will find it very useful to have an assistant support the free end. Tap the rail into place with a rubber mallet, locating all the slats before applying the cramps. Make sure the ends are aligned and the assembly is square, and leave to dry.

12 Mark the positions of the connecting bolts and dowels on the inner faces of the end frames. Note that the back is inclined outward at the top to provide a more comfortable seating position. The 50mm (2in) legs allow an angle of about 3 degrees within their width, which makes all the difference. Use a bevel gauge to set out the positions of the back rails.

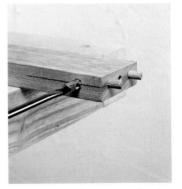

13 Each end of each rail is fitted with two 8mm (5/16in) diameter wooden dowels to locate it accurately and prevent it from twisting when the bolt is tightened. The central hole is drilled to suit the diameter of the bolt. Use centre-points to mark the hole positions on each rail – note the block of scrap wood clamped to the bench to hold the rail square.

14 Clamp the rails horizontally to drill the holes in the ends. The holes for the connecting bolts should be drilled to a full 75mm (3in) depth to allow plenty of clearance. Get someone to help you by standing to one side to check that your drill bit is truly horizontal.

15 Drill a hole for the cross-dowel, intersecting the bolt hole, and insert the cross-dowel from beneath the rail. Note the slot in the end of the dowel, which is used to align the hole to receive the bolt. When the slot is parallel to the sides of the rail, the bolt should enter the dowel easily.

**16** Countersink the holes for the bolts in the outer faces of the legs so that the heads sit just below the surface. Align the wooden dowels, tap the end frames into place and tighten the bolts with the key provided. The result is a discreet and immensely strong connection.

**17** Cut two battens to the full length of the front and back rails, and screw them in place to support the seat. The seat can be made of any suitable sheet material – in this case, 12mm (½in) plywood strips were used to provide a degree of flexibility.

**18** The two endmost strips should be notched to fit around the legs. Note that the top edges of the plywood have been radiused with a rounding-over cutter to prevent splinters from catching on the upholstered seat cushions. Sand all the strips smooth before fixing.

**19** Screw the plywood strips to the battens, using a block of wood to ensure regular spacing. Make sure that the screw heads are countersunk well to prevent them from snagging on the cushion material.

# KITCHEN BASE UNIT

A FITTED KITCHEN DEPENDS ON a series of base units, built to standard sizes, to support a work counter and provide storage space. The easy option is to buy ready-made units in flat-pack form for self-assembly. Although economical, their main disadvantage is that the panels are made of chipboard or similar man-made materials, which are not durable. This project shows how to make your own units in solid timber (lumber), which will last longer and be more attractive. This example was made from good-quality pine, varnished to give a waterproof, easy-clean finish.

## Materials

- 3.8m (12ft 6in) of 75 x 25mm (3 x 1in) softwood for the door and draw front
- 3m (10ft) of 90 x 10mm (3½ x ⅜in) tongued-and-grooved cladding boards for the door
- 2.1m (7ft) of 100 x 25mm (4 x 1in) softwood for the drawer
- 6mm (¼in) plywood for the drawer bottom
- 5.2m (17ft) of 75 x 25mm (3 x 1in) softwood for the sides
- 5.2m (17ft) of 90 x 10mm (3½ x ⅜in) tongued-and-grooved cladding boards for the side panels
- 2.2m (7ft 3in) of 100 x 25mm (4 x 1in) softwood for the plinth
- 1.25m (48in) of 50 x 25mm (2 x 1in) softwood for the rails
- 610mm (24in) of 50 x 19mm (2 x ¾in) softwood for the bottom panel trim
- 610 x 500mm (24 x 20in) of 19mm (¾in) MDF (medium-density fibreboard) for the bottom panel
- 760 x 610mm (30 x 24in) of 6mm (¼in) MDF for the back panel
- 8 bolts and cross-dowels
- 6mm (¼in) dowels
- 2 drawer runners
- 2 handles
- 2 concealed hinges
- PVA wood glue
- Panel pins (brads)
- Wooden or plastic joint blocks

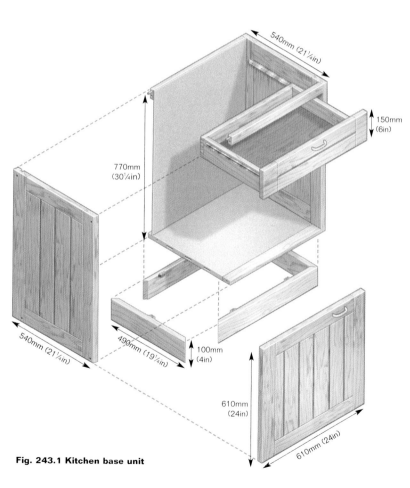

540mm (21¼in)

150mm (6in)

770mm (30¼in)

540mm (21¼in)

490mm (19¼in)

100mm (4in)

610mm (24in)

610mm (24in)

**Fig. 243.1 Kitchen base unit**

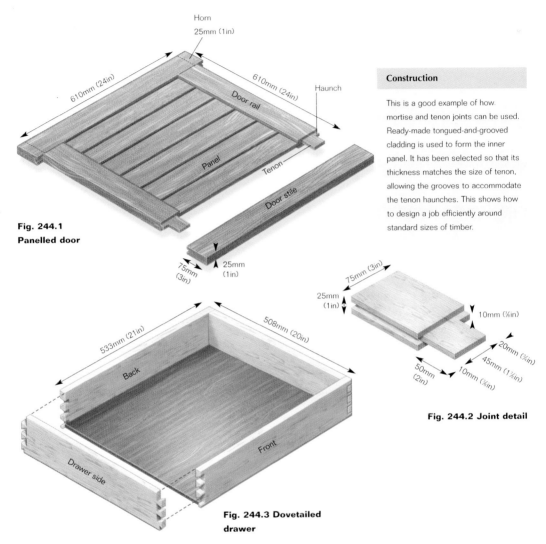

**Fig. 244.1**
**Panelled door**

Horn
25mm (1in)

610mm (24in)

Door rail

610mm (24in)

Haunch

Panel

Tenon

Door stile

75mm (3in)

25mm (1in)

## Construction

This is a good example of how mortise and tenon joints can be used. Ready-made tongued-and-grooved cladding is used to form the inner panel. It has been selected so that its thickness matches the size of tenon, allowing the grooves to accommodate the tenon haunches. This shows how to design a job efficiently around standard sizes of timber.

**Fig. 244.2 Joint detail**

75mm (3in)

25mm (1in)

10mm (⅜in)

20mm (⅞in)

45mm (1¾in)

50mm (2in)

10mm (⅜in)

**Fig. 244.3 Dovetailed drawer**

533mm (21in)

508mm (20in)

Back

Front

Drawer side

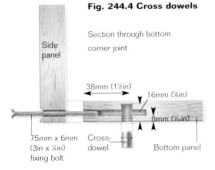

**Fig. 244.4 Cross dowels**

Side panel

Section through bottom corner joint

38mm (1½in)

16mm (⅝in)

8mm (⅜in)

75mm x 6mm (3in x ¼in) fixing bolt

Cross-dowel

Bottom panel

## Construction

The rails and panels are connected with the same type of knock-down fitting as found in professionally made units, simplifying accurate assembly and holding the unit square and rigid, even though no glue is used. These small cross-dowel fittings (see figure 244.4) are available from hardware suppliers.

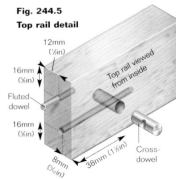

**Fig. 244.5**
**Top rail detail**

12mm (½in)

16mm (⅝in)

Fluted dowel

16mm (⅝in)

Top rail viewed from inside

8mm (⅜in)

38mm (1½in)

Cross-dowel

## Making the cabinet door

1 Set out the positions for the mortises on the door stiles, clamping them together for accuracy. Note how the stiles are left long at this stage. The extra 25mm (1in) at each end is called the horn.

2 Set the mortise gauge to the thickness of the panelling, which will also determine the size of the tenons. Scribe all along the inner face of each stile to mark out the groove and mortises in one operation.

3 Cut the mortises at each end of the stiles, but before cutting the tenons, use a plough (bullnose) plane to form the grooves 10mm (⅜in) deep. Check the panelling for a good fit before proceeding.

4 Cut the tenons on the rails, and form the haunches as shown. The depth of each haunch should match the depth of the grooves in the stiles – 10mm (⅜in) in this case.

5 Form the grooves in the rails to the same depth as those in the stiles. Dry fit the door together and pare the tenons for a snug joint.

6 Cut the strips of wood panelling to length, tap them together and square up with a try (cominbation) square. Trim the edges flush with a block plane and number the strips.

7 Trim the width of the panel to suit the door size. Measure out from the centre and mark the outer strips accordingly. This makes the layout of the panel symmetrical.

8 Remove waste with a ripsaw or jigsaw. Use a bench plane to trim the edges of the two strips to their finished width. Leave an extra 10mm (⅜in) to fit into the grooves in the stiles.

9 Apply wood glue to the joints of one stile, insert both rails and carefully slide the panelling into place. The panelling itself is not glued, allowing each strip to expand or contract slightly without distorting the panel.

10 Gently tap the remaining stile into place and clamp the assembly on a flat surface. The horn at the end of the stile is clearly visible; it can be cut off when the glue is dry.

## Making the drawer

1 When working in soft-wood, a shallower angle is required for the dovetails to ensure sufficient strength. An angle of about 10 degrees (pitch of 1:6) works well – draw up a simple scale on a piece of scrap wood to set the bevel gauge, and keep it safe for future use.

2 Mark the top face and edge of each drawer side and set out the tails. Note how the standard dovetail profile has to be altered to allow for a rebate (rabbet) for the bottom panel. Only the lower dovetail has a 12mm (½in) haunch that enters the rebate in the drawer front.

3 Cut out the tails and use a small bevelled chisel to pare down to the shoulder line. Mark the position of the bottom panel's rebate along the inner edge of each drawer side.

4 Apply chalk to the ends of the drawer back and front, align the sides and mark out the pins. The bottom pin must be cut short to accommodate the haunch on the dovetail. Here, the bottom rebate is being marked to suit.

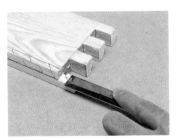

5 Cut out the pins, paring the bottom pin to suit the rebate depth.

6 Use a plough (bullnose) plane to rebate the inner edges of the drawer for the bottom panel.

7 Glue the joints and gently tap the drawer together. Use a rubber mallet to avoid bruising the wood.

8 Clamp the drawer together with a pair of sash cramps, using scraps of wood to protect the drawer sides. Wipe off excess glue and check for square with a try square.

9 When the glue is dry, fit the plywood bottom panel into the rebates and attach with panel pins (brads).

10 Finally, tidy up the ends of the dovetails with a block plane and smooth with sandpaper. Fit the front panel to the drawer after installing it in the cabinet.

## Making the carcass

1 Make up the side panels in exactly the same way as instructed for the panelled cabinet door. Mark and cut out the mortises in the stiles as shown. The key to making the panels flat is to make sure that the cheeks of each mortise are cut accurately, providing parallel sides to receive the tenons.

2 The blind tenons do not pass completely through the rails. A useful tip when fitting a blind tenon is to nip off the corners to clear any obstructions at the very bottom of the mortise. Note the haunch on the tenon, which fits in the groove of the rail to help prevent twisting in the panel.

3 Use tongued-and-grooved cladding to form panel infills that match the door. This is particularly important for a freestanding unit where the sides will be visible. Cut the cladding to length and slot it together within the frame, as for the door. Glue and clamp the panels together in turn, making sure that they are kept flat and square.

4 Score across the ends of the stiles with a sharp knife and remove the horns with a tenon saw. Tidy up the end grain with a sharp block plane, and sand the panels before preparing them for assembly.

5 Use a router fitted with a 6mm (¼in) cutter to form a groove for the back in the inner face of each side panel. The groove should be set in from the back edge by exactly the thickness of the top rail, in this case 25mm (1in).

6 Cut the bottom panel to size, and rout a 6mm (¼in) groove in the back edge to match the side panels. Note how the depth of the panel is reduced by 50mm (2in) to allow the fitting of the front trim piece. Glue and clamp this in position so that it is flush with the surface of the panel, using biscuits to reinforce the joint.

### Practical tip

A drawer box is a good project for practising dovetailing. The dovetail is a favourite joint for drawers, as it stands up well to the pulling action when the drawer is opened.

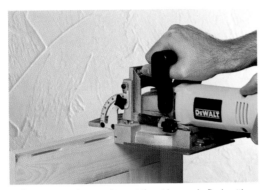

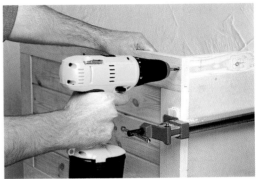

7 Biscuits are also used to set the side panels flush with the bottom of the unit. Cut three slots in the bottom rail of each side panel, keeping clear of the ends. Form corresponding slots in the edges of the bottom panel and insert the biscuits. No glue is needed.

8 Clamp the sides and bottom together so that the cross-dowels can be fitted at the corners. The cross-dowel is a neat device that allows small-section components to be bolted together to make a really strong assembly. Mark up each joint, using the dimensions given in the diagram (see figure 244.4), and drill a bolt hole through the side and into the rail.

9 Take the unit apart to fit the cross-dowels. Drill a blind hole of the correct diameter and depth to receive the metal cross-dowel. Note the tape wrapped around the drill bit to act as a depth gauge.

10 The top rails also need fitting with a 6mm (¼in) round wooden dowel to prevent them from twisting out of line when the bolts are tightened. Drill holes in the ends of the rails as shown in the diagram (see figure 244.5), use centre-points to mark the dowel positions on the side panels, and insert a dowel at each top corner.

11 Before finally assembling the unit, attach the fittings for the door. These adjustable base plates are required for the concealed hinges, allowing the door to be simply clipped into place. The exact fixing dimensions will be supplied with the hinges.

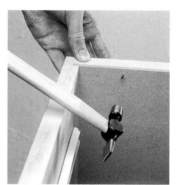

12 It is also easier to attach the drawer runners at this stage. They will be left and right handed, and must be fitted exactly square using a try square to the front edges so that the drawer runs level.

13 Connect the two sides to the bottom panel and the top rails, using the countersunk bolts and cross-dowels. The picture shows clearly how the connector operates – note how the slot in the top of the cross-dowel is used to align the threaded hole with the bolt.

14 Slide the back panel into its groove and attach it to the back rail with short panel pins. At this stage, the unit can be sanded and finished before attaching the plinth and adding the door and drawer.

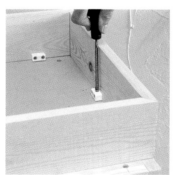

15 Cut four lengths of timber to make a simple plinth, mitring the ends with a mitre saw. Fit a biscuit at each corner to aid alignment, then glue and clamp together, adding a couple of panel pins. Check that the assembly is square and leave to dry.

16 Note how the plinth runs the full width of the unit, but is slightly recessed at the front. Turn the cabinet upside down and attach the plinth to the bottom, using small wooden blocks or plastic joint blocks, as shown here.

17 Drill two holes in the door with a wood boring bit of a size to suit the concealed hinges. Position the holes following the instructions supplied with the hinges. Attach the hinges to the door, clip them into place on their backing plates and adjust until the door hangs squarely in its opening.

### Practical tip

You can use MDF (medium-density fibreboard) for the internal panels of this unit provided you seal the edges for extra waterproofing. The sides, however, are solid wooden panels, properly jointed and finished for the extra quality that no man-made materials can match.

# GLOSSARY

Some of the less familiar woodworking terms encountered in this book are listed here. Turn to the sections on tools and wood for more information on tools and materials.

**bare-faced**    A type of tenon joint where the shoulder is formed on only one face of the tenon.

**batten**    A length of timber (lumber), usually square in section, for joining or strengthening.

**baulk**    A squared log from which smaller sections of timber (lumber) are converted in the sawmill.

**bench hook**    A portable stop, often home-made, which fits over the edge of a bench for steadying the workpiece.

**bevel**    The angled edge or end of a piece of wood – measured and marked with a bevel gauge.

**biscuit**    A small flat lozenge-shaped dowel for edge or corner jointing – fitted with a biscuit jointer.

**botanical name**    The Latin name that uniquely identifies the genus and species of timber (lumber).

**burr (burl)**    The part of a tree with twisted and complex grain formation, prized for its decorative appearance.

**carcass**    The basic box assembly of any construction, such as a cabinet or shelving unit.

**chamfer**    To remove the sharp corner of a section of wood and produce a smooth bevelled edge. (vb & n)

**chuck**    The adjustable jaws of a power drill or hand brace.

**clearance hole**    A hole drilled through a panel to allow clearance for the shank of a wood screw.

**conversion**    A method of cutting timber (lumber) from the baulk to produce boards for woodworking.

**counterbore**    A cylindrical hole at the top of the clearance hole to recess the head of a screw below the surface.

**cross-dowel**    A threaded metal rod inserted across the grain of a wooden member to receive a connecting bolt.

**density**    The relative weight of a substance, expressed as kg per cubic metre, or pounds per cubic foot.

**dowel**    A cylindrical length of wood used for connecting a joint, sometimes fluted to allow good adhesion.

**face and edge marks**    Pencil marks to identify the square and straight edges of a length of wood before working it.

**flute**    A semicircular groove in a piece of wood; also, the description of the cutting tool to produce it.

**follower (fence)**    A circular fitting for the base of a router used to follow the curved edge of a template.

**growth rings**    Layers of annual growth in the tree, clearly visible in cross section.

**hardwood**    Wood from broad-leaved trees, usually harder and more close-grained than coniferous softwoods, ideal for fine finishing or joinery.

**haunch**    A shortened section of a tenon, formed at the outside edge of a joint to prevent twisting.

**heartwood (core)**    The inner part of the tree below the sapwood layer, yielding the most usable timber (lumber).

**hockey stick (corner bead)**    A moulding used to trim the edges of a panel, with a J-shaped section in the profile of a hockey-stick to produce a finished edge.

**horn**    The end of frame member in a door or panel, which projects past the mortise for added strength.

**housing**    A grooved joint, square in section, which receives the end of another component.

**jig**    A woodworking aid for controlling the tool or locating the workpiece, for added safety or accuracy.

**kiln-dried**    Seasoned timber (lumber) that has been dried in the kiln to a low moisture content of approximately 10%.

**laminate**    A thin layer of wood or other material, used for forming curves or building up a decorative surface. *(vb & n)*

**liming wax**    Finishing wax that imparts a delicate white colour to the grain of the wood, especially oak.

**MDF**    Medium-density fibreboard – all-purpose sheet material, available in a range of thicknesses with a smooth sanded surface, suitable for home woodworking projects of all kinds.

**mitre**    Halving the angle of a corner joint where two members intersect: in a right angle, two 45 degree angles. *(vb & n)*

**moisture content**    A measure of how dry a sample of wood may be – low moisture content means the wood is stable and well-seasoned.

**mortise**    The square socket that receives a tenon for the classic woodworker's mortise and tenon joint. The mortise is the female part of the joint.

**moulding**    Decorative profiled edge of a length of wood, formed either by hand or with machine tools.

**movement**    The tendency of wood to shrink or expand with the changing atmospheric conditions of its surroundings.

**nominal**    The size of a section of timber after sawing, before machining further to an exact dimension.

**pare (shave)**    To remove thin layers of wood by hand with a flat chisel blade.

**pilot hole**    A hole drilled to receive the threaded end of a wood screw, to assist location and prevent the wood from splitting.

**plinth (kick)**    A raised base of a cupboard or floor unit, usually detachable.

**prepared**    Describes planed timber (lumber) with smooth faces and square edges.

**profile**    Any shape produced from a square blank of timber (lumber).

**profile cutter**    A special cutter fitted to a router, used to follow a template for reproducing a particular profile.

**rail**    The upper or lower horizontal member in a door or panel.

**rebate (rabbet)**    To cut a rectangular, stepped recess along the edge of a section of wood. *(vb & n)*

**relish**    A cutaway section of a tenon joint to avoid the edge or corner of a frame, and thus avoid weakening the joint.

**sapwood**    The outer layer of the tree, just below the bark; softer and more perishable than heartwood.

**scribe**    To mark or shape the end of a section of wood to fit around a moulding or profile for a neat joint. *(vb & n)*

**shooting board (stop)**    A home-made jig used with a bench plane to square the end or the edges of a length of wood.

**shorts/short ends (cuts)**    Shorter lengths of wood as sold by a timber (lumber) yard, often suitable for home woodworking projects at lower cost.

**shoulder**    The edge of a tenon joint that mates with the surface of another component, keeping it square.

**softwood**    Relatively inexpensive, general-purpose timber, from pine or other coniferous trees.

**sole plate**    The smooth base plate of a plane, which makes contact with the wood when in use.

**stretcher**    Part of a wooden frame, usually between two rails, to maintain a fixed distance between them.

**TCT**    Tungsten-carbide tipped: better quality but more expensive cutters and sawblades.

**template**    A pattern, usually of wood, used as a guide to form complex shapes or for repetitive, accurate work.

**tenon**    The male part of a mortise and tenon joint.

**veneer**    Very thin slices of wood for high quality decorative work.

**wane**    The uneven edge of a board, where the outside edges of the tree have not been cut away during conversion.

# Suppliers

## United Kingdom

**Axminster Power Tool Centre**
Chard Street
Axminster
Devon EX13 5HU
Tel: 01297 33656
*Power tools supplier*

**Blumson Fine Timber**
36–38 River Road
Barking
Essex IG11 0DN
Tel: 020 8594 5175
*Timber (lumber) suppliers*

**Chestergate Wood Supplies Ltd.**
Porron Street
Portwood, Stockport
Greater Manchester SK1 2JD
*Timber (lumber) suppliers*

**Crown Fasteners and Fixings Ltd.**
Watermill House
Restmor Way, Hackridge
Surrey SM6 7AH
Tel: 020 8773 3993
*Hardware supplier*

**Dewalt**
210 Bath Road
Slough
Berkshire SL1 3YD
Tel: 01753 567055
*Power tools supplier*

**Foxell and James**
Farringdon Road
London EC1M 3JB
Tel: 020 7405 0152
*Wax, oil, varnish, and finishing products.*

**FR Shadbolt & Sons Ltd.**
North Circular Road
South Chingford
London E4 8PZ
Tel: 020 8527 6441
*Veneer suppliers*

**James Latham**
Leeside Wharf
Mount Pleasant Hill
Clapton E5
Tel: 020 8806 3333
*Timber (lumber) suppliers*

**John Boddy's Wood and Tool Store**
Riverside Sawmills
Boroughbridge
North Yorkshire YO51 9LJ
Tel: 01423 322370
e-mail: info@john-boddy-timber.ltd.uk
*Timber (lumber) suppliers*

**Machin Bros. Ltd.**
79 Sceptre Road
Bethnal Green
London E2 0JU
Tel: 020 7790 3575
*Veneer suppliers*

**North Wales Timber Ltd.**
Industrial Estate
Pinfold Lane
Buckley
Flintshire CH7 3PL
*Timber (lumber) suppliers*

**Record Tools Ltd.**
Parkway Works
Kettlebridge Road
Sheffield S9 3BL
Tel: 0114 244 9066
*Hand tools supplier*

**Spear & Jackson
Neill Tools Ltd.**
Atlas Way
Atlas North
Sheffield S4 7QQ
Tel: 0114 261 4242
*Tools supplier*

**Stanley Tools UK Ltd.**
Beighton Road East
Drakehouse
Sheffield S20 7JZ
Tel: 0114 276 8888
*Tools supplier*

**West and Heaton Timber Ltd.**
4 North Back Lane
Bridlington
East Yorkshire YO16 5BA
*Timber (lumber) suppliers*

**Winther Browne & Co.**
Nobel Road
Eley Estate
Edmonton
London N18 3DX
Tel: 020 8803 3434
*Fine wood carvings and mouldings*

**Woodfit Ltd.**
Kem Mill
Whittle-le-Woods
Chorley
Lancashire PR6 7EA
Tel: 01257 266421
*Furniture fittings supplier*

**Y Goldburg & Sons**
3–5 Waterloo Road
Uxbridge
Middlesex UB8 2QX
Tel: 01895 253491
*Timber (lumber) suppliers*

**United States**

**California Redwood Association**
405 Enfrente Drive
Suite 200
Novato, CA 94949
Tel: (415) 382-0662
Fax: (415) 382-8531
www.calredwood.org/

**Colonial Hardwoods Inc.**
7953 Cameron Brown Ct.
Springfield, VA 22153
Tel: (703) 451-9217
www.colonialhardwoods@rica.com

**Diamond Machining Technology Inc.**
85 Hayes Memorial Drive
Malborough, MA 01752
Tel: (800) 666-4368
Fax: (508) 485-3924
www.dmtsharp.com
*Woodworking tool supplier*

**North Atlantic Timber Corporation**
South Road
Chilmark, MA 0235
Tel: (508) 696-8939
Fax: (508) 696-8232
www.northatlantictimber.com

**Southern Pine Council**
P.O. Box 641700
Kenner
Louisiana, 70064-1700
Tel: (504) 443-4464
Fax: (504) 443-6612
www.SouthernPine.com

**Talarico Hardwoods**
Route 3, Box 3268
Mohnton, PA 19540

**Tropical Exotic Hardwoods of Latin America**
2579 State Street
Carlsbad, CA 92008-1624
Tel: (760) 434-3030
Fax: (760) 434-5423
www.anexotichardwood.com

**Viking Woodcrafts Inc.**
1317 8th Street SE
Waseca, MN 56093
Tel: (507) 835 8043
www.vikingwoodcrafts.com

**Australia**
**Anagote Timbers**
144 Renwick Street
Marrickville
New South Wales 2204
Tel: 02 9558 8444

**Trend Timbers Pty Ltd.**
Cunneen Street, McGraths Hill
New South Wales 2756
Tel: 02 4577 5277

**The Wood Works**
8 Railway Road, Meadowbank
New South Wales 2114
Tel: 02 9807 7244

**Lazarides Timber Agencies**
PO Box 440, Ferny Hills
Queensland 4055
Tel: 07 3851 1400

**Veneers**
37 Alexandra Road
East Ringwood
Victoria 3135
Tel: 03 9870 8733

**Useful addresses**

**United Kingdom**
**British Antique Furniture Restorers' Association**
BAFRA Head Office
The Old Rectory
Warmwell
Dorchester
Dorset DT2 8HQ
Tel: 01305 854822
Fax: 01305 852104
www.bafra.org.uk

**British Woodturners' Association**
Treetops
78 St. Mark's Avenue
Salisbury
Wiltshire SP1 3DW
Tel: 01722 328032
Fax: 01722 333558

**Forest Stewardship Council**
FSC UK Working Group
Unit D, Station Building
Llanidloes SY18 6EB
Wales
Tel: 01686 413916
Fax: 01686 412176
www.fsc-uk.demon.co.uk

**Timber Research and Development Association Technology Ltd**
Stocking Lane
Hughenden Valley
High Wycombe
Buckinghamshire HP14 4ND
Tel: 01494 563091
Fax: 01494 565487
www.tradatechnology.co.uk

**United States**
**Forests Forever**
973 Market Street
Suite 450
San Francisco, CA 94103
Tel: (415) 974-3636
Fax: (415) 974-3664
www.forestsforever.org

**Timber Reclamation International**
3011 Killarny Drive
Cary, Illinois 60013
Tel: (847) 516-3804
Fax: (847) 516-2313

# INDEX

# Acknowledgements

The publisher would like to thank the following individuals and suppliers for loaning equipment and their help with photography.

**Bob Cleveland**
111 Stillingfleet Road
London SW13 9AF
Tel: 020 8748 9726
*For the loan of the rocking horse, and for the carving demonstration.*

**Andrew Gillmore**
*For making the three-legged chair and computer cupboard projects.*

John Bruch
**Woodfit**
*For the loan of fixtures and fittings.*

**Stanley UK Tools Ltd.**
*For the loan of tools.*

**Spear & Jackson**
*For the loan of saws.*

**Dewalt**
*For the loan of power tools.*

Marcus Jervis Hughes
**Y Goldburg & Sons**
(Timber Importers).

**Volume**
21 St. Alban's Place
London N1 0NX
Tel: 020 7359 0224
*For the loan of the glass table (page 186) and wooden table (page 236).*

**Fothergills**
79 Salmon Lane
Limehouse
London E14 7NA
Tel: 020 7790 7774
*For the loan of the music case and scarf (page 230).*

**Farbo Nairn Ltd.**
PO Box 1
Kircaldy
Fife KY1 2SB
Tel: 01592 643777
*For the loan of kitchen flooring (page 242).*

**Chromacolor by Perstorp**
Perstorp Customer Hotline
Tel: 01325 303303
*For the loan of the worksurface (page 204).*

**The Old Tool Chest**
41 Cross Street
Islington
London N1 2BB
Tel: 020 7359 9313
*For the loan of tools for the jacket cover image.*

**James Latham**
Leeside Wharf
Mount Pleasant Hill
Clapton E5
Tel: 020 8806 3333
*For the loan of the wooden background for the jacket cover image.*

**Grahams Hi Fi**
Canonbury Yard
190a New North Road
London N1 7BS
Tel: 020 7226 5500
http://www.grahams.co.uk
*For the loan of the stereo system (page 158).*

**Egg**
36 Kinnerton Street
London SW1Z 8ES
Tel: 020 7235 9315
*For the loan of ceramics (page 178 and 190).*

**Gill Wing Cookshop**
190 Upper Street
Islington
London N1 1RQ
Tel: 020 7226 5392
*For the loan of kitchen products.*

Alan Stiles
**Axminster Power Tool Centre**
Chard Street
Axminster
Devon EX13 5HU
*For the loan of tools and images.*

Mr Wright
**Blumsom Timber Centre**
*For helping with photography.*

Liz Boddy
**John Boddy's Wood and Tool Store**
*For the loan of images.*

Justin Browne
**Winther Browne & Co.
Fine Wood Carvings & Mouldings**
*For the loan of mouldings.*

Paul Machin
**Machin Bros. Ltd.**
*For the loan of veneers.*

Suzanna Tabor
**FR Shadbolt & Sons**
*For the loan of veneers.*

Vin Vara
**The Tool Shop**
97 Lower Marsh
London SE1
Tel: 020 7207 2077
*For the loan of tools.*

Glyn Storey
William Marples
**Record Tools. Ltd.**
*For the loan of chisels.*

Drew Geldart
**Spear & Jackson
Neill Tools Ltd.**
*For the loan of tools.*

**Picture credits**
DIY Photo Library p28br; p29br; p132bl; p134tr, br. Forest Life Picture Library pp6tr, bl; 10tr, 11tl, b; 21cl. Imagebank p14b. Liz and John Boddy p14tr; 15tr, br; 18c. Ian Durrant p133, 135br.

The publisher would like to thank FSC for allowing the reproduction of their logo on page 20; Graham Bruford at Forests Forever for permission to reproduce text on page 21; Ian Durrant for his help on woodturning and permission to reproduce the image on pages 133 and 135bl; to Tony McMullen for permission to use images on page 133tr, cr; to Anthony Bryant for permission to use images on page 132tr, 135bl, tr and to Kenneth Wilson for permission to use the image on page 136 bl. The author would like to thank Steven Differ for image on the back jacket.

# NOTES

# NOTES

# NOTES

# NOTES

# NOTES

NOTES

# NOTES

# NOTES